ALSO BY
Sara Foster

SARA FOSTER'S
CASUAL COOKING

FRESH EVERY DAY

THE FOSTER'S
MARKET COOKBOOK

Sara Foster's Southern Kitchen

soulful, traditional, seasonal

Sara Foster's Southern Kitchen

SARA FOSTER

with *Tema Larter*

FOREWORD BY LEE SMITH

PHOTOGRAPHY BY PETER FRANK EDWARDS

RANDOM HOUSE | NEW YORK

Copyright © 2011 by Sara Foster

Published in the United States by Random House,
an imprint of The Random House Publishing Group,
a division of Random House, Inc., New York.

RANDOM HOUSE and colophon are
registered trademarks of Random House, Inc.

Photographs courtesy of Peter Frank Edwards Photography.
Photograph of Sara Foster on page xii courtesy of Quentin Bacon.

LIBRARY OF CONGRESS CATALOGING-IN-PUBLICATION DATA

Foster, Sara.
[Southern kitchen]
Sara Foster's Southern kitchen / Sara Foster with Tema Larter.
p.   cm.
ISBN 978-1-4000-6859-3
eBook ISBN 978-0-679-60457-0
1. Cooking, American—Southern style.   2. Cookery—Southern States.   I. Title.
TX715.2.S68F677 2011
641.5975—dc22   2010029328

Printed in China on acid-free paper

www.atrandom.com

2 4 6 8 9 7 5 3 1

FIRST EDITION

Book design by Barbara M. Bachman

*To my sister, Judy,
for sharing life,
recipes, and more*

Sara Foster has always been the perfect hostess—warm, welcoming, relaxed—and I have been a grateful guest for over twenty years at her innovative Foster's Markets in North Carolina, comfortable cafés where you can read a newspaper, write a novel, meet the girls for lunch (hint: choose the famous Tarragon Chicken Salad), conduct a power breakfast (sticky buns will make the meeting go your way), dissect a love affair (chocolate helps), or simply pick up a pan of vegetable lasagna for that last-minute dinner party at your house. I go to Foster's for therapy and community as well as food; there's not much that Sara's chicken pot pie can't fix. There was nothing like Foster's until Sara came to town—whoever heard of *bruschetta,* for God's sake? Or fennel? Or even *wraps*? We were pretty provincial. So I've always thought of Sara herself as very cutting-edge and ultrasophisticated, and have been a bit mystified as to why I feel so much at ease in her aura.

Now, with this wonderful new cookbook, I get it! Sara is coming out of the closet—er, the pantry, I guess—as a secret Southerner! Well, not *exactly* secret, when I look back to consider her trademark cheesy grits casserole, those big fluffy biscuits, and the fact that some of her best recipes (like Say's Bread Pudding with Bourbon Icing) have come from her mother. But whoever imagined that Sara Foster actually grew up in Jackson, Tennessee, with a pig named Pig, grandparents who owned two country cooking restaurants and, best of all, a big working farm, plus a pitmaster dad and mom who operated a barbecue stand on the Fourth of July and Labor Day? Sara tells all here, in charming narrative style—a very personal approach to cooking and life that is as much fun to read as it is to cook from (which I have been doing, nonstop, ever since I got my hands on this book).

Sara points out that many of these recipes are not even "New Southern," they're actually "Old Southern" (albeit simplified, faster, and healthier)—classic dishes such as pimiento cheese, Brunswick stew, cornbread (yes, she uses sugar), gumbo, hummingbird cake, and boiled custard. I'm especially glad to have this last one: in my own family, we always took boiled custard to the sick, and a ham in the case of death. I thought it was the law! The taste of Sara's skillet-fried corn (cast-iron skillet required) takes me right back to my own grandmother's Virginia kitchen in the 1950s, eating from the old Blue Willow china at the oilcloth-covered farm table, her window ledge lined with Mason jars containing pickles, vegetables, and fruits glowing like jewels within. Oh yes, Sara's back to canning, too, and makes the process so simple that even I can do it—so far, I've put up blueberry preserves and chow-chow.

Sara's "Know-how" boxes and sidebar tips may be the most valuable part of this book, in fact: not only how to can, but also how to do all those other things you think you ought to know how to do but don't. Things you've always been too embarrassed to ask anybody: how to grill a steak, cut a chicken into ten pieces, carve a standing rib roast, make your own mayonnaise, make cracklings, and even deep-fry a turkey and produce your very own wood-smoked barbecued pig in your very own backyard. In fact, Chapter 7—"Pig: A Food Group All Its Own"—is my favorite, as Sara demystifies many of these traditionally sacred processes and uses up every part of the pig but the squeal.

Dedicated to local food and seasonal eating, Sara's approach is especially helpful now that most of us have ready access to fresh vegetables at farm stands and farmer's markets. We can get them, but what are we going to do with them? Here's a simple yet comprehensive catalog and guide, plus recipes that range from the simplest preparations to traditional dishes such as stewed field peas or that sweet potato casserole, which you just have to have at Thanksgiving, to brand-new ideas like Grilled Peach Salad with Shaved Country Ham and Summer Herbs, Arugula Pesto Snap Beans, and Watermelon-Tomato Salad with Shaved Feta and Handfuls of Mint (this is unbelievably delicious).

Sara is not afraid of intense flavor or innovation. She has gone back to her Tennessee past to produce a vibrant new Southern-style cuisine, rooted in love, family, and memory, yet open to all life's bounty.

lee smith

AUGUST 5, 2010

contents

There is deep satisfaction in eating locally and seasonally.

gOOD COOKING, GOOD EATING, *and* GOOD LIVING

I've wanted to write a book about Southern food for a long time, but it took me a little while to figure out how to begin. My first three books welcomed readers to my Foster's Market cafés, shared my philosophy on fresh, seasonal eating, and talked about how to make room in busy schedules for good, simple home cooking. Each of my books has been personal, but with this one, I am finally going home—back to Tennessee, to the South, and to the Southern upbringing and regional dishes that first inspired and shaped my love of food.

Even though much of my cooking has Southern roots, I love to mix it up. I'm not shy about adding my own twist to classic dishes with ingredients like chipotle chiles, soy sauce, and fresh mozzarella, which my grandmother would say have no business being in Southern food. I also prefer to cook my greens closer to four minutes than four hours, and I'm always trying to find ways to cut some of the fat in my everyday, go-to recipes.

But no matter how far I stray in my cooking repertoire, Southern food is my home base. With my Tennessee origins, there was simply no way around it. Southern cooking is and always has been firmly rooted in place, a potent stew of culinary traditions arising from a region both geographical and cultural. Once you have it in your bones, it doesn't matter where you are; in that sense, Southern cooking is a state of mind. Accordingly, my deepest feelings and memories about food are all rooted in Southern traditions: the Friday-night fish fries; the Sunday fried-chicken suppers; the holiday dinners; and the picnics, potlucks, and tailgating parties that I relished as a child and that I continue to look forward to when I visit my family in Tennessee.

We Southerners love our fried chicken and our whole hog and our greens cooked in bacon fat, but these are only one side of Southern food. There's a whole other side to it, too—one that's all about farm-fresh produce, long growing seasons, simple preparations, and homemade *everything*. It was this side of Southern cooking that I came to know best on my grandparents' farm, where I spent the majority of my weekends and summers throughout my childhood. It took culinary school and a career in cooking to learn the techniques behind perfectly translucent consommés, gravity-defying soufflés, and other fancy dishes that tend to separate home cooks from restaurant chefs. But I learned the most important lessons on that farm—that

there is deep satisfaction in eating locally and seasonally, that feeding family and friends is an essential act of love, and that you can never have too many vegetable sides.

Like most Southern farm women of her generation, Granny Foster filled her entire days with tasks related to food preparation. Aside from the actual cooking, she worked from dawn to bedtime fetching eggs and cleaning the henhouse, tending her garden, feeding the pigs, shelling peas, and making all kinds of pickles, preserves, and relishes from the fruits and vegetables in her garden. She would also buy and put up huge quantities of corn and peaches from neighboring farmers. This, along with the meat in the smokehouse and the freezer, ensured they had high-quality, homegrown food year-round.

My grandparents were wonderful cooks, and their food anchored our family by virtue of the magnetic effect it had on all of us. The pull was strongest during the holidays, when the

whole extended family would descend on the farm. Papa Foster always made the traditional Christmas ham, replete with pineapple rings, cloves, and maraschino cherries, and Granny Foster would always roast a turkey. Occasionally, this might be supplemented by a piece of goat. The rest of us were tasked with bringing the many sides, from mashed potatoes, molded cranberry aspics, flaky biscuits, and airy dinner rolls to green bean casserole, candied sweet potatoes, ambrosia salad, and dressing. This was followed by an equally impressive array of pies, which were placed in a pretty row on the sideboard.

Even on a normal day, the food, though often simple, reflected the matter-of-fact care and hard work that went into each element of each meal. Warm, fresh-from-the-oven biscuits topped with butter and mashed fresh strawberries, meats from Papa Foster's smokehouse, and just-harvested greens simmering in their own pot likker were all part of daily life. Summers were the best time of all, of course; my sister and I would go out to the fields and pick sweet white corn so tender and sugary that we would eat it raw, right off the stalks. And when Granny Foster sent me out to her garden to gather tomatoes for lunch, they were so flavorful and warm from the sun that I always ate one like an apple on the way back to the house.

In retrospect, it was a sort of culinary utopia. Of course, it took a long time and a lot of distance before I came to understand just how profoundly the farm and, by extension, my Southern heritage had shaped me—and my cooking.

Today Southern cooking is all about mixing and matching old favorites with new ingredients and techniques, and vice versa. I wouldn't have it any other way, but I don't think of my style as "New Southern"—a phrase that is often used to describe any Southern cooking that isn't deep-fried in lard or molded and gelled. Instead, I like to think of my cooking as *old* Southern, because it's about going back to the basics that have long underpinned Southern cooking: fresh, local ingredients, simple preparations, and a deep appreciation for pork. Accordingly, in this book I offer all my favorite Southern recipes, traditional and with a twist.

In today's South, most of us eat differently than

did previous generations, so it follows that we cook differently, too. Unlike my mother, for instance, I don't consider deep-fried okra a "green vegetable." We Southerners are good at keeping alive the best of our traditions, but Southern food has never stayed the same for long. After all, its very roots are a mash-up of globally diverse people, cultures, and geographies, an ever-changing melting pot that continues to shape Southern food. These influences are part of a natural evolution, one that today accounts for locally grown Asian greens stewed in fatback and doused with vinegar, Spanish *churros con chocolate* (sweet fritters with chocolate dipping sauce) on the menus of high-end Southern restaurants, and pork tamales and hominy-studded posole for sale from Mexican tacquerias and tiendas on Southern street corners.

This evolution—and the appetizing tension it creates between old and new—is what makes Southern food so exciting. The recipes in this cookbook are a testament to this process as it has played out in my own life, reflecting both the Southern food from my childhood and Southern food as I see it today. It is my "little slice of Southern," and I hope you like it.

Sara
Foster's
Southern
Kitchen

come on in

hors d'oeuvres and cocktails

*S*outhern hospitality may be a cliché, but there's a reason people talk about it. Southerners love to entertain at least as much as they love to eat and drink, maybe even more. After all, entertaining is not just an opportunity to connect with friends and family; it's an excuse to dust off the nice dishes, fix everyone's favorite recipes, and, if one is so inclined, open the liquor cabinet just a crack.

To be sure, good entertaining doesn't hinge on cocktails and hors d'oeuvres. As for me, I never feel obliged to precede a nice dinner with appetizers and aperitifs—especially not when the recipes are more complicated than the main dish—but there *is* something cozy and congenial about easing into dinner that way. And, of course, the pleasures of whiling away an afternoon or early evening with friends, drinks, finger food, and a bocce ball or badminton set shouldn't be discounted.

In keeping with my belief in stress-free entertaining, the recipes in this chapter—from Herb Deviled Eggs (page 10), and Pimiento Cheese with Cornbread Toasts (page 18) to Sazeracs (page 28), Salty Dogs (page 27), and Wendy's Bloody Marys (page 28)—are easy in both spirit and practice, and many can be made in advance. Meaning the only thing left for you to do is welcome your guests to come on in.

sweet and spicy pecans

These flavor-infused pecans somehow manage to be crunchy, sweet, savory, and spicy—all at the same time. It's a dangerously addictive combination that also happens to play well with just about every cocktail it meets. For pretty party favors or stocking stuffers, package these fragrant nibbles in sheer organza or cellophane bags tied with colored ribbons. **shake it up with a MINT JULEP (see page 27)** MAKES ABOUT 4 CUPS

- 4 **cups pecan halves**
- 1/3 **cup natural cane sugar**
- 2 **tablespoons fresh rosemary**
- 1 **tablespoon sea salt, plus more to taste**
- 1/2 **teaspoon freshly ground black pepper**
- 1/2 **teaspoon ground cayenne pepper**
- 4 **tablespoons (1/2 stick) unsalted butter, melted**
- 1 **tablespoon pure vanilla extract**

Preheat the oven to 400°F.

Spread the pecans on a rimmed baking sheet and place in the oven to lightly toast, 5 to 7 minutes.

While the pecans are toasting, combine the cane sugar, rosemary, salt, black pepper, and cayenne in a bowl and stir to mix. Place the butter and vanilla in a separate bowl, remove the pecans from the oven and add them to the butter and vanilla mixture, tossing to coat. Add the spice mixture and toss again to coat evenly.

Return the pecans to the baking sheet, spread them evenly, and bake for 8 to 10 minutes more, until toasted and fragrant, stirring halfway through. Sprinkle with additional salt, if desired. Let cool completely—they will get crispy after they cool—before storing in an airtight container until ready to serve, or for up to 1 week.

SARA'S SWAPS Mix things up by flavoring the nuts with different combinations of herbs and spices. For a spiced orange rendition, omit the rosemary and add ground cardamom and orange zest. Or, to showcase Indian flavors, replace the rosemary with crushed red pepper flakes, ground cumin, and ground coriander. For more savory pecans, use Worcestershire sauce in place of the vanilla.

rosemary cheese crackers

Most every Southerner has a favorite recipe for cheese biscuits, cheese crackers, or cheese straws, those staples of holiday gifting and year-round entertaining. With the addition of rosemary and chile peppers, I give this version of these buttery crackers unexpected heat and flavor that makes them extra habit-forming. Serve topped with fresh goat cheese and pepper jelly along with a round or two of Sazeracs (page 28) or Wendy's Bloody Marys (page 28). **shake it up with a *SALTY DOG* (see page 27)**

MAKES ABOUT 2½ DOZEN 2-INCH-SQUARE OR ROUND CRACKERS

2	cups (8 ounces) grated sharp Cheddar cheese
8	tablespoons (1 stick) unsalted butter, softened
1½	cups all-purpose flour
2	teaspoons dried rosemary
1	teaspoon sea salt, plus more for sprinkling on top
1	teaspoon crushed red pepper flakes
¼	teaspoon ground cayenne pepper

Cream the cheese and butter together in a large bowl with an electric mixer or a wooden spoon until smooth and well combined. Stir together the flour, rosemary, salt, red pepper flakes, and cayenne in a separate bowl. Add the flour mixture to the cheese mixture and stir to combine thoroughly.

Turn the dough onto a piece of wax or parchment paper. Roll into a log shape for round crackers; for square crackers, gently tap each side of the log on the counter several times to form a long rectangle. Wrap the dough in the paper and refrigerate for several hours or overnight, until the dough is firm and sliceable.

When ready to bake, preheat the oven to 375°F.

Remove the dough from the refrigerator. Cut the log into ¼-inch-thick slices and arrange them on a baking sheet. Using a fork, prick the center of each cracker several times and sprinkle with salt. Bake for 12 to 15 minutes, until golden brown around the edges.

Remove from the oven and allow to cool completely before serving or storing in an airtight container for up to 3 days.

Know-how: planning ahead

The dough for these crackers can be made a day or two in advance and refrigerated until you are ready to bake and serve. Once baked, the crackers can be frozen and then reheated in the oven for a few minutes before serving—great for unexpected company.

herb deviled eggs

With their outsize flavor and perfectly bite-size proportions, deviled eggs never go out of style. The best part is that they're one of the few dishes fit for entertaining that's also so simple, you can probably throw them together on a moment's notice without even going to the grocery store. All you need are some eggs and a little something to give them zip, from chopped pickles or pickle relish to cayenne pepper or spicy pepper relish. I like this version, which is topped with fresh herbs and cornichons or other pickled vegetables, like okra or asparagus. MAKES 1 DOZEN

6	large eggs
2	tablespoons your favorite or Homemade Mayonnaise (page 280)
4	cornichons or mini dill pickles, 3 minced and 1 thinly sliced
2	teaspoons Dijon mustard
1	teaspoon white wine vinegar
1	tablespoon chopped fresh dill, plus more for garnish, if desired
1	teaspoon chopped fresh chives, plus more for garnish, if desired
1/8	teaspoon ground cayenne pepper
	Sea salt and freshly ground black pepper

Place the eggs in a saucepan with enough water to cover by about 2 inches. Bring the water to a low boil over medium-high heat. As soon as the water comes to a boil, turn off the heat, cover, and let the eggs sit in the water for about 10 minutes longer.

Drain the eggs, rinse under cold running water, gently crack the shells, and let sit in cold or ice water until completely cool. Remove the eggs from the water and carefully remove the shells. Place on a paper towel to drain.

Cut the eggs in half lengthwise. Scoop the yolks into a medium bowl, being careful to keep the whites intact. Place the whites on a plate and set aside.

Add the mayonnaise, minced pickles, mustard, vinegar, dill, chives, cayenne, and salt and black pepper to taste to the egg yolks and mash with a fork to form a smooth paste.

Spoon about 1 heaping teaspoon of the yolk mixture back into each egg half and refrigerate, covered, until ready to serve, or for several hours.

Top each egg with a thin slice of pickle and a sprinkling of fresh dill or chives and season with additional salt and pepper, if desired, just before serving.

deviled ham salad

Think of fresh deviled ham as pork's answer to chicken salad. Creamy and savory, it makes a great dip for crackers or crostini. For a light lunch, try scooping it into cups of butter lettuce with sliced tomatoes.   MAKES ABOUT 4 CUPS

1	pound smoked ham, chopped
¾	cup your favorite or Homemade Mayonnaise (page 280)
2	small dill pickles, chopped (about ½ cup)
¼	cup your favorite or Sweet Pickle Relish (page 299)
2	tablespoons grated onion
2	tablespoons Dijon mustard
1	teaspoon Worcestershire sauce
	Dash of hot sauce
	Sea salt and freshly ground black pepper

Place the ham in the food processor and pulse six to eight times, until finely chopped, being careful not to overprocess.

Transfer to a bowl and add the mayonnaise, dill pickles, pickle relish, onion, mustard, Worcestershire sauce, hot sauce, and salt (ham may already be salty, so taste before adding salt) and pepper to taste and stir to combine. Refrigerate until ready to serve.

IN SEASON   Here are a few of my favorite finger sandwiches for all seasons:

SPRING

Fresh watercress or pea shoots, unsalted butter, and thinly sliced cucumbers

Roasted asparagus and Horseradish-Mustard Vinaigrette (page 92)

SUMMER

Ripe tomatoes and Homemade Mayonnaise (page 280)

Pimiento Cheese (page 18) with sprouts

FALL

Slivered apples, grainy mustard, Cheddar cheese, and turkey

Pork Rillettes (page 169)

WINTER

Deviled Ham Salad (recipe above)

Brandied Chicken Liver Pâté (page 23) with Pickled Okra (page 298)

spring pea toasts with lemon olive oil and fresh pea shoots

Fresh green peas and their curlicue shoots are one of the first signs of spring at my local farmer's markets, and I can never resist combining the two in these refreshing and delicately flavored toasts or Meyer Lemonade. ***shake it up with a MEYER LEMONADE*** (*see page 27*)   MAKES ABOUT 2 CUPS, ENOUGH FOR ABOUT 2 DOZEN CROSTINI

½	**pound shelled fresh green peas (in the South we call these English peas)**
	Zest and juice of 1 lemon
4	**garlic cloves, smashed**
8	**to 10 fresh mint leaves**
1	**tablespoon chopped fresh chives**
¼	**cup extra-virgin olive oil**
½	**cup (1½ ounces) freshly grated Parmesan cheese**
	Sea salt and freshly ground black pepper
24	**crostini (see Know-how, page 19)**
	Lemon Olive Oil (recipe follows), for drizzling on top
24	**fresh pea shoots or baby watercress or arugula (about 1 cup)**

Rinse and drain the peas, discarding any blemished peas or bits of pod. Place in a food processor along with the lemon zest and juice, garlic, mint, and chives and pulse four or five times to chop. With the motor running slowly, add the olive oil to puree and make a paste, stopping to scrape down the sides of the bowl several times. Add the Parmesan cheese and pulse several more times to mix. Season with salt and pepper to taste and pulse to mix.

Spread a heaping teaspoon of the pea mixture on top of each crostini, drizzle with Lemon Olive Oil, top each with 1 pea shoot, and serve at room temperature.

lemon olive oil

You can buy lemon-flavored olive oil, but to ensure freshness, why not make your own? Like making vinaigrette, it's so easy.   MAKES ABOUT 1 CUP

Combine **1 cup fruity green extra-virgin olive oil** and the **zest and juice of 1 lemon** in a glass jar, screw on the lid, and shake to combine. Refrigerate until ready to use, or for up to 2 weeks.

caramelized red onion tarts

I make these sweet and savory tarts all year round as a first course or served with a salad as a light lunch. The onions take on a lovely blushing red color when they caramelize. **shake it up with a SAZERAC (see page 28)** MAKES ABOUT FOURTEEN 3-INCH TARTS

1	**tablespoon olive oil**
1	**tablespoon unsalted butter**
1	**red onion, thinly sliced into rounds**
2	**tablespoons balsamic vinegar**
2	**tablespoons sugar**
2	**tablespoons fresh rosemary**
	Sea salt and freshly ground black pepper
1	**sheet frozen puff pastry, such as Pepperidge Farm or Dufour Pastry Kitchens, thawed in the refrigerator**
1	**cup (4 ounces) crumbled soft goat cheese**
2	**tablespoons chopped fresh parsley**

Preheat the oven to 375°F. Lightly grease a rimmed baking sheet or line with parchment paper.

Heat the olive oil and butter in a large skillet over medium-high heat until sizzling hot (see Know-how, page 100). Add the onions, vinegar, sugar, and rosemary and season with salt and pepper to taste. Reduce the heat to low and cook for about 15 minutes, stirring occasionally, until most of the liquid has evaporated and the onions are caramelized. Remove from the heat to cool slightly.

While the onions are cooking, flatten the pastry on a lightly floured surface and roll several times, smoothing out the folds, to create a 12-inch square. Cut into 3-inch rounds using a biscuit or round cookie cutter. Transfer to the prepared baking sheet and, using a 2¾-inch-round cutter, make an indented border on the cut pastry rounds, being careful not to cut all the way through. Refrigerate for about 30 minutes.

Combine the goat cheese and parsley in a small bowl, stir to soften and combine, and season with salt and pepper to taste.

Bake the pastry rounds for 10 minutes. Remove from the oven, depress and remove the top layer of the puffed centers with a small knife, and spread a heaping teaspoon of the cheese mixture into the center of each. Return to the oven and bake for 5 minutes more, until the pastry is golden brown and puffy and the cheese is warm. Remove from the oven and top each tart with 3 or 4 rings of the caramelized onions. Serve warm.

caramelized fig crostini with country ham and goat cheese

Like many Southerners, I have a fig tree—huge, old, gnarled, and prized—that bears bucketfuls of plump, grassy-sweet figs each summer. So sweet, in fact, that they draw not only the usual birds and squirrels, but also a certain stealthy neighbor who must surely keep as close a watch on the fruits' ripening as we do. *shake it up with a SAZERAC (see page 28)* MAKES 2 DOZEN CROSTINI

1	tablespoon unsalted butter
	Splash of olive oil
12	small fresh figs, such as Alma, Carolina Dark, or Celeste, halved lengthwise
2	tablespoons balsamic vinegar
1/4	cup sugar
	Sea salt and freshly ground black pepper
8	paper-thin slices country ham (about 8 ounces)
24	crostini (see Know-how, page 19)
1 1/2	cups (6 ounces) soft goat cheese
2	tablespoons chopped fresh parsley

Heat the butter and olive oil in a large skillet over medium-high heat until the butter is sizzling hot (see Know-how, page 100). Place the figs in the skillet, cut side down, and cook for about 1 minute, until they begin to brown around the edges. Add the vinegar and sprinkle the sugar on top, shaking the pan to distribute evenly.

Bring to a boil, shaking the pan back and forth to keep the figs moving, and cook until the liquid reduces to a sticky syrup, about 2 minutes. Sprinkle with salt and pepper to taste and set aside to cool slightly.

Heat the country ham in a large skillet over medium-high heat until heated through and crispy around the edges; cut each slice into thirds. In a small bowl, combine the goat cheese and parsley Spread each crostini with about 1 tablespoon of the goat cheese mixture and top with a small slice of country ham and half a caramelized fig. Serve warm or at room temperature.

SARA'S SWAPS Experiment with the flavor and texture of these two-bite dainties by using different kinds of cheese. Some of my favorites are mascarpone, Saint-André, Gorgonzola, fresh ricotta, and fresh burrata mozzarella. You can successfully substitute cooked bacon or prosciutto for the country ham as needed.

pimiento cheese with cornbread toasts

see photograph on page 2

Whether spread on saltines, white bread, or "celery boats," tangy, creamy Pimiento Cheese is seriously habit-forming. A simple mix of mayonnaise or cream cheese, shredded Cheddar, and jarred red peppers, Pimiento Cheese is one of those unassuming Southern classics that can sometimes be a hard sell for people who didn't grow up on it. But when it's made right, it's easy to see why Southerners are so passionate about it. Try it—it may just become your new obsession. *Shake it up with a WENDY'S BLOODY MARY (see page 28)* MAKES ABOUT 2 CUPS

> 2 **cups (8 ounces) grated extra-sharp Cheddar cheese**
> 1 **cup (3 ounces) freshly grated Parmesan cheese**
> **One 4-ounce jar pimiento peppers, drained and chopped**
> ½ **cup your favorite or Homemade Mayonnaise (page 280)**
> 1 **tablespoon apple cider vinegar**
> 1 **teaspoon honey**
> **Pinch of ground cayenne pepper**
> **Sea salt and freshly ground black pepper**

Combine the Cheddar and Parmesan cheeses, pimiento peppers, mayonnaise, vinegar, honey, cayenne, and salt and black pepper to taste in a bowl and stir to blend. Cover and refrigerate until ready to serve, or for up to 1 week. For best flavor, make 1 day ahead.

When ready to serve, remove from the refrigerator and let come to room temperature.

cornbread toasts

These crunchy, savory toasts are the upside of cornbread's short shelf life. Scrumptious and versatile, they can be used in dozens of dishes and snacks—but I'm especially partial to the way they complement zingy Pimiento Cheese

Preheat the oven to 400°F.

Cut **day-old cornbread** into slices about ¼ inch thick and 2 inches long. Brush lightly with **olive oil** and place in the oven for 10 to 12 minutes, until golden brown around the edges.

Remove from the oven and cool slightly. Spoon a dollop of **Pimiento Cheese** (recipe above) on one end of each toast and garnish with an **arugula or celery leaf.** Serve warm or at room temperature.

Know-how: making crostini and toast points

Crostini and toast points are practically the same thing made with different kinds of bread, and both make great vehicles for cheeses, spreads, and dips. Toast points are usually made from thin white sandwich bread cut into triangles, while crostini are made from small, crusty baguettes sliced into rounds. Follow your inspiration and experiment with different types of bread—most any kind will work, from crusty sourdough to whole wheat—and different combinations of herbs and spices.

For toast points, trim the crusts from slices of thin white sandwich bread and cut diagonally into quarters to form triangles. Brush lightly with melted unsalted butter and place in a preheated 400°F oven to lightly toast.

For crostini, slice a baguette into ½-inch-thick rounds. Brush lightly with extra-virgin olive oil; sprinkle with chopped herbs, such as parsley, oregano, and thyme, and salt and pepper, if desired; and place in a preheated 400°F oven to lightly toast.

IN SEASON Cornbread toasts are so versatile, I couldn't resist providing a few more of my favorite accompaniments for all seasons.

SPRING

Serve in place of crostini with Spring Pea Toasts with Lemon Olive Oil and Fresh Pea Shoots (page 13) or make oversized herby croutons by sprinkling the day-old bread with chopped fresh herbs, then float them on Garden Tomato Soup with Creamy Goat Cheese (page 35).

SUMMER

Top with Fried Green Tomatoes with Buttermilk Green Goddess Dressing (page 284) or serve with scoops of Simple Lump Crab Salad (page 111) and sliced avocado.

FALL

Top with cream and sherry-spiked sautéed wild mushrooms and fresh thyme or spread with roasted sweet potatoes or butternut squash and a drizzle of molasses.

WINTER

Serve with cream cheese and pepper jelly or spread with Deviled Ham Salad (page 11).

salty oysters on the half-shell four ways

It used to be that Southerners ate oysters only in months with the letter *r* in them because it was just too hot from May to August to ensure their safety and freshness. Today, thanks to the wonders of modern refrigeration, they can be eaten year-round. Keep in mind that oysters must be cooked or eaten alive, so freshness is paramount when using oysters, mussels, clams, and scallops. Fresh, properly stored oysters should smell clean and briny, with no hint of fishiness. Any that remain open when tapped prior to cooking or closed after cooking should be discarded. SERVES 2 TO 4

OYSTERS MIGNONETTE Combine ½ cup red wine vinegar, juice of ½ lemon, 1 minced shallot, and **sea salt and freshly ground black pepper to taste.** Stir to mix. Shuck **2 dozen oysters** (see Know-how, page 22) and spoon a small amount of the vinegar sauce on top of each oyster. Place on ice to keep chilled and serve immediately.

OYSTERS CASINO Preheat the oven to 475°F. Sprinkle rock salt on a rimmed baking sheet and heat in the oven for about 10 minutes. Shuck **2 dozen oysters** (see Know-how, page 22) and top each oyster with one **2-inch slice half-cooked bacon,** a **sprinkle of chopped fresh parsley,** and a **squeeze of fresh lemon juice.** Season with **sea salt and freshly ground black pepper to taste,** transfer to the prepared baking sheet, and bake until the bacon is crispy, about 3 minutes. Remove from the oven and serve warm.

OYSTERS BIENVILLE Preheat the oven to 475°F. Sprinkle rock salt on a rimmed baking sheet and heat in the oven for about 10 minutes. Combine **1 cup fresh bread crumbs** (see Know-how, page 134) with **4 tablespoons (½ stick) melted butter, 2 tablespoons heavy cream,** and the **zest of 1 lemon.** Shuck **2 dozen oysters** (see Know-how, page 22) and top each oyster with a **few pieces of lump crabmeat** and a spoonful of the bread crumb mixture. Season with **sea salt and freshly ground black pepper to taste,** transfer to the prepared baking sheet, and bake for 5 to 7 minutes, until the topping is golden brown and slightly bubbly. Remove from the oven and serve warm.

OYSTERS ROCKEFELLER Preheat the oven to 475°F. Sprinkle rock salt on a rimmed baking sheet and heat in the oven for about 10 minutes. Sauté **2 cups fresh spinach, washed and drained,** with **2 minced garlic cloves in 1 tablespoon olive oil** for about 1 minute, until the spinach wilts and turns bright green. Shuck **2 dozen oysters** (see Know-how, page 22) and top each oyster with a few leaves of the garlic spinach, a **splash of Pernod,** and a **sprinkling of freshly grated Parmesan cheese.** Season with **sea salt and freshly ground black pepper to taste** and transfer to the prepared baking sheet. Bake for 5 to 7 minutes, until the cheese is golden and slightly bubbly. Remove from the oven and serve warm.

Know-how: shucking oysters

To shuck an oyster, first stabilize the oyster by placing it between two dishtowels on the counter. This is an important precaution so you won't cut yourself if the knife or the oyster slips. Once the oyster is stabilized, insert an oyster knife (a regular kitchen knife will likely break) between the two shells directly to the side of the place in the back where the shells hinge together. Twist the knife around until the shells pop open. Use the knife to slice through the bit of muscle connecting the oyster to the top shell, then snap off and discard the top shell. To ensure that the oyster slips right off the shell when you eat it, run the blade of the knife under the oyster itself, severing the connective tissue that keeps it in place. Another method that works for all but raw preparations is to first roast the oysters on a rimmed baking sheet in a preheated 400°F oven or on a hot grill just until the shells begin to loosen and separate; pop the tops right off by hand and proceed with your recipe. Just handle the hot oysters with tongs or a kitchen towel to avoid burns.

chew on this: about southern oysters

The oysters found along the East and Gulf coasts are almost all the same variety, commonly called Eastern or Atlantic oysters, but you wouldn't know it from eating them. Because oysters filter their food from the water in which they live, they vary considerably from place to place based on local conditions. Thus, oysters from Apalachicola, Florida—where wild oysters are still harvested from little boats using long tongs—are known for their plump, meaty flesh and mild, coppery flavor, while Chesapeake oysters are famously sweet, a result of the many freshwater tributaries that make their watery home less salty. The oysters from Chincoteague Inlet, in Virginia, are made salty by the waxing and waning Atlantic tide that continually washes over them, and Breton Sound oysters are sweetest in the spring, when the Louisiana marshes are flooded with fresh water.

This same filtration process makes oysters one of the most vulnerable of all sea creatures; given polluted water, they are among the first to suffer. And because oyster reefs play a key role in maintaining estuaries—the nurseries of the sea—the consequences of their destruction are manifold. As consumers, our best bet is to support local, sustainably operated oyster fisheries and—most urgently—ongoing efforts to restore the national treasures that are Southern oyster reefs.

brandied chicken liver pâté

A nice splash of brandy adds depth of flavor to this creamy pâté, which is just right served on crostini, toast points (see Know-how, page 19), or Cornbread Toasts (page 18) topped with Sweet Pickle Relish (page 299). For the best results, start with fresh livers from the butcher or farmer's market that haven't been frozen. Note that the chicken livers must soak in buttermilk for several hours prior to cooking. SERVES 4 TO 6

1	pound chicken livers, trimmed and connective tissue removed
1/2	cup well-shaken buttermilk
8	tablespoons (1 stick) unsalted butter, softened
1	tablespoon olive oil
2	shallots, chopped
2	garlic cloves, smashed
	Sea salt and freshly ground black pepper
1/3	cup brandy
1	tablespoon chopped fresh parsley
2	teaspoons fresh thyme, plus 3 or 4 sprigs for garnish
1/4	cup heavy cream
2	tablespoons melted butter, chicken fat, or duck fat

Rinse and drain the chicken livers. Place in a bowl with the buttermilk, cover, and let sit, refrigerated, for several hours or overnight. Drain and pat dry.

Heat 2 tablespoons of the butter and the olive oil in a large skillet over medium-high heat until sizzling hot (see Know-how, page 100). Add the shallots and cook and stir for about 3 minutes, until they begin to soften. Add the garlic and continue to cook and stir for 1 minute more.

Add the chicken livers, season with salt and pepper to taste, and cook and stir for 3 to 4 minutes, until the livers are brown all over but still slightly pink on the inside. Add the brandy, parsley, and thyme and cook and stir for about 1 minute, until the brandy reduces slightly. Remove from the heat and let cool to room temperature.

Combine the liver mixture and cooking liquid in a food processor and add the cream. With the motor running, add the remaining 6 tablespoons softened butter, 1 tablespoon at a time, until smooth and incorporated.

Spoon the mixture into a 2-cup mold and spread evenly. Pour the melted butter over the top and add a few sprigs of thyme for garnish. Refrigerate for at least 2 hours or overnight, until firmly set.

Destination: **MOBILE, ALABAMA**

WORTH THE DETOUR

WINTZELL'S OYSTER HOUSE'S

fresh oysters on the half shell

(251) 432-4605

wintzellsoysterhouse.com

FIRST STARTED GOING TO WINTZELL'S OYSTER HOUSE, A FUNKY LITTLE GEM of a place in historic downtown Mobile, many years ago, when I was in college and my sister, Judy, and her husband, Pat, still lived in the area. I loved the crumbling white storefront with its quirky, hand-lettered signs; the worn old butcher block that could be glimpsed behind the oyster bar and that bore the deep scars of so many oyster knives; and the myriad sayings from the restaurant's original owner, J. Oliver Wintzell, that papered the walls in a bright patchwork of homespun wit and wisdom. Most of all, I loved the briny-sweet oysters that emerged from the kitchen in an unbroken stream. They could be ordered by the dozen, "fried, stewed, or nude," but I quickly came to see that with oysters as flavorful as theirs, "nude" was the way to go. Slurping a dozen of Wintzell's lemony oysters from their pearly shells while sipping a cold beer and chewing the fat became a favorite ritual of ours, and it was how we passed many slow evenings in Mobile.

Since that time, the ownership has changed hands and several new locations have opened, but Wintzell's is still the same as ever, staying true to the six-stool oyster bar it started out as in 1938. That means that not only do old Mr. Wintzell's sayings remain the primary form of decoration, but also that the oysters are as succulent, plump, and fresh as they've always been. And *that* means a visit to Wintzell's is still my first order of business anytime I find myself anywhere near Mobile—and you should make it yours, too.

Most of all, I loved the briny-sweet oysters that emerged from the kitchen in an unbroken stream.

mint juleps

Thanks to the Kentucky Derby, mint juleps are the best known—and perhaps best loved—of all Southern cocktails. The details are much debated, but the basics are these: fresh spearmint, lightly bruised; smoky-sweet bourbon; cane sugar; and crushed ice. A combination so good, there isn't much that can be done to improve it. MAKES 4 COCKTAILS

Divide **2 tablespoons natural cane sugar** and **1 cup fresh mint** evenly between 4 glasses and crush well with a wooden spoon, muddler, or pestle. Divide **2 cups crushed ice** and **4 ounces (½ cup) bourbon** evenly between the glasses and stir to mix well. Garnish the glasses with **mint sprigs** and serve cold.

salty dogs

The combination of bittersweet grapefruit, lime, and salt in this refreshing cocktail is a true palate cleanser. MAKES 4 COCKTAILS

Scatter **2 tablespoons sea salt** on a small plate. Cut **3 pink grapefruits** in half. Run the cut edges of the grapefruit around the rims of 4 glasses and dip the rims into the salt to coat. Fill the glasses with ice.

Squeeze the juice from the grapefruit halves and place in a cocktail shaker with a small amount of ice, **4 ounces (½ cup) vodka,** and the **juice of 1 lime.** Shake a few times and pour over the ice into the glasses. Top each glass with a **splash of seltzer.** Squeeze a **lime or grapefruit wedge** into each drink and serve.

meyer lemonade

The delicate, orangelike flavor of Meyer lemons is what sets this mellow lemonade apart. For a cocktail version, spike the punch bowl with a glug or two of Jack Daniel's.
MAKES ABOUT 2 QUARTS

Place **1½ cups freshly squeezed Meyer lemon juice (from 10 to 12 lemons),** ½ cup **natural cane sugar,** ¼ **cup honey,** and a **pinch of sea salt** in a large glass pitcher with **6 cups water** and stir until the sugar and honey dissolve. Add **lemon slices from 1 Meyer lemon** and **4 fresh mint sprigs** and refrigerate until ready to serve. Serve chilled with **additional Meyer lemon slices or mint for garnish.**

sazeracs

Now the official cocktail of New Orleans, this spicy, heady concoction was the creation of a Creole apothecary named Peychaud whose medicinal tinctures became after-hours cocktails with the addition of whiskey and sugar.   MAKES 4 COCKTAILS

Place a **splash of absinthe or Herbsaint** in each of 4 glasses and coat the insides of the glasses by swirling the absinthe around; fill the glasses with ice.

Fill a cocktail shaker halfway with ice. Add **4 ounces (½ cup) rye whiskey or bourbon, 2 tablespoons natural cane sugar,** the **juice of ½ lemon,** and **8 dashes of Peychaud bitters;** shake to mix until the sugar dissolves. Pour over the ice-filled glasses and serve garnished with **lemon twists.**

wendy's bloody marys

My friend Wendy makes the best Bloody Marys—full of punchy, spicy flavor. Serve them with little dishes of pickles as well as the usual cucumber and celery spears for fun mix-and-match garnishes.   MAKES 4 TO 6 COCKTAILS

Combine **4 cups tomato juice, 8 ounces (1 cup) vodka, ⅓ cup prepared horseradish, ¼ cup Worcestershire sauce,** the **juice of 3 limes, 1 tablespoon hot sauce, 2 teaspoons sea salt,** and **1 teaspoon freshly ground black pepper** in a large pitcher and stir to mix. Taste for seasoning, adding more salt and pepper, if desired, and pour over ice. Garnish with **assorted pickles** and serve chilled.

minted sweet tea

When Southerners say "tea," they mean basic black—as in Lipton or Tetley, not English Breakfast or Earl Grey—iced and sweet. It is the ubiquitous, unofficial drink of the South.   MAKES 2 QUARTS

Bring **4 cups water** to a boil in a saucepan and remove from the heat. Halve and squeeze **3 lemons,** setting aside the juice and reserving the squeezed halves. Add **8 bags black tea, 6 to 8 fresh mint sprigs,** the reserved squeezed lemon halves, and **½ cup sugar** and stir to mix and submerge the mint and tea bags. Cover and let steep for 15 to 20 minutes. Remove and discard the bags, mint, and lemon halves. Add **4 more cups water** and the reserved lemon juice and stir to mix. Taste for sweetness and add up to ¼ **cup additional sugar to taste,** if desired, stirring to mix until the sugar dissolves. Serve cold over ice, garnished with **sprigs of mint and wedges of lemon.**

soups, stews, and gumbo

When I was growing up, my mom made soup all the time.

Her vegetable soup, a hearty mix of corn, lima beans, potatoes, and whatever else was in season, was delicious, but she was famous for her meaty, chunky Brunswick Stew (page 38). Mom made her stew in huge batches for the Fourth of July, Labor Day, and family gatherings in one of those enormous black cast-iron kettles over a wood fire in the backyard.

In my view, there is nothing in the world homier than soup. What could be cozier than a simmering, fragrant pot bubbling away on the stove? It's the ultimate comfort food. It's practically impossible to make a batch of soup that feeds fewer than four people (just ask my mom!); more likely, you end up with a huge pot that lasts the better part of a week, with enough left over to freeze or give away. Because of this, and because soup usually calls for less (and usually less expensive) meat and is forgiving enough to absorb bits of this and that from the pantry, it embodies and encourages resourcefulness, thrift, and generosity.

With ample yields and equally big flavors, as well as a healthy appetite for improvisation, the Southern approach to soups and stews epitomizes this sensibility. In developing the recipes for this chapter, I have tried to do the same. I often come up with ideas for soups and stews when trying to figure out how to use leftovers. As with Ham Bone Soup (page 37), the best creations are often the accidental by-products of just this sort of practical experimentation. Seasonal abundance is another motivating factor; the transformation of daunting piles of garden-ripe squash and tomatoes into Summer Squash Soup (page 36) and Garden Tomato Soup with Creamy Goat Cheese (page 35), respectively, prove that necessity is, indeed, the mother of invention. I encourage you to use these recipes as templates or jumping-off points. Like me, you can follow the seasons, your inspiration, your pantry—and perhaps last night's dinner—to make these recipes work for you with great results.

garden tomato soup with creamy goat cheese

No matter how many tomato sandwiches, salads, or platters of thick, salted slices we eat, come August we can never seem to keep up with the overabundance of tender-ripe Beefsteaks, Early Girls, Cherokee Purples, and Arkansas Travelers taking up semi-permanent residence on the kitchen counter. Everyone develops a strategy for the happy problem of too many tomatoes: in some people it inspires bouts of generous and indiscriminate gift giving; in others, a frenzy of canning and freezing. This light and satisfying take on cream of tomato soup is my favorite solution. MAKES ABOUT 2 QUARTS / SERVES 6 TO 8

2	tablespoons olive oil
2	tablespoons unsalted butter
2	onions, chopped
2	garlic cloves, smashed and chopped
8	garden-ripe tomatoes (about 4 pounds), peeled
2	teaspoons sea salt, plus more to taste
½	teaspoon freshly ground black pepper, plus more to taste
6	cups low-sodium chicken or vegetable broth
2	bay leaves
1	teaspoon crushed red pepper flakes
1	cup fresh basil leaves, plus shredded basil for garnish (optional)
1	cup (4 ounces) crumbled soft goat cheese, plus more for garnish (optional)
	Crusty baguette, sliced and toasted, for serving (optional)

Heat the olive oil and butter in a large saucepan or Dutch oven over medium heat until hot. Add the onions and cook and stir for about 10 minutes, until soft and light brown. Add the garlic and cook for 1 minute more, stirring constantly.

Core and roughly chop the tomatoes and add, along with their juices, to the onions. Season with salt and black pepper to taste and cook, stirring occasionally, for about 10 minutes. Add the broth, bay leaves, and red pepper flakes and bring the soup to a low boil. Reduce the heat and simmer for 20 to 30 minutes, until the tomatoes break down and the flavors meld.

Remove the soup from the heat, remove and discard the bay leaves, and stir in the basil and goat cheese. Using an immersion blender, standing blender, or food processor, puree the soup until smooth. (If using a blender or food processor, allow the soup to cool slightly before blending in batches.) Taste for seasoning and add more salt and pepper, if desired.

Serve hot with toasted baguette slices or chilled with a sprinkling of crumbled goat cheese and shredded basil, if desired.

summer squash soup

My friend Phyllis from Mississippi makes this vibrant and creamy squash soup when she comes to visit us in the summer. It's such a quick and easy way to make use of fast-growing summer squash that it's bound to become one of your summer staples, too.

MAKES ABOUT 3 QUARTS / SERVES 8 TO 10

4	tablespoons (½ stick) unsalted butter
2	tablespoons olive oil
1	onion, diced
3	celery stalks, chopped
2	garlic cloves, smashed and minced
4	cups low-sodium chicken broth
6	medium to large summer squash (about 3 pounds), trimmed and sliced
2	teaspoons sea salt, plus more to taste
½	teaspoon freshly ground white pepper or black pepper, plus more to taste
1	cup half-and-half
8	fresh basil leaves, thinly sliced, plus more for garnish
2	tablespoons chopped fresh parsley

Heat the butter and olive oil in a large saucepan over medium heat until hot. Add the onion and celery and cook, stirring, until the onion is soft and golden, about 5 minutes. Add the garlic and cook and stir for 1 minute more.

Add the broth, squash, salt, and pepper and stir to combine. Bring to a low boil, reduce the heat, and simmer until the squash is tender, stirring occasionally, about 15 minutes. Remove from the heat and add the half-and-half, basil, and parsley.

Using an immersion blender, standing blender, or food processor, puree the soup until smooth. (If using a blender or food processor, allow the soup to cool slightly before blending in batches.) Taste for seasoning and add more salt and pepper, if desired. Serve hot or cold, garnished with basil.

ON THE SIDE   For a filling and summery supper, try serving this soup with Fried Green Tomato BLT (page 79) or Grilled Peach Salad with Shaved Country Ham and Summer Herbs (page 273) and Watercress Angel Biscuits (page 54) or slices of crusty bread.

ham bone soup

A few years ago, at Easter, in addition to the usual spread of ham and sides, I made a gratin of white beans, country ham, and collards from Frank Stitt's very fine *Southern Table* cookbook. That dish, which everyone raved about, and the leftover ham bone—a prized ingredient that should never, ever be put to waste—inspired this low-on-the-hog soup. MAKES 3 TO 4 QUARTS / SERVES 10 TO 12

2½	cups (about 1 pound) dried flageolet or navy beans
2	tablespoons olive oil
2	onions, chopped
4	carrots, chopped
2	celery stalks, chopped
4	garlic cloves, smashed and minced
	Leftover ham bone, with some meat left on the bone
4	quarts cold water
2	bay leaves
2	teaspoons sea salt, plus more to taste
1	teaspoon crushed red pepper flakes
½	teaspoon freshly ground black pepper, plus more to taste
1	bunch collard greens (about 1 pound), washed and drained, stems removed and roughly chopped
	White onion, sliced, for garnish
	Hot sauce, for garnish

Soak the beans overnight or, for a quick soak, place in a pot, cover with water, add salt, and boil for about 45 minutes, just until they begin to soften. Drain and rinse.

Heat the olive oil in a large saucepan or Dutch oven over medium heat until hot. Add the onions, reduce the heat to low, and cook and stir for about 10 minutes, until soft and light brown. Add the carrots and celery and continue to cook and stir for about 5 minutes longer, until the vegetables are tender. Add the garlic and continue to cook, stirring constantly, for about 1 minute.

Add the ham bone, beans, and cold water. Season with the bay leaves, salt, red pepper flakes, and black pepper and stir to mix. Bring to a low boil, then reduce the heat to low and simmer for about 2 hours, skimming the scum that rises to the top as needed, until the ham is falling off the bone and the beans are tender.

Remove the bone from the pot and remove and discard the bay leaves. When cool enough to handle, pick the meat from the bone, shred it, and return the meat to the soup, discarding the bone.

Stir in the collard greens and simmer for another 15 to 20 minutes, until the greens are wilted and tender. Taste for seasoning and add more salt and pepper, if desired. Serve warm with lots of onion and hot sauce on the side.

brunswick stew

Rich and meaty Brunswick stew is a true Southern classic. This streamlined rendition of my mom's perfect version makes a huge amount of food—but to my thinking, that's the point of stew. It tastes even better the next day, so it's a great make-ahead meal if you are planning to have weekend visitors or feed a big crowd. You can also pop some in the freezer for a quick-fix weeknight supper another time.

MAKES 5½ TO 6 QUARTS / SERVES 16 TO 20

	One 3½- to 4-pound chicken
4	bay leaves
6	quarts cold water
	Sea salt and freshly ground black pepper
2	tablespoons olive oil
2	tablespoons unsalted butter
2	pounds beef stew meat, cut into 1-inch chunks
2	pounds pork butt, cut into 1-inch chunks
2	onions, chopped, skins and trimmings reserved
4	celery stalks, chopped, leaves reserved
4	carrots, chopped, peels and trimmings reserved
	One 28-ounce can diced tomatoes and their juice
½	cup ketchup
¼	cup Worcestershire sauce
2	teaspoons crushed red pepper flakes
3	large potatoes (about 1½ pounds), peeled and chopped
4	cups fresh or frozen corn kernels (about 1 pound)
4	cups fresh or frozen butter beans or lima beans (about 1 pound)
	Hot sauce, for serving

Rinse the chicken and remove any excess fat. Place the chicken and 2 of the bay leaves in a large soup or stockpot and cover with the cold water. Season with salt and black pepper to taste and bring to a low boil. Add the vegetable trimmings as you prep the vegetables. Reduce the heat and simmer for about 1 hour, skimming the top of the broth as needed, until the juices run clear when the chicken is pierced with the tip of a small knife.

Remove the chicken and set aside to cool. Strain the broth into a large bowl, discarding the bay leaves and vegetable trimmings. Skim and discard the fat from the top of the broth with a large spoon.

When the chicken has cooled enough to handle, pull the meat from the bones, discarding the skin and bones.

Place the olive oil and butter in the same pot and heat over medium heat until the butter is sizzling hot (see Know-how, page 100). Season the stew meat and pork butt with salt and black pepper to taste, add to the pot, and cook, stirring occasionally, until brown all over, 10 to 12 minutes. Remove the meat from the pan and set aside.

Place the onions in the same pot, reduce the heat to low, and cook and stir for about 10 minutes, until soft and light brown. Add the celery and carrots and cook and stir for 5 minutes more. Add the reserved broth, the remaining bay leaves, the beef, pork, tomatoes, ketchup, Worcestershire sauce, and red pepper flakes. Season with salt and black pepper and bring to a low boil. Reduce the heat and simmer, uncovered, for 1 hour.

Add the chicken and potatoes and continue to cook, stirring occasionally, for 30 minutes longer, until the stew meat is very tender. Remove and discard the bay leaves. Add the corn and butter beans and continue to cook for 15 to 20 minutes more, until the beans are tender. Taste for seasoning and add more salt and pepper, if desired. Serve hot with hot sauce on the side to give it a kick.

ON THE SIDE   Celebrate Labor Day or the Fourth of July in high Southern style by serving Brunswick Stew with Crispy Crusty Jalapeño Cornbread Sticks (page 58) or Squash Puppies (page 65) and Watermelon-Tomato Salad with Shaved Feta and Handfuls of Mint (page 270). Don't forget the Mint Juleps (page 27) and Meyer Lemonade (page 27)!

chew on this: ***about brunswick stew***

With Brunswick, Georgia, and Brunswick County, Virginia, laying competing claims, the exact origins of Brunswick stew remain a mystery, but it hardly matters—either way, the stew is a staple of Southern cuisine. It can be found year-round in restaurants—barbecue joints, mainly—but it's traditionally served on Labor Day, the start of hunting season, as a way to clean last year's meat out of the freezer. Consequently, this vegetable-based stew is made using every kind of meat you could possibly think of—and some you might not want to think of—including chicken, pork, beef, rabbit, and squirrel.

carolina shrimp chowder

Every summer when the Carolina shrimp are in season, Nana's, which is one of my favorite restaurants in Durham, makes a delicious shrimp chowder that is the inspiration for this light and succulent soup. Nana's version is rich and creamy—closer to a traditional potato chowder—but because I love the sweetness of the corn and shrimp together, I make mine thinner, more like a corn chowder. To give this dish extra oomph, I add the shrimp at the very end, so they are tender and extra sweet, and top with Crispy Fried Oysters Four Ways (page 117). MAKES ABOUT 3 QUARTS / SERVES 8 TO 10

6	ears corn, shucked, cobs and trimmings reserved for broth
2	tablespoons olive oil
1	onion, diced
3	russet potatoes (about 1½ pounds), chopped
2	celery stalks, diced
1	red bell pepper, cored, seeded, and diced
1	jalapeño pepper, cored, seeded, and diced
3	garlic cloves, smashed and minced
2	quarts Fast and Fresh Broth (recipe follows)
2	tablespoons fresh thyme, plus more for garnish
2	bay leaves
2	teaspoons sea salt, plus more to taste
½	teaspoon freshly ground black pepper, plus more to taste
10	fresh basil leaves, thinly sliced, plus more for garnish
2	pounds large shrimp, peeled and deveined, shells reserved for broth

Cut the corn from the cobs into a large bowl and scrape the stripped cobs with the back of the knife to release the juices into the bowl. Reserve 3 of the cobs.

Heat the olive oil in a large saucepan or Dutch oven over medium heat until hot. Add the onion and cook for about 10 minutes, stirring frequently, until soft and light brown. Add the potatoes, celery, bell pepper, and jalapeño and cook, stirring frequently, for another 5 minutes. Add the garlic and continue to cook and stir for 1 minute more.

Add the broth, reserved corn cobs, thyme, bay leaves, salt, and black pepper and bring the soup to a low boil. Reduce the heat to low and simmer for about 30 minutes, until the potatoes are tender.

Add the corn kernels and basil and cook, stirring occasionally, for 5 minutes more. Remove and discard the corn cobs and bay leaves and, using an immersion blender, standing blender, or food processor, puree half the soup until smooth. (If using a blender or food processor, allow the soup to cool slightly before blending in batches.) Return the pureed mixture to the saucepan and stir to mix and thicken the soup.

(continued)

Add the shrimp and let simmer for about 3 minutes, until the shrimp are bright pink and just cooked through. Taste for seasoning and add more salt and pepper, if desired. Serve immediately garnished with thyme and basil.

fast and fresh broth

This flexible broth is one of the things I always try to teach when I'm giving cooking classes because it's *easy* to throw together a fast, flavor-enhancing broth using whatever you already have on hand—the trimmings from the herbs, aromatics, and vegetables you are cooking with and the bones or shells from any meat or seafood on the menu. Just throw a pot of water on first thing when you start to cook and add to it as the ingredients are prepped. Here's a basic recipe made with the shrimp shells and trimmings from the preceding recipe, but remember: you can apply the concept to any of the soup recipes in this chapter. Most anything goes, but stay away from vegetable trimmings that might become bitter or have an overly strong flavor, like eggplant and broccoli.   MAKES ABOUT 2½ QUARTS

Place the **reserved shrimp shells; corn cobs; onion, celery, pepper trimmings;** and **herb stems** in a large pot with **about 3 quarts cold water** and bring to a low boil.

Reduce the heat to low and simmer for about 30 minutes. Note that most of the flavors from shrimp shells and vegetables cook out after about 30 minutes, but bones take a little more time. If using bones in place of shells, let the broth cook about 30 minutes longer.

Strain the broth, discarding the shells and trimmings, and proceed with your soup recipe.

SARA'S SWAPS   To give this soup a more traditional, smoky chowder flavor, add 2 slices chopped, thick-cut bacon when you add the onion. Alternatively, put the focus on oysters rather than shrimp by omitting the shrimp from the chowder and garnishing with Crispy Fried Oysters Four Ways (page 117). Or, take a simpler, fresher route and garnish with chopped summer tomatoes or Simple Lump Crab Salad (page 111).

oyster stew, rockefeller style

Traditional oyster stew was one of my dad's favorites, and he used to make it all the time, especially when we visited my sister in Biloxi, Mississippi, where we could get really fresh oysters. Taking a cue from oysters Rockefeller, another hallmark dish from Antoine's Restaurant in New Orleans, I brighten my version with fresh spinach. And, to achieve the same smooth, creamy texture with less fat, I blend potatoes with just a touch of heavy cream to make the broth. Taste for seasoning and add more salt and pepper, if desired. This soup should be served hot as soon as it's done, lest the oysters continue to cook in the broth. MAKES ABOUT 2 QUARTS / SERVES 6 TO 8

3	tablespoons unsalted butter
1	tablespoon olive oil
2	russet potatoes (about 1 pound), peeled and chopped
1	onion, chopped
3	celery stalks, chopped
1/4	cup all-purpose flour
2	teaspoons sea salt, plus more to taste
1/2	teaspoon freshly ground black pepper, plus more to taste
	Pinch of ground cayenne pepper
1/4	cup chopped fresh parsley, plus more for garnish
4	garlic cloves, smashed and minced
1	tablespoon chopped fresh marjoram or basil
3	cups low-sodium chicken broth
1	pint fresh shucked oysters, such as Apalachicola or Breton Sound, strained with the liquor reserved, picked through and shells removed
1	cup heavy cream
4	cups roughly chopped spinach, washed and drained

Heat the butter and olive oil in a large saucepan over medium heat until hot. Add the potatoes and onion and cook, stirring frequently, for about 10 minutes, until the onion is soft and light brown. Add the celery and cook, stirring occasionally, for 5 minutes more. Add the flour, salt, black pepper, and cayenne and cook, stirring constantly, until golden brown, about 3 minutes. Add the parsley, garlic, and marjoram and cook and stir for 1 minute more.

Stir in the broth and reserved oyster liquor and cook, stirring occasionally, until the mixture is slightly thick and the potatoes are soft, about 15 minutes. Add the cream, stir to mix, and reduce the heat to low. Using a potato masher, mash the potatoes to help thicken the soup. Add the oysters and spinach and cook for about 3 minutes, stirring frequently, until the oysters are just cooked (the edges will begin to curl up) and the spinach is wilted.

Remove from the heat to avoid overcooking the oysters. Serve warm, sprinkled with parsley.

quick seafood and chicken sausage gumbo

see photograph on page 30

When Paul Prudhomme's first cookbook, Chef Paul Prudhomme's Louisiana *Kitchen,* came out, I think I made every last one of his gumbos in the span of a few weeks. To this day, his are the recipes I always refer to when I make gumbo. More often than not, however, I don't have time to make ultratraditional, slow-cooking gumbo, so I've adapted my own quicker—and often lighter—versions that take a fraction of the time but still pack loads of soulful flavor. Served over rice with ice-cold beer, it's all the excuse you need to throw a block party. MAKES ABOUT 4 QUARTS / SERVES 10 TO 12

1/3	cup canola oil
1/2	cup all-purpose flour
2	onions, chopped, skins and trimmings reserved for broth
1	bell pepper, cored, seeded, and chopped, trimmings reserved for stock
1	poblano chile or 2 jalapeño peppers, cored, seeded, and diced
4	celery stalks, diced, trimmings reserved for stock
2	tablespoons unsalted butter
1	pound spicy chicken sausage links, cut into 3-inch pieces
4	garlic cloves, smashed and minced
2	bay leaves
1	teaspoon sea salt, plus more to taste
1/2	teaspoon dried thyme
1/2	teaspoon ground cayenne pepper
1/2	teaspoon freshly ground black pepper, plus more to taste
2 1/2	quarts Fast and Fresh Broth (page 42)
2	cups chopped fresh or canned tomatoes, with juice
2	pounds large shrimp, peeled and deveined, shells reserved for broth
2	cups chopped okra
1/2	pound fresh lump crabmeat, picked through for shells
2	tablespoons fresh thyme, plus more for garnish
8	fresh basil leaves, plus more for garnish
	Steamed white or Creamed Vegetable Rice (page 216), for serving

Heat the canola oil in a large Dutch oven or heavy cast-iron skillet over medium-high heat until sizzling hot (see Know-how, page 100). To make a roux, reduce the heat to medium-low, add the flour, and cook, stirring constantly with a long-handled whisk, until the mixture changes from light to golden brown, 8 to 10 minutes, adjusting the heat if the flour starts browning too quickly.

Add the onions, bell pepper, poblano chile, celery, and butter and cook, stirring frequently, for about 10 minutes, until the vegetables are tender. Add the sausage and garlic and cook and stir for 2 to 3 minutes more. Add the bay leaves, salt, dried thyme, cayenne, and black pepper and stir to mix. Add the broth and tomatoes and their juice, stir to combine, and bring the mixture to a low boil. Reduce the heat and simmer for about 40 minutes, stirring occasionally.

Stir in the shrimp, okra, crab, fresh thyme, and basil and simmer for about 5 minutes, until the shrimp are just cooked and the okra is tender, stirring occasionally. Taste for seasoning and add salt and pepper, if desired. Remove and discard bay leaves. Serve warm over steamed white or Creamed Vegetable Rice, garnished with thyme and basil.

Know-how: about roux

The paste of oil, butter, and flour that begins this recipe is called a roux, and it forms the base of gumbo and other stews. The key to cooking roux—which is made from approximately one part fat to one part flour—is to constantly tend the pot, stirring and adjusting the temperature as necessary to avoid burning. The length of time you cook the roux affects the color and flavor of the final dish; the longer you cook it, the darker and smokier the stew. Roux cooked for a shorter period of time are golden to reddish brown in color, resulting in blonder gumbos and stews with full-bodied, but slightly subtler, flavor. Roux that are cooked longer, until dark red to dark brown—even blackish—create gumbos and stews with a distinctive rich, deep, smoky flavor. Oil or butter (or a combination of the two) may be used, but butter is better suited to lighter roux than darker roux, as it tends to burn more readily than oil.

SARA'S SWAPS This seafood gumbo can be easily adapted depending on what's in season or what your fishmonger has in good supply. Some of my favorite additions include soft-shell crabs, oysters, and crawfish. Just make sure to adjust the cooking time as necessary for any variations in seafood. You can also experiment with different kinds of meat, from smoked tasso ham to sausages of all kinds, including boudin, andouille, chorizo, linguiça, and kielbasa.

chew on this: *gumbo and potato salad*

Although gumbo is most often served on a bed of white rice, there is a little-known Creole tradition of serving it over a bed of good, old-fashioned potato salad. If you're feeling adventurous, give it a try by serving this gumbo over Creamy Potato Salad (page 266).

CHAPTER *three*

biscuits, cornbread, and rolls

I can't think of a single meal that came out of Granny Foster's kitchen, whether it was breakfast, lunch, dinner, or something in between, that wasn't punctuated by a side of biscuits, cornbread, or dinner rolls—and sometimes all three. This tendency was most extreme during the holidays, when three kinds of biscuits (angel, buttermilk, and cream), rolls, and cornbread all jostled for space at the same crowded table. We'd smother them in sweet butter and whatever else was on our plates, but each type of bread was individually prized for its particular affinities with other foods. Cornbread we loved for its compatibility with chili, succotash, barbecue, and greens with pot likker; rolls, for the soft pillows they made for fried chicken, mashed potatoes, and gravy; and biscuits, as a vessel for all these things, plus country ham, fresh fruit, preserves, molasses, fried eggs, and just about everything else we ate.

Most of the women in my family—not just Granny Foster—had made these special breads so often that their recipes had long since been memorized and then forgotten in favor of some sixth culinary sense that allowed them to skillfully eyeball the ingredients: dumping, pinching, and dashing until everything looked and felt just right. I'll never forget how my grandmother mixed her biscuits right on the countertop, no bowl in sight, by forming a little well with the flour to catch the buttermilk.

Although most Southerners today no longer eat these traditional breads on a daily basis, their near-magical hold on the Southern palate and imagination hasn't waned. For Southerners, biscuits, cornbread, and—to a lesser extent—yeast rolls are more than mere accompaniments; they are the comfort of home and gracious hospitality in tangible form.

The uniformly simple recipes in this chapter, from my Favorite Buttermilk Biscuits (page 51) to Kate's Sweet Potato Refrigerator Rolls (page 66) and Squash Puppies (page 65), are the easiest way I know to elevate an ordinary meal into something more—and always something better.

favorite buttermilk biscuits

As anyone who has actually made biscuits from scratch will tell you, they are fast and oh-so-easy—no culinary wizardry required. Of course, you needn't go out of your way to divulge that fact when serving these rich, flaky biscuits to a chorus of *oohs* and *ahhs.* Sometimes, certain things are better left unsaid. Serve warm with lots of sweet butter, honey, molasses, or jam.   MAKES ABOUT 1 DOZEN 2- TO 2½-INCH BISCUITS

2½ cups self-rising flour (see Know-how, page 53)
   Pinch of kosher salt
   Pinch of sugar
8 tablespoons (1 stick) cold unsalted butter, cut into small pieces
2 tablespoons vegetable shortening or lard
1 cup well-shaken buttermilk
2 tablespoons unsalted butter, melted

Preheat the oven to 425°F. Lightly grease a baking sheet.

Place the flour, salt, and sugar in a large bowl and stir to mix. Cut the butter and the shortening into the flour mixture using a pastry blender or two knives in a crosscutting motion until the mixture resembles coarse meal. Work quickly so the butter remains cool and doesn't melt into the flour.

Create a well in the center of the flour-butter mixture. Pour the buttermilk into the well and stir together just until all the flour is incorporated; do not overmix.

Turn the dough onto a lightly floured surface and knead two or three times, just until it comes together, and form into a flat disk. Using a lightly floured rolling pin or your hands, roll or pat the dough ½ to ¾ inch thick. Lightly flour a 2- to 2½-inch biscuit cutter and cut the biscuits, leaving as little space between each cut as possible and pressing down just once for each biscuit; do not twist the cutter. If the dough begins to stick to the cutter, dip the cutter in a little flour. Gather the excess biscuit dough, reroll once, and cut as many biscuits from it as possible.

Arrange the biscuits on the prepared baking sheet and bake for 15 to 18 minutes, until the biscuits have risen and are golden brown. Remove from the oven and brush the tops with the melted butter.

---

chew on this: *about flour and fat*

Because biscuits are made with so few ingredients, the quality of each one is of utmost importance. That probably accounts for why Southerners are so famously particular about the kind of flour and shortening they use in their biscuits. My mother swears by Martha White flour and Crisco, whereas I—and many others—favor White Lily flour, a brand that is practically synonymous with Southern baking. As for shortening, there are factions that favor lard, those that favor vegetable shortening, and those that favor butter. I use mostly butter for its superior flavor, but I typically add just a little bit of vegetable shortening or lard for extra flakiness.

Know-how: *making no-fail biscuits*

Here are some quick tips that practically guarantee perfect biscuits every time.

• For the softest biscuits, always use flour that has a low gluten content. All-purpose flour is a safe bet, and certain brands, such as White Lily and Martha White, are known for being extra soft. Steer clear of whole-wheat or bread flour.

• Do not add more flour than is needed to keep the dough from sticking together; if you add too much, the dough will be tough.

• Do not mix or work the dough any more than is necessary to bring it together.

• Never roll biscuit dough more than twice or your biscuits will be tough. Any scraps left over from the second rolling can be wrapped around cooked sausage links and baked as pigs-in-blankets (see Sara's Swaps, page 68) or baked as they are—they won't look as nice but they'll taste just as good!

• Dip the biscuit cutter in flour to keep the dough from sticking to the cutter.

• To allow your biscuits to more fully rise, cut straight down with the biscuit cutter and resist the urge to twist.

• For biscuits with soft sides, bake them nestled up next to each other so the sides are touching. For crispy sides, leave a one-inch space between the biscuits.

• For a fail-proof way of cutting the butter into the flour without any danger of the butter melting, freeze the butter for several hours or overnight and then simply use a grater to grate the butter into the flour.

• Rotate the pan halfway through baking for even cooking and color.

cream biscuits with sugared strawberries

Growing up, my sister, Judy, and I coveted one simple dish above all others for breakfast: hot biscuits topped with lightly mashed strawberries and lots of sweet butter. I use a dead-simple recipe for cream biscuits adapted here from the *Times-Picayune* of New Orleans. MAKES ABOUT 1 DOZEN 2- TO 2½-INCH BISCUITS

2½ cups self-rising flour (see Know-how, below)
Pinch of kosher salt
1½ cups heavy cream, plus more for brushing on the biscuits
¼ cup sugar (less if the strawberries are really sweet),
plus more for sprinkling on the biscuits
2 pints (about 4 cups) ripe strawberries, hulled and sliced
2 tablespoons unsalted butter, cut into slices

Preheat the oven to 450°F. Lightly grease a baking sheet.

Place the flour and salt in a large bowl and stir to mix. Add the cream and stir to mix just until the flour is moist.

Turn the dough onto a lightly floured surface and knead three or four times, just until it comes together, and form into a flat disk. Using a lightly floured rolling pin or your hands, roll or pat the dough about ½ inch thick. Lightly flour a 2- to 2½-inch biscuit cutter and cut the biscuits, leaving as little space between each cut as possible and pressing down just once for each biscuit; do not twist the cutter. If the dough begins to stick to the cutter, dip the cutter in a little flour. Gather the excess biscuit dough, reroll once, and cut as many biscuits from it as possible.

Arrange the biscuits on the prepared baking sheet. Brush the tops with cream, sprinkle with sugar, and bake until golden brown, 10 to 12 minutes.

While the biscuits are baking, combine the strawberries and remaining ¼ cup of the sugar in a bowl and mash lightly with a fork or your hand to release some of the juices.

Remove the biscuits from the oven, split in half, and place a pat of butter in the middle, allowing the butter to melt. Spoon the strawberries over and serve warm.

Know-how: making self-rising flour

If you don't have self-rising flour in your pantry, you can still avoid a trip to the store by making your own. Add 2 teaspoons baking powder or 1½ teaspoons baking powder plus ½ teaspoon baking soda to every 3 cups of all-purpose flour. If the recipe does not call for salt, add ½ teaspoon to the mix as well.

---

watercress angel biscuits

With the airiness of dinner rolls and the flaky, buttery layers of traditional biscuits, angel biscuits—which get their extra lift from a little yeast—truly deserve their celestial name. I add chopped watercress for its mild peppery flavor and a pop of color.

MAKES ABOUT 1 DOZEN 2- TO 2½-INCH BISCUITS

2   teaspoons active dry yeast (from one ¼-ounce envelope)
1   teaspoon sugar
¼   cup warm water (105°F to 115°F)
3   cups self-rising flour (see Know-how, page 53)
½   teaspoon kosher salt
8   tablespoons (1 stick) cold unsalted butter, cut into small pieces
¼   cup vegetable shortening
½   cup chopped fresh watercress leaves or arugula, washed and drained
1   cup well-shaken buttermilk
2   tablespoons unsalted butter, melted

Lightly grease a baking sheet.

Combine the yeast and sugar in a small bowl. Stir in the warm water and set aside in a warm place for about 5 minutes, until the yeast froths and doubles in size.

Meanwhile, stir together the flour and salt in a large bowl. Cut the butter and the shortening into the flour mixture using a pastry blender or two knives in a crosscutting motion until the mixture resembles coarse meal. Work quickly so the butter remains cool and doesn't melt into the flour. Stir in the watercress.

Add the buttermilk to the yeast mixture and stir to combine. Create a well in the center of the flour-butter mixture. Pour the buttermilk mixture into the flour mixture and stir just until the dough starts to stick together.

Turn the dough onto a lightly floured surface, knead several times, and form into a flat disk. Using a lightly floured rolling pin or your hands, roll or pat the dough ½ to ¾ inch thick. Lightly flour a 2- to 2½-inch biscuit cutter and cut the biscuits, leaving as little space between each cut as possible and pressing down just once for each biscuit; do not twist the cutter. If the dough begins to stick to the cutter, dip the cutter in a little flour. Gather the excess biscuit dough, reroll once, and cut as many biscuits from it as possible.

Preheat the oven to 425°F.

Arrange the biscuits on the prepared baking sheet and brush the tops lightly with the melted butter. Cover loosely with a clean cloth and let rise in a warm place until doubled in size, about 30 minutes. Uncover and bake for 15 to 18 minutes, until the biscuits rise and are golden brown. Remove from the oven and serve warm.

salt and pepper skillet cornbread

Some Southerners will happily argue till they are blue in the face defending the honor of unsweetened cornbread, a preference that tends to divide the South from the North. But I find that a touch of sugar adds a layer of complexity that is well worth breaking the rules. More important to me is the baking vessel: specifically, a cast-iron skillet, preferably one that is slicked with bacon grease. MAKES ONE 9- OR 10-INCH SKILLET

2	tablespoons bacon grease or olive oil
1½	cups yellow cornmeal
½	cup all-purpose flour
¼	cup sugar
2	teaspoons baking powder
2	teaspoons sea salt, plus more for sprinkling on top
1	teaspoon freshly ground black pepper, plus more for sprinkling on top
½	teaspoon baking soda
2	cups well-shaken buttermilk
2	large eggs, lightly beaten
2	tablespoons unsalted butter, melted

Preheat the oven to 425°F. Coat a 9- or 10-inch cast-iron skillet with the bacon grease and place it in the oven to heat while you mix the batter.

Combine the cornmeal, flour, sugar, baking powder, salt, pepper, and baking soda in a large bowl and stir to mix. Add the buttermilk, eggs, and butter and stir until just combined; do not overmix. The batter should be lumpy.

Pour the batter into the hot skillet and sprinkle the top with a little salt and pepper. Bake until the top is golden brown and a wooden skewer inserted in the center comes out clean, about 25 minutes.

Remove from the oven, turn the cornbread out of the skillet, slice into wedges, and serve warm.

CORNBREAD CROUTONS Preheat the oven to 400°F. Drizzle **2 cups ½-inch cubes of day-old Salt and Pepper Skillet Cornbread** with **2 tablespoons melted butter** and **1 tablespoon olive oil** and toss gently to coat. Season with **sea salt and freshly ground black pepper to taste** and any **fresh or dried herbs, such as parsley or oregano,** you have on hand. Spread the cornbread cubes in a single layer on a rimmed baking sheet and bake, uncovered, for 15 to 20 minutes, turning several times, until golden brown and crispy. Remove from the oven and use immediately or cool completely before storing in an airtight container for up to 2 weeks.

crispy crusty jalapeño cornbread sticks

Cornbread sticks are a Southern specialty and an example of function following form. I imagine that whoever dreamed them up was probably just trying to be cute by fashioning a corn-shaped mold for cornbread, but the end product, with its high ratio of crispy crust to soft innards and perfect shape for dipping in chili or pot likker, is a whole different animal. In this version, I kick things up a notch by adding sharp Cheddar cheese and spicy jalapeño pepper. If you don't have (or care to purchase) a corn stick pan—cast-iron only— you can, of course, use a skillet. MAKES ABOUT 14 CORN STICKS / ONE 9- OR 10-INCH SKILLET

1	cup yellow cornmeal
1/2	cup all-purpose flour
1	cup (4 ounces) grated sharp Cheddar cheese
1	jalapeño pepper, cored, seeded, and minced (about 2 tablespoons)
2	tablespoons sugar
2	teaspoons baking powder
1	teaspoon kosher salt
1/2	teaspoon freshly ground black pepper
1/2	teaspoon baking soda
1 1/4	cups well-shaken buttermilk
4	tablespoons (1/2 stick) unsalted butter, melted
2	large eggs, lightly beaten

Preheat the oven to 425°F.

Lightly grease 2 cast-iron corn stick pans and place in the oven to heat while you mix the batter. (If you have only one pan, halve the recipe or bake in batches, taking care to preheat the pan again before baking the second batch. The batter will be fine left at room temperature while the first batch bakes.)

Stir together the cornmeal, flour, cheese, jalapeño, sugar, baking powder, salt, black pepper, and baking soda in a large bowl. Whisk the buttermilk, butter, and eggs in a separate bowl. Add the buttermilk mixture to the flour mixture and stir just to combine. Do not overmix; the batter should have a lumpy appearance.

Remove the pans from the oven and spoon about 2 heaping tablespoons of batter into each mold. Return the pans to the oven and bake until the sticks are slightly puffed and golden, about 15 minutes (20 to 25 minutes if using a skillet). Remove from the oven and serve warm.

holiday cornbread dressing

This moist and flavorful cornbread dressing—or what you non-Southerners may call stuffing—appeared in *Martha Stewart Living,* and it remains one of our most requested recipes at the Market. The mix of pillowy egg bread and crusty, grainy cornbread is a real winner. Try stirring in leeks and wild mushrooms in spring or oysters and hot Italian sausage in winter. SERVES 10 TO 12

1/2	pound (2 sticks) unsalted butter
1	onion, chopped
6	celery stalks, chopped, with 1/4 cup leaves chopped and reserved
1	loaf challah, brioche, or other soft egg bread, cut into 1-inch cubes (about 12 cups)
	Salt and Pepper Skillet Cornbread (page 57), cut into 1-inch cubes (about 8 cups)
2	tablespoons chopped fresh sage
2	tablespoons chopped fresh marjoram
1 1/2	teaspoons sea salt
1	teaspoon dried crumbled sage
1/2	teaspoon freshly ground black pepper
2	cups low-sodium chicken broth
4	large eggs

Preheat the oven to 350°F.

Melt the butter in a large, deep ovenproof skillet over medium heat. Add the onion and celery and cook, stirring occasionally, for about 5 minutes, until the onion is soft and golden.

Remove from the heat, add the bread, cornbread, reserved celery leaves, fresh sage, marjoram, salt, dried sage, and pepper, and stir to mix. Add the broth and eggs and stir to combine and moisten the bread. The dressing can be mixed in the same skillet if it is large enough; if not, transfer to a large bowl to mix and return to the skillet to bake.

Bake, uncovered, until golden brown on top, 45 minutes to 1 hour. If it begins to brown too quickly, cover with foil and continue to bake. Remove from the oven and serve warm.

ON THE SIDE   Put on a truly impressive holiday spread by serving this dressing alongside Carl's Deep-Fried Turkey (page 149), Buttermilk Mashed Creamers (page 238), and Sweet Potato Casserole (page 254).

summer corn cakes with
chopped tomato and avocado salsa

The contrasting flavors, textures, and colors make this vibrant summertime dish a feast for the eyes as well as the mouth. It is tops served with a fried egg for breakfast, and you can turn it into a filling lunch or dinner by scattering the cakes with grilled shrimp or chicken breast. MAKES ABOUT 1 DOZEN CAKES / SERVES 6 TO 8

3	ears corn, shucked
1	cup all-purpose flour
½	cup yellow cornmeal
¼	cup diced red onion
¼	cup thinly sliced fresh basil
1	teaspoon baking powder
½	teaspoon baking soda
	Sea salt and freshly ground black pepper
2	large eggs, lightly beaten
2	tablespoons well-shaken buttermilk
2	tablespoons unsalted butter, melted
	Canola oil, for frying
	Chopped Tomato and Avocado Salsa (recipe follows)

Preheat the oven to 200°F. Line a baking sheet with a brown paper bag.

Cut the corn from the cobs into a large bowl and scrape the stripped cobs with the back of the knife to release the juices into the bowl.

Place 2 cups of the corn kernels in a food processor or blender and pulse several times, until the corn is slightly pureed but still chunky. Scrape into the bowl with the remaining corn kernels and add the flour, cornmeal, onion, basil, baking powder, baking soda, and salt and pepper to taste and stir to mix. Add the eggs, buttermilk, and butter and stir just to combine; do not overmix.

Place a large skillet over medium heat, add just enough canola oil to barely cover the bottom, and heat until sizzling hot (see Know-how, page 100). One heaping tablespoon at a time, scoop the batter into the skillet. Cooking in batches of 4 or 5 to avoid overcrowding, fry the cakes 1 to 2 minutes per side, until golden brown. Drain on the lined baking sheet and place in the oven to keep warm while cooking the remaining corn cakes. Serve warm topped with a heap of Chopped Tomato and Avocado Salsa.

chopped tomato and avocado salsa

MAKES ABOUT 2 CUPS

1	large tomato, cored and chopped
1	scallion, trimmed and minced

¹/₂	jalapeño pepper, cored, seeded, and diced
1	tablespoon chopped fresh cilantro
1	tablespoon chopped fresh basil
1	garlic clove, smashed and minced
	Juice of ¹/₂ lime
1¹/₂	teaspoons extra-virgin olive oil
1¹/₂	teaspoons white balsamic vinegar or white wine vinegar
	Sea salt and freshly ground black pepper
1	avocado, peeled, pitted, and diced

Place the tomato, scallion, jalapeño, cilantro, basil, garlic, lime juice, olive oil, vinegar, and salt and black pepper to taste in a bowl and stir to mix. Refrigerate in an airtight container until ready to serve, or for up to 2 days. Just before serving, add the avocado and mix gently.

squash puppies

The addition of tender yellow squash lends nice texture and sweetness to these savory little balls of fried goodness. If you plan to serve them in the traditional manner—with fried fish—try frying them in the same oil as the fish; this will add an extra layer of flavor *and* make for less cleanup. **MAKES ABOUT 2 DOZEN PUPPIES**

2	cups self-rising yellow cornmeal
3/4	cup self-rising flour (see Know-how, page 53)
1	tablespoon sugar
1	teaspoon sea salt
1/2	teaspoon freshly ground black pepper
2	medium yellow squash (about 1 pound), minced
3/4	cup well-shaken buttermilk
2	large eggs, lightly beaten
3	tablespoons grated onion
1	jalapeño pepper, cored, seeded, and minced
	Canola oil, for deep-frying
1	cup Roasted Jalapeño Mayonnaise (page 281) or Phyllis's Comeback Sauce (page 282), for dipping

Preheat the oven to 200°F. Line a baking sheet with a brown paper bag.

Combine the cornmeal, flour, sugar, salt, and black pepper in a large bowl and stir to mix. Stir the squash, buttermilk, eggs, onion, and jalapeño in a separate bowl until combined.

Pour the buttermilk mixture into the cornmeal mixture and stir just until combined; do not overmix. Let the batter sit for 15 minutes, undisturbed, at room temperature.

Fill a saucepan with canola oil 3 to 4 inches deep and heat over medium-high heat to between 350°F and 375°F. Spoon the batter into the hot oil about 1 tablespoon at a time, using the back of another spoon to push the batter into the oil. Working in batches of 6 to 8 squash puppies to avoid overcrowding, fry, turning several times, until crispy and golden brown all over, 2 to 3 minutes. Using a slotted spoon, carefully remove the squash puppies from the pan and drain on the prepared baking sheet. Place in the oven to keep warm while cooking the remaining puppies. Serve hot with Roasted Jalapeño Mayonnaise or Phyllis's Comeback Sauce for dipping.

kate's sweet potato refrigerator rolls

When my friend Kate joins us for Thanksgiving, she brings these yummy refrigerator rolls. The best thing about them is that you can throw together the dough up to a week ahead of time, store it in the fridge, and bake the rolls whenever you want, which helps make for stress-free holiday planning. When I make them, I like to add sweet potato for the beautiful color and flavor it imparts. And, since I've always been a fan of the combination of sweet potatoes and pork, I often use this version of the rolls to make pulled pork sandwiches, tucking Slow-Roasted Pulled Pork Butt (page 177) and Quick Cucumber Pickles (page 287) inside. Note that you'll need to let the dough rise for two hours between mixing and baking.

MAKES ABOUT 4 DOZEN 2- TO 2½-INCH ROLLS

1	cup milk
12	tablespoons (1½ sticks) unsalted butter
¾	cup plus 1 teaspoon sugar
2	teaspoons sea salt
1	tablespoon plus 1 teaspoon active dry yeast (from two ¼-ounce envelopes)
½	cup warm water (105°F to 115°F)
2	cups mashed sweet potato (1 large or 2 small sweet potatoes, baked, peeled, and mashed)
2	large eggs, lightly beaten
6½ to 7	cups all-purpose flour
3	tablespoons unsalted butter, melted

Lightly grease a large bowl with vegetable oil and set aside.

Heat the milk and butter in a large saucepan over medium heat, stirring regularly, just until the butter melts and the milk is scalded. Add ¾ cup of the sugar and the salt and stir until the sugar dissolves. Remove from the heat and let cool to lukewarm.

Combine the yeast and remaining 1 teaspoon sugar in a bowl. Stir in the warm water and set aside in a warm place for about 5 minutes, until the yeast froths and doubles in size. Add the yeast mixture to the milk-butter mixture and stir to combine.

Place the potato and eggs in the bowl of an electric mixer fitted with the dough hook and beat until smooth and well combined. (Or place them in a large bowl and mix with a wooden spoon.) Add the milk-yeast mixture to the potato mixture and beat to mix.

Slowly add 6½ cups of the flour and mix until incorporated, stopping several times to scrape down the sides and bottom of the bowl. If the dough is too sticky, add the remaining ½ cup flour, 1 tablespoon at a time, until the desired consistency is reached. Beat or knead 3 to 4 minutes more; the dough will be sticky (it will firm up after being chilled).

With lightly floured hands, turn the dough into the oiled bowl, turning several times to coat the dough lightly with the oil. Cover loosely with a clean cloth and let rise in a warm place for about 2 hours, or in the refrigerator overnight, until doubled in size.

(continued)

Lightly grease 2 rimmed baking sheets.

If the dough has been refrigerated, let rest at room temperature for 15 to 20 minutes before proceeding. Punch down the dough, turn it onto a lightly floured surface, and cut in half. Roll half the dough about ½ inch thick. Lightly flour a 2- to 2½-inch biscuit cutter and cut the rolls, leaving as little space between each cut as possible and pressing down just once for each roll; do not twist the cutter. If the dough begins to stick to the cutter, dip the cutter in a little flour. Gather the excess dough, reroll once, and cut as many rolls from it as possible. Repeat with the remaining half of the dough or refrigerate until ready to use.

Preheat the oven to 400°F.

Arrange the rolls on the prepared baking sheets so they just barely touch. Brush the tops lightly with the melted butter. Fold the rolls in half, pressing gently at the center point so they stick together.

Cover loosely with a clean cloth and let rise in a warm place until doubled in size, 30 to 40 minutes. Uncover the rolls and bake for 12 to 14 minutes, until golden brown. Remove from the oven and serve warm.

Know-how: parbaking rolls

A nice trick that makes for easy entertaining but still results in hot-out-of-the-oven rolls is to parbake the rolls ahead of time. Up to 5 or 6 hours in advance, bake the rolls at 375°F for 8 to 10 minutes, until firm but not golden brown. Store at room temperature and then, when ready to serve, return the rolls to a preheated 400°F oven and bake for 4 to 5 minutes, just until light brown. Remove from the oven and serve warm.

SARA'S SWAPS Phoebe Lawless of Scratch bakery makes the most incredible farmstead "pigs-in-blankets" with really fresh local sausage wrapped and baked in buttery pastry. It's a great use for the little bits of dough left from rolling and cutting biscuits and rolls that you wouldn't otherwise use. Wrap the dough around 2- to 3-inch sausage links, arrange on a rimmed baking sheet, and bake in a preheated 375°F oven just until the dough is puffy and light brown, 12 to 15 minutes. Serve warm with spicy mustard for dipping.

buttermilk-sage dinner rolls

These splendidly soft dinner rolls, which my aunt June used to make for special occasions, are the Southern equivalent of brioche, minus the egg. I've added fresh sage for an aromatic boost. MAKES ABOUT 2 DOZEN CLOVERLEAF ROLLS

8	tablespoons (1 stick) unsalted butter, cut into cubes
10	fresh sage leaves, chopped
3	tablespoons sugar
1½	cups well-shaken buttermilk
1	tablespoon plus 1 teaspoon active dry yeast (from two ¼-ounce envelopes)
½	cup warm water (105°F to 115°F)
4½	cups all-purpose flour
2	teaspoons kosher salt
½	teaspoon baking soda
2	tablespoons unsalted butter, melted

Lightly grease 2 muffin tins and set aside.

Place the butter, sage, and 2 tablespoons of the sugar in a saucepan over medium-high heat, stirring regularly, just until the butter melts. Stir in the buttermilk and heat just until warmed; do not let it come to a boil. Remove from the heat and let cool to room temperature.

Combine the yeast and remaining 1 tablespoon sugar in a bowl. Stir in the warm water and set aside in a warm place for about 5 minutes, until the yeast froths and doubles in size. Add the yeast mixture to the buttermilk mixture and stir to combine.

In a separate large bowl, stir together the flour, salt, and baking soda. Add the buttermilk-yeast mixture and stir to combine and form a sticky dough. Cover the bowl loosely with a clean cloth and let sit in a warm place for about 30 minutes, until the dough has risen slightly. (At this point, the dough can be refrigerated in an airtight container if you want to make it up to 1 day ahead; remove from the refrigerator and let rest for 15 to 20 minutes before proceeding with the recipe.)

Preheat the oven to 375°F.

Turn the mixture onto a lightly floured surface and knead several times, until the dough is easy to work with. Pinch off pieces of dough and form balls about ½ inch in diameter. Shape the rolls into "clover leaves" by nestling 3 small balls in each muffin tin. Cover loosely with a clean cloth and let rise in a warm place until doubled in size, 30 to 45 minutes.

Uncover the rolls, brush lightly with the melted butter, and bake for about 15 minutes, until golden brown. Remove from the oven and serve warm.

hearty breakfasts

It's something I've always known, but working on this book has made me truly appreciate how distinctively Southerners approach the first meal of the day. For example, only in the South, it seems, do "dinner" meats like pork tenderloin, beef, quail, and oysters regularly share a starring role with eggs and other, more universally familiar breakfast foods. Moreover, some of my all-time favorite foods—like country ham, fried green tomatoes, and, of course, grits—are staples of the Southern breakfast table.

When I was growing up, my family's breakfast traditions reflected the Southern approach. This meant that we not only ate a hot meal together nearly every morning but also depended on simple preparations whose success relied on the quality of fresh, seasonal ingredients. Favorite Buttermilk Biscuits (page 51) spread with Granny Foster's peach and blackberry preserves and fried eggs from the chicken coop were daily fare.

But as good as they were, those everyday meals didn't hold a candle to holiday breakfasts. The usual eggs, biscuits, and grits were there, as always, but that was only the beginning. During hunting season in the fall and winter, we made room on our plates for pan-fried quail or dove smothered in gravy. And in the summer, we would spoon lightly mashed and sugared strawberries on hot biscuits and set out big platters of sliced tomatoes, bowls of ripe peaches, and little dishes of homemade pickles, relishes, and chili sauce. To this day, I still love the combination of pickles, relish, and eggs.

The recipes in this chapter are my take on my favorite Southern breakfast dishes, from easy and satisfying basics like Foster's Sausage and Egg Biscuit (page 74) and Buttermilk Waffles (page 91) to sumptuous treats like Roasted Asparagus with Country Ham, Red-Eye Gravy, and Poached Eggs (page 84), which are equally perfect for slow weekend mornings at home and for entertaining guests any time of day.

If you're like me, breakfast sometimes gets put on the back burner in the weekday rush; there are mornings when coffee and toast are as far as I get before lunch. But I always try to take time, especially on the weekends, to make something special for breakfast and savor it with family and friends. I hope these comforting Southern dishes will become a part of your own breakfast traditions.

foster's sausage and egg biscuit

Southerners take sausage and egg biscuits for granted. They are just about everywhere in the South—we make them at Foster's, and you can even buy them at country convenience stores, where you might find a stack wrapped in cellophane in a basket by the register. If you haven't already had sausage and egg biscuits yourself, I hope this recipe will make you a convert. For extra flavor, cook the eggs the way my dad did, by frying them directly in the sausage grease left in the skillet rather than using butter. Feel free to scramble rather than fry the eggs if you prefer. SERVES 4 TO 8

1	pound ground pork sausage
8	Favorite Buttermilk Biscuits (page 51)
8	slices sharp Cheddar cheese (optional)
1	tablespoon unsalted butter (optional)
1 or 2	large eggs per person
	Sea salt and freshly ground black pepper

Preheat the oven to 350°F.

Form the sausage into 8 patties (about 2 ounces each). Heat a large, dry nonstick or cast-iron skillet over medium-high heat and cook the patties for 4 to 5 minutes per side. (There should be enough fat in the patties that you will not need to oil the pan.) Remove the sausage, drain on a paper towel, and cover loosely to keep warm.

Split the biscuits in half. Open the biscuits, arrange on a baking sheet, and cover the top halves with cheese slices, if using. Place in the oven just until the biscuits are warm and the cheese is melted, 3 to 4 minutes.

While the biscuits are in the oven, return the skillet to the stove over medium heat. If using butter instead of the sausage grease, wipe the skillet with a paper towel and add the butter. Heat the fat until sizzling hot (see Know-how, page 100). Crack the eggs into the skillet, one at a time, taking care not to break the yolks or overcrowd the skillet. Reduce the heat to medium and fry until the whites are set, about 1 minute. Using a spatula, carefully flip the eggs and fry the other sides until they are done to your liking, 30 seconds to 1 minute more. Season the eggs with salt and pepper to taste.

Remove the biscuits from the oven and place a sausage patty on each bottom half. Top each with a fried egg and a biscuit top. Serve warm.

judy's warm ham and cheese rolls

My sister used to make these rich rolls for her husband and kids when they went duck hunting. She would prepare them the night before, wrap them in foil, and refrigerate. Then, when Pat and the kids got up to go hunting—sometimes as early as four in the morning—they would just pop the rolls in the oven to melt the cheese and hit the road. The way everything melds together on the soft, steamed rolls is so irresistible, I'm pretty sure the rolls never made it to the duck camp, or even out of the driveway. For nonhunters like me, these rolls, served warm or at room temperature, are great for tailgating, picnics, and road trips. MAKES 2 DOZEN ROLLS

Twenty-four 2-inch potato rolls, or Buttermilk-Sage
Dinner Rolls (page 69), or Kate's Sweet Potato
Refrigerator Rolls (page 66)

8   tablespoons (1 stick) unsalted butter

3   tablespoons grated onion

2   tablespoons Dijon mustard

2   tablespoons poppy seeds

1   tablespoon Worcestershire sauce

8   ounces smoked ham, thinly sliced

8   ounces Gruyère cheese, thinly sliced

Preheat the oven to 350°F.

Split the rolls in half horizontally. Combine the butter, onion, mustard, poppy seeds, and Worcestershire sauce in a small saucepan and place over low heat until the butter melts, stirring to blend.

Brush the butter mixture evenly on both cut sides of the rolls. Place the ham on the bottom halves and top with the cheese. Place the top halves on the sandwiches and press lightly. Nestle the sandwiches together on a large piece of foil, wrap tightly, and seal the edges.

Place the wrapped rolls on a baking sheet and bake for 20 to 25 minutes, until the cheese is melted and the rolls are warmed through. Remove from the oven and let sit for about 5 minutes before unwrapping and serving warm or let cool to room temperature.

Know-how: planning ahead

Like Judy, you can assemble these sandwiches ahead of time and keep them in the refrigerator until you are ready to heat and serve. They can even be frozen for up to 2 weeks. Just be sure to wrap them tightly and heat thoroughly before serving.

Destination: **OXFORD, MISSISSIPPI**

WORTH THE DETOUR
BIG BAD BREAKFAST'S
Southern breakfast plates

(662) 236-2666

bigbadbreakfast.com

THE SOUTH IS HOME TO COUNTLESS EXCELLENT BREAKFAST SPOTS—FAR TOO many to list—but how many of them boast house-made bacon and andouille sausage cured in their very own smokehouse? Big Bad Breakfast, a cozy diner in Oxford, Mississippi, offers that and more, all served up with a side helping of Southern wit and irreverence. The brainchild of award-winning chef John Currence, co-owner of the famed City Grocery and other beloved Oxford institutions, Big Bad Breakfast opened in 2008, but it already feels like it's been around forever.

I think this is because the place is so thoroughly steeped in Oxford culture and personalities. Most items on the menu pay winking homage to Southern literature and the many esteemed writers who have lived in or passed through Oxford. Even the restaurant's own name is an allusion to a local writer, Larry Brown, and his short story collection turned movie, *Big Bad Love.*

Like many of the best new Southern restaurants, Big Bad Breakfast focuses on local ingredients—eggs from cage-free local chickens, dairy from Billy Ray's Farm in nearby Yocona, fresh herbs from the chef's organic garden, Mississippi state cheese, and catfish that "you can bet your ass" comes straight from the Mississippi Delta. All of this emerges from the kitchen in the form of homey, hearty plates of fried eggs; tender cathead biscuits with homemade jam; creamy grits; country ham or andouille sausage drizzled with red-eye, tomato, or sausage gravy; and short stacks of buttermilk or buckwheat pancakes served with fresh cream and berries. With fresh-squeezed orange juice or a mug of steaming-hot chicory coffee, this is Southern breakfast food at its finest.

Most items on the menu pay winking homage to Southern literature.

fried green tomato blt

Fried green tomatoes are one of those Southern classics that inspire fanatical devotion. For good reason: green tomatoes have a lovely tart flavor that mellows and warms in the heat of the frying pan, and, because they are so firm, they keep their shape and texture even after they're cooked. They are most often eaten on their own, as a side dish, so it wasn't until I visited a small grocery store in Greenwood, Mississippi, that I tried a fried green tomato BLT for the first time. It immediately struck me as such an obvious combination that I couldn't believe I hadn't already thought of it myself. SERVES 4

½	cup Quick Basil Mayo (page 280)
4 to 8	slices whole-grain sandwich bread, toasted or grilled
½	recipe Fried Green Tomatoes (page 249)
12	slices thick-cut bacon, fried or baked until crisp
8	large Bibb lettuce leaves, washed and drained

Spread the mayo on half the bread slices and top evenly with the tomatoes, bacon, and lettuce, and serve open-face or top with the remaining bread to form sandwiches. Serve warm or at room temperature.

SARA'S SWAPS Turn these hearty breakfast sandwiches into bite-size appetizers or hors d'oeuvres by making them mini. Cut the bread into quarters and spread with the mayonnaise. Cut the tomatoes, lettuce, and bacon to fit the quartered bread and stack them on top, making open-face sandwiches. Secure with a toothpick or small wooden skewer and serve warm. Add a fried egg to make a hearty breakfast and serve open-face.

pork tenderloin and buttermilk biscuits with roasted tomato-thyme gravy

My mom always made this hearty breakfast when my husband, Peter, and I came to visit her in Memphis; it is so Southern that eating it always made me feel I was really *home*. (I don't think Peter, who is from New York, had ever had either pork tenderloin or gravy for breakfast.) The roasted tomato gravy is what makes it so special; roasting the tomatoes cuts and deepens their bright acidity, adding complex layers of flavor to the savory sauce. You can mix things up by making this dish with sausage patties or leftover slices of Grilled and Roasted Filet of Beef with Crispy Roasted Shallots (page 193) instead of the pork tenderloin. Either way, you'll want to use the biscuits to sop up the last drops of gravy.

SERVES 4 TO 6

3	plum tomatoes, cored and halved
2	tablespoons olive oil
1	tablespoon balsamic vinegar
	Sea salt and freshly ground black pepper
	One 1-pound pork tenderloin, trimmed
2	tablespoons fresh thyme
1/3	cup all-purpose flour
1	tablespoon unsalted butter
2	cups low-sodium chicken broth
	Favorite Buttermilk Biscuits (page 51)

Preheat the oven to 400°F.

Place the tomatoes on a rimmed baking sheet and toss with 1 tablespoon of the olive oil and the vinegar. Season with salt and pepper to taste and bake for about 30 minutes, until the skins begin to shrivel and the tomatoes start to caramelize. Remove from the oven and set aside until cool enough to handle. Remove and discard the skins (they will slip right off) and roughly chop the tomatoes.

While the tomatoes are cooking, rinse the pork, pat dry, and remove any silver skin (see Know-how on next page). Heat the remaining 1 tablespoon olive oil in a large skillet over medium-high heat until sizzling hot (see Know-how, page 100). Slice the tenderloin into rounds about 1/4 inch thick (12 to 15 slices) and sprinkle with the thyme and salt and pepper to taste, pressing lightly so the seasonings adhere. Dip the rounds in the flour to coat both sides lightly; reserve the remaining flour. Place the pork in the skillet and sauté for about 2 minutes per side, until light brown around the edges. Remove the meat from the skillet, place on a plate, and cover loosely.

Add the butter to the same skillet and melt until sizzling hot. Add 2 tablespoons of the reserved dredging flour and stir to scrape any brown bits from the bottom of the skillet. Cook, stirring constantly, for about 1 minute, just until the flour cooks slightly and turns light brown. Whisk in the broth and stir until the gravy is slightly thick and smooth. Add the tomatoes and cook, stirring frequently, until the gravy comes to a boil and thickens, 3 to 5 minutes.

Reduce the heat to low and return the tenderloin slices to the skillet with the gravy just to warm through. Remove from the heat and serve warm over the biscuits.

ON THE SIDE Although this dish is certainly filling enough by itself, a side of scrambled eggs and Green Tomato Chow-Chow (page 300) or Tomato Jam (page 302) transforms it into a true feast.

Know-how: removing silver skin

Silver skin is the name for the thin silvery membrane that covers the top of the tenderloin. It tends to be tough when cooked, so you want to remove it. To do this, slip a sharp knife under the silver skin toward the thin tail end of the tenderloin. Hold on to the loosened end of silver skin and move the tip of the knife forward and upward (to keep from cutting into the underlying meat) to remove the silver skin in strips. Repeat the process several times until all the silver skin is removed.

Know-how: cooking pork

I think people tend to believe that cooking pork is the same as cooking chicken. The problem with that line of thinking is that it usually results in overcooked meat. The pork will be nice and juicy if it is slightly pink in the center when you take it off the heat; this is how you know it's done to perfection. Keep in mind that the temperature for medium-done pork is between 140°F and 145°F, much lower than for chicken, and it will continue to rise another 5 degrees while the meat is resting. If you still want it more well done, cook to about 160°F.

country ham and hominy hash

A good hash is like soup: you can toss together all the odds and ends from your fridge and pantry and end up with something rustic and hearty that is much more than the sum of its parts.   SERVES 4 TO 6

HASH

One 4-ounce piece country ham

1   **bay leaf**

3 or 4   **black peppercorns**

2   **russet potatoes (about 1 pound), peeled and chopped**

2   **cups cooked hominy, rinsed and drained**

1   **onion, chopped**

2   **tablespoons chopped fresh parsley**

Sea salt and freshly ground black pepper

2   **tablespoons olive oil, plus more if needed**

1   **tablespoon unsalted butter**

EGGS

2   **teaspoons distilled white vinegar**

Pinch of sea salt

1 or 2   **large eggs per person**

HASH | Place the ham in a pot with the bay leaf and peppercorns. Cover with water and simmer for about 1 hour, until the ham is fork-tender (see Know-how, page 172). Add the potatoes and simmer for 10 minutes more, until the potatoes are just beginning to get tender. Strain the ham and potatoes from the pot, reserving about ¼ cup of the liquid, removing and discarding the bay leaf, and set aside.

Using two forks, shred the ham into bite-size pieces and place in a large bowl. Add the potatoes, hominy, and onion. Stir in the reserved cooking liquid and parsley and season to taste with salt and pepper. (Country ham is salty, so be sure to taste before adding any extra salt.)

Heat the olive oil and butter in a large nonstick or cast-iron skillet over medium-high heat until hot. Add the ham-potato mixture and spread into a flat cake. Cover with a splatter screen or lid and cook until crispy, 4 to 5 minutes. Flip and re-form the cake. Cover and cook, adding a little more oil if needed, until crispy on the other side. Remove from the heat and cover.

EGGS | Fill a large skillet with water about 2 inches deep and bring to a boil. Add the vinegar and salt and reduce the heat to a simmer.

Add the eggs one at a time and poach for 2 to 3 minutes, until the whites set and a thin, translucent film forms over the yolks (see Know-how, page 86). Use a slotted spoon to gently transfer the eggs to a paper towel–lined platter to drain.

ASSEMBLY | Divide the hash evenly between individual serving plates, place 1 or 2 eggs on top of each, and serve hot.

SARA'S SWAPS For a more rustic interpretation of this dish, make a hole in the hash, crack the eggs in the hole, and cover to fry, rather than poach, to your liking. For a sweet-and-savory combination, substitute sweet potatoes for the russets, and for a crispy finish, scatter fried oysters on top. Or, make a cheesy variation by layering the hash mixture with Gruyère cheese in a skillet to form one large cake and sauté until brown and crispy. Slide the cake out of the skillet and cut into 4 to 6 wedges, then assemble the dish as for the main recipe.

chew on this: **about hominy**

Hominy is the name for corn kernels that have been hulled to remove the bran and germ. Lye hominy is hulled by soaking the corn kernels in a weak lye solution—a very traditional, centuries-old Native American method—and pearl hominy is hulled mechanically. It is then dried and either ground to make our beloved hominy grits or boiled whole to make what New Orleanians call "big hominy." You can buy hominy canned, meaning precooked, or dried, in which case it will need to be presoaked and boiled in the same manner as dried beans.

roasted asparagus with country ham, red-eye gravy, and poached eggs

Red-eye gravy——which for most Southerners is the only acceptable sauce for country ham—is a savory and slightly bitter mixture of black coffee and the pan drippings left behind from frying country ham. I'm not sure how the coffee first made its way into the pan, but I like to imagine it was one of those happy accidents born of necessity. It rings true, anyway, because Southerners love gravy so much that they will find a way to eke some out of a greasy pan no matter what. I lighten my version of this quintessentially Southern dish with a bright shock of fresh, green asparagus, which plays perfectly off the saltiness of the red-eye gravy and the richness of the runny egg yolks. SERVES 4

ASPARAGUS
1 **pound asparagus, trimmed or peeled**
2 **tablespoons olive oil**
   Sea salt and freshly ground black pepper

HAM AND GRAVY
4 **thin slices country ham (about 6 ounces)**
1 **cup strong black coffee**
1 **tablespoon unsalted butter**

EGGS
2 **teaspoons distilled white vinegar**
   Pinch of sea salt
1 or 2 **large eggs per person**

2 **tablespoons chopped fresh tarragon, for garnish**

ASPARAGUS | Preheat the oven to 400°F.

Arrange the asparagus on a rimmed baking sheet, drizzle with the olive oil, and sprinkle with salt and pepper to taste. Roast until the color intensifies to a bright green and the asparagus spears are tender with crispy edges, 8 to 10 minutes. Remove from the oven and cover loosely to keep warm.

HAM AND GRAVY | While the asparagus is in the oven, heat a dry cast-iron skillet over medium-high heat. Add the ham and cook until the meat is warmed through and begins to brown slightly, about 2 minutes per side. Remove from the skillet and cover loosely to keep warm.

Without cleaning the skillet, return it to the heat and add the coffee and butter. Stir to mix, scraping the bottom and sides to incorporate any bits of meat. Cook until the gravy reduces slightly, 3 to 5 minutes. Reduce the heat to low and simmer until the dish is assembled.

(continued)

EGGS | Fill another large skillet with water about 2 inches deep and bring to a boil. Add the vinegar and salt and reduce the heat to a simmer.

Add the eggs one at a time and poach for 2 to 3 minutes, until the whites set and a thin, translucent film forms over the yolks (see Know-how, below). Use a slotted spoon to gently transfer the eggs to a paper towel–lined platter to drain.

ASSEMBLY | Divide the asparagus evenly between individual serving plates or place on a large serving platter and top with the ham. Place 1 or 2 eggs on each slice of ham and spoon the gravy on top. Sprinkle with the tarragon and additional salt and pepper, if desired, and serve hot.

IN SEASON In North Carolina, asparagus is a short-lived springtime treat, so I have to get creative when I make this dish at other times of the year. Here are some of the best vegetable substitutes I've found.

SUMMER

Roasted tomatoes or summer squash

FALL

Roasted fennel, mushrooms, or sautéed spinach

WINTER

Roasted sweet potatoes and onions

Know-how: making poached eggs

Poached eggs are as healthy as hard-boiled eggs because they are cooked in water, and as versatile as fried eggs, with yolks as runny or firm as you please. They are easy to make, too. The touch of vinegar added to the water helps the eggs keep their shape while they cook.

Fill a large skillet with water about 2 inches deep and bring to a boil. Add 2 teaspoons vinegar and a pinch of sea salt and reduce the heat to a simmer.

Break 1 egg into a small bowl or measuring cup, taking care not to break the yolk. Quickly turn the egg out of the bowl into the simmering water so the egg keeps its shape when it hits the water. Repeat with the remaining eggs, working in batches, if necessary, to avoid overcrowding the skillet. Cook for 2 to 3 minutes, or until the whites set and a thin, translucent film forms over the yolks. For a firmer yolk, cook 1 to 2 minutes longer. Use a slotted spoon to gently transfer the eggs to a paper towel–lined platter to drain.

---

mott's breakfast soufflé

Every Southern cook has his or her own version of this stratalike breakfast soufflé, but I'm willing to bet that each and every one begins with white sandwich bread. In the past, I've tried to fancy it up using challah or brioche or some other bread, but it was never quite as good. I first had this particular variation on a visit to Meridian, Mississippi, catering my cousin's rehearsal dinner. My crew and I were working so hard we hadn't even stopped to eat. One of the local ladies, Mott, brought us this soufflé, ready to bake. Hot out of the oven, it was utterly delicious. Note that it should be prepared the night before, allowed to soak overnight, and baked the following morning. SERVES 6 TO 8

1	pound ground pork breakfast sausage
8	slices white bread (I like Pepperidge Farm)
6	tablespoons (³/₄ stick) unsalted butter, softened
2	cups (8 ounces) grated sharp Cheddar cheese
3	cups milk
6	large eggs
2	teaspoons dry mustard
1	teaspoon hot sauce
	Sea salt and freshly ground black pepper

Generously butter a 7 x 11-inch baking dish.

Heat a cast-iron skillet over medium heat to just before the smoking point (see Know-how, page 147). Add the sausage and break into small pieces. Cook and stir until brown all over, 7 to 8 minutes.

Trim the crusts from the bread and spread the slices with the butter. Cut each slice into 3 fingers and layer half the fingers over the bottom of the baking dish. Sprinkle with half the sausage and half the cheese. Repeat with the remaining bread, sausage, and cheese.

Combine the milk, eggs, mustard, hot sauce, and salt and pepper to taste in a large bowl and whisk to mix. Pour the egg mixture over the bread, sausage, and cheese. Press the bread down to submerge. Cover with aluminum foil and refrigerate overnight.

When ready to bake, preheat the oven to 350°F.

Bake for about 30 minutes, covered, until the edges are set and the center is slightly jiggly. Uncover and bake for another 10 to 15 minutes, until the top is golden brown and puffy. Remove from the oven and let sit for about 10 minutes before serving warm.

pot roast potato cakes with poached eggs, fresh greens, and horseradish-mustard vinaigrette

This hearty dish, which is a great way to reinvigorate leftover Foster Family's Pot Roast with Herb-Roasted Vegetables (page 199), is inspired by Southern dishes featuring "low" cuts of meat. With savory layers of potato, roast, and poached eggs finished with the cool heat of the Horseradish-Mustard Vinaigrette and brightened with fresh greens, this crowd-pleaser makes for a decadent Sunday brunch, but it can just as comfortably double as the main event at dinner. Serve with warm, crusty toast for a complete meal.   SERVES 4

POTATO CAKES

4 to 5	Yukon Gold potatoes (about 1 pound), peeled and halved
2	cups cooked, shredded pot roast
3	tablespoons minced onion
1	large egg
2	tablespoons all-purpose flour
1	tablespoon chopped fresh parsley
	Sea salt and freshly ground black pepper
1	tablespoon olive oil
1	tablespoon unsalted butter

EGGS

2	teaspoons distilled white vinegar
	Pinch of sea salt
1 or 2	large eggs per person

GREENS

4	cups baby spinach or arugula, washed and drained
	Horseradish-Mustard Vinaigrette (recipe follows)
2	tablespoons chopped chives

POTATO CAKES | Preheat the oven to 200°F.

Place the potatoes in a large pot with enough water to cover by about 1 inch and bring to a boil. Reduce the heat to a simmer, cover, and cook until the potatoes are tender, 20 to 30 minutes. Drain and mash roughly with a potato masher; the potatoes do not have to be smooth.

Combine the potatoes, 1 cup of the pot roast, the onion, egg, flour, and parsley in a large bowl and stir to thoroughly combine. Season with salt and pepper to taste and stir to mix. Form into four 3-inch-round, ½-inch-thick patties and refrigerate for about 15 minutes.

(continued)

Heat the olive oil and butter in a large nonstick or cast-iron skillet over medium heat until hot. Add the cakes and cook for about 3 minutes per side, until golden brown and crispy. Place in the oven to keep warm.

EGGS | Fill another large skillet with water about 2 inches deep and bring to a boil. Add the vinegar and salt and reduce the heat to a simmer.

Add the eggs one at a time and poach for 2 to 3 minutes, until the whites set and a thin, translucent film forms over the yolks (see Know-how, page 86). Use a slotted spoon to gently transfer the eggs to a paper towel–lined platter to drain.

GREENS | Just before serving, toss the greens with ¼ cup of the vinaigrette.

ASSEMBLY | Place 1 potato cake on each plate and top with 1 or 2 poached eggs and about ¼ cup of the remaining pot roast. Drizzle about ¼ cup of the remaining dressing on and around the eggs and top with a handful of the dressed greens. Season with salt and pepper to taste and serve warm, garnished with the chives.

horseradish-mustard vinaigrette

MAKES ABOUT ½ CUP

¼	cup extra-virgin olive oil
2	tablespoons distilled white vinegar
1	shallot, minced
1	tablespoon prepared horseradish
1	teaspoon Dijon mustard
	Sea salt and freshly ground black pepper

Combine the olive oil, vinegar, shallot, horseradish, and mustard in a small bowl or a jar with a tight-fitting lid. Whisk or shake until well combined, season with salt and pepper to taste, and serve or refrigerate in an airtight container until ready to serve.

SARA'S SWAPS If you're itching to make this dish but don't have leftover pot roast on hand, try substituting corned beef—it has a similarly flaky texture and good beef flavor. This recipe is also great as a vegetarian dish, without the meat.

buttermilk waffles

When I was young, we ate pancakes or waffles for breakfast almost every Saturday morning, and my dad was the self-appointed commander of the waffle iron. Dad's waffles were crispy, light, and puffy, perfect with a drizzle of honey or—his pick—molasses. My version of our old weekend favorite does my dad's waffles justice. They are wonderfully crispy with a slightly tangy bite imparted by the buttermilk. Serve warm with butter and honey or sweetened cream and fresh fruit. MAKES 6 WAFFLES / SERVES 4 TO 6

1½	**cups all-purpose flour**
½	**cup yellow cornmeal**
2	**tablespoons sugar**
1	**tablespoon baking powder**
1	**teaspoon baking soda**
	Pinch of kosher salt
1½	**cups well-shaken buttermilk**
8	**tablespoons (1 stick) unsalted butter, melted**
3	**large eggs**

Preheat the oven to 200°F. Preheat a waffle iron and spray lightly with vegetable oil.

Combine the flour, cornmeal, sugar, baking powder, baking soda, and salt in a large bowl and stir to mix. Whisk the buttermilk, butter, and eggs in a separate bowl. Add the buttermilk-egg mixture to the flour mixture and stir just to combine; do not overmix.

Pour about ¾ cup of the batter into the bottom of the waffle iron, close the lid, and cook for about 4 minutes, until the waffle is golden brown and crisp. Transfer to a baking sheet and place in the oven to keep warm while cooking the remaining waffles.

---

chew on this: **waffles and fried chicken**

There is a long and noble Southern tradition of serving buttermilk waffles with—you guessed it—fried chicken. This seemingly strange combination has made appearances in Southern cookbooks (and among the Pennsylvania Dutch) since the nineteenth century. Try it for yourself and see how delicious it is. Just top each waffle with several pulled pieces of Granny Foster's Sunday Fried Chicken (page 127), drizzle with maple syrup, molasses, or Fried Chicken Gravy (page 128), and serve warm.

from catfish
to crawfish

One of my parents' favorite pastimes, and one of my best childhood memories, is fishing on the Tennessee River. Every summer we would go to the same fishing spot and catch a mess of brim and crappie for frying. Much of the time our catch was reserved for Friday night, when my parents would have a bunch of friends over for cocktails and a fish fry.

In preparation, my dad would spend all day cleaning the fish. Then, because my mom didn't like the way it made the house smell, he would take the whole frying operation outside. He used one of those great big butane-powered deep fryers, which he set up in the yard before dredging the fish in cornmeal batter and frying them whole. The considerable bounty of fried fish—which we ate with lemon wedges, thick slices of white onion, and dabs of my mom's homemade tartar sauce—was supplemented with hushpuppies, corn on the cob, and vinegar slaw.

I still love a good fish fry, but I don't typically have the time to put on such a spread. When I make fish for supper it's usually because I want something delicious that can be thrown together with a handful of pantry staples and fresh ingredients in under twenty minutes. Many of the dishes in this chapter—including my lighter, faster take on my parents' fish fry, Skillet-Fried Catfish with Herb Tartar Sauce (page 97), and quick-fix suppers like Grilled Grouper with Heirloom Tomato Salsa (page 102) and Louisiana BBQ Shrimp (page 103), were created with just that goal in mind.

This lighter, easier style is closer to the way we eat fish at home on a daily basis, making "seasonal" and "regional" more relevant than "breaded" and "fried." I've included recipes that run the gamut from market-inspired, such as Soft-Shell Crabs with Salty Tomato Butter (page 108) to versions of old standards like Salmon Croquettes (page 107) and Crispy Fried Oysters Four Ways (page 117). Have fun and make these recipes your own—the only absolute requirement is that you start with the freshest possible seafood, whether it's the kind the recipe calls for or whatever your local fishmonger has to offer.

skillet-fried catfish with herb tartar sauce

It may not be deep-fried, but with a satisfyingly crunchy cornmeal crust, this skillet-fried catfish has all the flavors and textures that you would expect from fried fish. Most important, served with a healthy dollop of Herb Tartar Sauce or a heap of Roxy's Grated Coleslaw (page 260), lemon wedges, and cold beer, it is just as sure to draw a crowd. This recipe can also be made with snapper, flounder, or any other flaky white fish. SERVES 4 TO 6

> Four 6- to 8-ounce catfish fillets, about $1/2$ inch thick
> (1$1/2$ to 2 pounds), or snapper or flounder
> Sea salt and freshly ground black pepper
> 1 cup well-shaken buttermilk
> 1 large egg
> Dash of hot sauce
> $2/3$ cup all-purpose flour
> $2/3$ cup yellow cornmeal
> Pinch of ground cayenne pepper
> Canola oil, for frying
> Herb Tartar Sauce (page 100)
> 1 white onion, thinly sliced
> 1 lemon, cut into wedges

Preheat the oven to 200°F. Line a baking sheet with a brown paper bag.

Rinse the catfish and pat dry. Slice each fillet lengthwise into 3 long strips and season with salt and black pepper to taste. Combine the buttermilk, egg, and hot sauce in a shallow bowl and stir to mix. In a separate bowl, combine the flour, cornmeal, and cayenne, season with salt and black pepper, and stir to mix.

Pour canola oil into a large skillet about $1/4$ inch deep and place over medium-high heat until sizzling hot (see Know-how, page 100).

Dip each piece of fish in the buttermilk mixture, then dredge in the flour mixture to evenly coat both sides, shaking off any excess flour. Without overcrowding the skillet—you may need to fry in batches—place the fish in the hot oil and cook for 2 to 3 minutes per side, turning only once, until golden brown and crispy. If the fish is browning too quickly, reduce the heat to medium.

Remove the fish from the skillet and drain on the lined baking sheet. Place the pan in the oven to keep warm while you fry the remaining fish, adding more oil to the skillet if needed. Season with additional salt and pepper, if desired, and serve hot with Herb Tartar Sauce, raw onion, and lemon wedges to squeeze over the fish.

ON THE SIDE   Make it a party with Squash Puppies (page 65), Creamy Potato Salad (page 266), and Spring Coleslaw with Fresh Herbs and Light Honey Citrus Vinaigrette (page 258).

Destination: TAYLOR, MISSISSIPPI

WORTH THE DETOUR
TAYLOR GROCERY'S
fried catfish with the works

(662) 236-1716

taylorgrocery.com

EVERY TIME I GO TO MISSISSIPPI I MAKE THE TIME-HONORED PILGRIMAGE to Taylor, a tiny hamlet eight miles south of Oxford that also happens to be a mecca of sorts for people with a hankering for fried catfish. Taylor Grocery has been around since 1889, but it didn't always deal in that holy trinity of fish, meal, and oil. Prior to the 1970s, locals frequented Taylor Grocery to stock up on dry goods and farm supplies, and—on special occasions—to get a shave and a trim from Elton McCain, the barber who set up shop in the back of the store on Saturday afternoons. Today, though, the crumbling brick building, resplendent with sagging front porch, rusty gas pump, and faded, weather-beaten sign, is the quirky home to what may well be the best fried catfish in the world.

The inside is as ramshackle as you might expect. The dining room, which is always packed, holds a gaggle of tables, some decked with old-timey red-and-white-checkered tablecloths and others with nothing but graffiti; they and the much-scribbled-upon walls bear the signatures and public proclamations of countless sated diners past.

The menu at Taylor Grocery isn't limited to catfish, but steak, chicken, shrimp, and pork are beside the point as far as most folks are concerned. It's not unusual to wait in a line stretching out the door for a plate of whole or filleted fish, lightly breaded and fried to a miraculously airy crisp and loaded with the works—baked beans, brown rice (that's dirty rice, not the whole-grain stuff), hushpuppies, and perfectly executed traditional Southern slaw, sweet and creamy. If you can't get to Taylor's, try my Skillet-Fried Catfish with Herb Tartar Sauce (page 97).

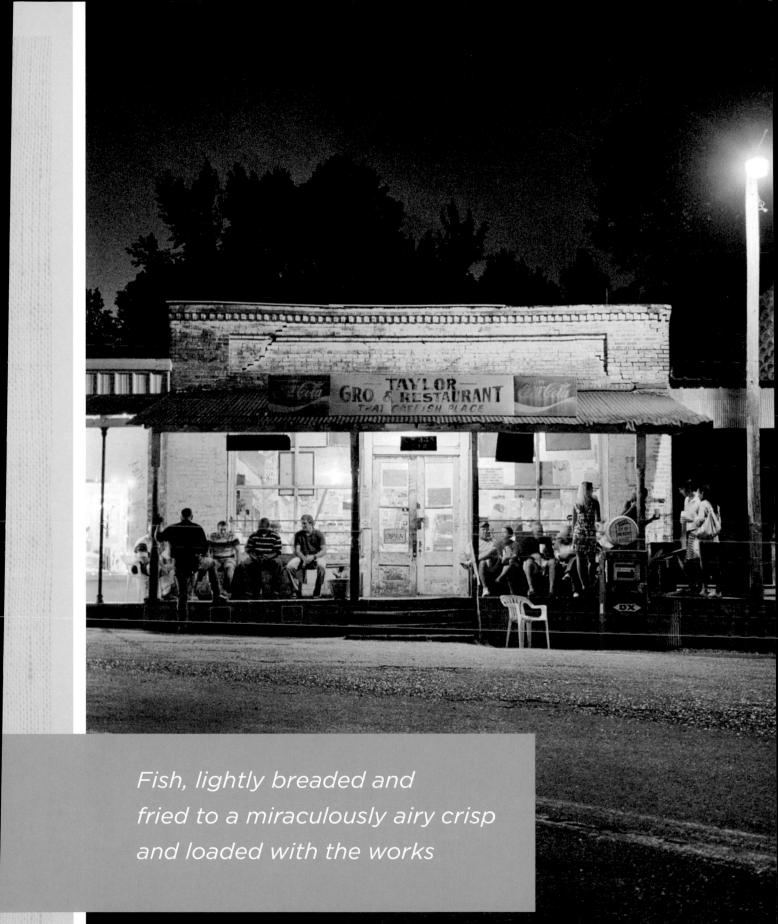

Fish, lightly breaded and fried to a miraculously airy crisp and loaded with the works

herb tartar sauce

1	cup your favorite or Homemade Mayonnaise (page 280)
½	cup fresh herbs, such as tarragon, basil, chives, parsley, cilantro, scallions, or a combination
2	tablespoons sour cream
2	small dill pickles, chopped
2	small sweet pickles, chopped
1	hard-boiled egg, chopped
1	jalapeño pepper, cored, seeded, and chopped
2	tablespoons grated red onion
2	tablespoons capers
1	tablespoon dill pickle juice
1	tablespoon fresh lemon juice
	Sea salt and freshly ground black pepper

Combine the mayonnaise, herbs, sour cream, dill pickles, sweet pickles, egg, jalapeño, onion, capers, pickle juice, lemon juice, and salt and pepper to taste in a blender or food processor and pulse to blend to a chunky sauce. Serve immediately or refrigerate in an airtight container until ready to serve, or for up to 4 days.

Know-how: how to tell when oil is sizzling hot

There are many instances in this book, especially for pan- and skillet-frying, where instructions call for heating oil or butter until sizzling hot. Instead of using a thermometer, check the oil's readiness by dropping in a pinch of salt or flour; if the oil sizzles when the salt hits the pan, it's ready to go. (When frying chicken and other slow-cooking foods, it's important to keep the oil at a consistent temperature to ensure they cook evenly; in recipes like these I always provide an exact temperature and suggest using a thermometer.)

grilled grouper with heirloom tomato salsa

Last time I was at the See Wee, an old-school seafood restaurant outside Charleston, I had an incredibly good plate of grilled grouper with fresh tomato salsa. Not only was the fish superfresh and perfectly cooked, but the salsa, a rough mix of vine-ripe tomatoes, white onion, and cilantro, was so simple and bright that it enhanced the flavor of the fish perfectly without overpowering it. I was so fond of it that I've been re-creating it at home ever since. It's just the sort of light, fresh supper you want in the dead of summer. SERVES 4 TO 6

SALSA
2   heirloom tomatoes (about 1 pound), cored and chopped
2   tablespoons diced white onion
2   tablespoons chopped fresh cilantro
     Juice of 1 lime
1   tablespoon extra-virgin olive oil
     Sea salt and freshly ground black pepper

FISH
     One 1½-pound grouper fillet, about 1 inch thick, skin on
1   tablespoon extra-virgin olive oil
1   tablespoon chopped fresh cilantro
     Sea salt and freshly ground black pepper
1   lime, cut into wedges

SALSA | Combine the tomatoes, onion, cilantro, lime juice, and olive oil in a bowl, season with salt and pepper to taste, and stir to mix. The salsa can be made up to 2 days in advance and refrigerated in an airtight container until ready to serve.

FISH | When ready to cook the fish, prepare a hot fire in a charcoal or gas grill and let the coals burn to gray ash with a bright red glow; if using a gas grill, heat the grill on high. Oil the grill grates.

Place the fillet on a plate, skin side down, and rub the olive oil on the fleshy side. Sprinkle with the cilantro and season with salt and pepper to taste, pressing lightly to adhere.

Place the fish, flesh side down, on the grill and cook for 3 to 4 minutes, depending on the thickness of the fillet. The fish will start to turn white around the edges and release from the grill easily when it is ready to be turned. Flip the fillet over onto a piece of aluminum foil on the grill. Cover the grill with the lid or cover the fish with another piece of foil and cook for another 3 to 4 minutes, until cooked through and flaky.

Remove the fish from the grill, place on a large serving platter or divide evenly between individual plates, and serve warm, topped with lots of fresh salsa and lime wedges for squeezing over the fish.

louisiana bbq shrimp

Despite its name, this traditional shrimp dish isn't so much barbecue as a savory, saucy stew. It gets its full-bodied flavor from Worcestershire sauce and dark beer, and a dose of fresh lemon gives it a bright, clean finish. SERVES 2 TO 4

8	tablespoons (1 stick) unsalted butter
½	onion, diced
4	garlic cloves, smashed and minced
1	tablespoon chopped fresh marjoram or parsley
2	bay leaves
2	lemons, cut in half
1	cup dark beer
¼	cup Worcestershire sauce
2	teaspoons hot sauce
2	teaspoons crushed red pepper flakes
2	pounds large shrimp, peeled, tails left on
	Sea salt and freshly ground black pepper
2	tablespoons chopped fresh parsley
	Crusty French bread, for dipping

Heat the butter in a large cast-iron skillet over medium heat until sizzling hot (see Know-how, page 100). Add the onion, garlic, marjoram, and bay leaves and cook and stir until the garlic releases an aroma, about 1 minute. Squeeze the juice from the lemons into the skillet, reserving 2 of the squeezed halves. Add the beer, Worcestershire sauce, hot sauce, and red pepper flakes and stir to mix. Thinly slice the reserved lemon halves and add to the skillet. Bring the mixture to a low boil and simmer for 3 to 4 minutes.

Season the shrimp all over with salt and pepper to taste and add to the skillet. Cook, stirring occasionally, until the shrimp are bright pink and cooked through, 4 to 5 minutes. Remove and discard the bay leaves. Season with additional salt and pepper, if desired, and sprinkle with the parsley. Serve warm with lots of crusty French bread for dipping in the sauce.

ON THE SIDE I like to serve these juicy, flavor-packed shrimp over Carolina Gold Rice (page 215) or Creamy Cheese Grits (page 208) for soaking up all that saucy goodness and a side of Roxy's Grated Cole Slaw (page 260).

sautéed flounder with garden vegetable ratatouille

I like to make this in early summer, when the first summer vegetables are coming in and the flounder, which can grow to as much as twenty-five pounds, are running small—what our fishmonger calls "plate size." They are so fresh and dainty at that time of year that I usually budget one whole fish per person. I sometimes serve this simple dish with a green salad or fluffy steamed rice, but you don't have to, as it's really a complete meal in and of itself—the vegetable ratatouille, made with smaller-than-usual dice, doubles as both a sauce and a vegetable side.   SERVES 4

RATATOUILLE

2	tablespoons olive oil
2	spring onions, 4 scallions, or 1 leek, thinly sliced
1	cup peeled, diced eggplant
4	small summer squash, such as yellow crookneck, Sundrop, or Zephyr zucchini, diced
1/2	red bell pepper, cored, seeded, and diced
2	tomatoes (about 1 pound), cored and diced
10	fresh basil leaves, thinly sliced
2	garlic cloves, smashed and minced
	Sea salt and freshly ground black pepper

FLOUNDER

	Four 6-ounce flounder fillets, about 1/4 inch thick
	Sea salt and freshly ground black pepper
1/2	cup all-purpose flour
	Pinch of ground cayenne pepper
	Canola oil, for sautéing

RATATOUILLE | Heat the olive oil in a large skillet over medium-high heat until hot. Add the onions and eggplant and cook, stirring, for about 3 minutes, until the onions are soft and translucent. Add the squash and bell pepper and cook, stirring occasionally, for another 5 minutes, until tender and light brown around the edges. Add the tomatoes, basil, garlic, and salt and pepper to taste and cook and stir until the tomatoes are just heated through, about 1 minute. Remove from the heat and cover loosely to keep warm.

FLOUNDER | Rinse the fillets, pat dry, and season with salt and black pepper to taste. Combine the flour and cayenne in a small shallow bowl. Add salt and black pepper to taste and stir to mix.

Pour enough canola oil to just cover the bottom of a separate large nonstick or cast-iron skillet and place over medium-high heat until sizzling hot (see Know-how, page 100).

(continued)

Dredge each fillet lightly in the flour mixture and sauté in the hot oil for 2 to 3 minutes per side, until golden brown, flaky, and cooked through. Cook in batches if necessary to avoid over-crowding the skillet.

ASSEMBLY | Reheat the ratatouille if necessary. Transfer the fillets to a large serving dish or individual serving plates and serve hot with the ratatouille spooned over and around the fish.

SARA'S SWAPS I love the way the nuttiness of the flounder brings out the sweetness of the vegetables in the ratatouille, but you can substitute any delicate, flaky white fish, like red or B-Line snapper, or catfish. The same goes for the ratatouille; try changing the mix of herbs (to include parsley, marjoram, or chives) and vegetables (such as cherry tomatoes, zucchini, red onions, and spinach) to make the most of whatever is garden-fresh.

IN SEASON Spring onions are similar to green onions, but with slightly larger bulbs that pack a stronger onion flavor and quite a bit more heat. As their name suggests, you should be able to find them at your local farmer's market or supermarket in the spring; you can use them as you would scallions or even large onions.

---

chew on this: **about local fish**

The North and South Carolina beaches have long been considered prime fishing destinations, and we are lucky to have access to high-quality fresh fish, even as far inland as the Piedmont, where I live. In addition to grouper, the most common local seafood includes plump shrimp, soft-shell crabs, snapper, redfish, bass, marlin, wahoo, and stripers. Freshwater fishing, on the other hand, yields catfish, trout, and more bass. I encourage you to make friends with your local fishmonger; by figuring out what sort of fish flourish in your area, you will be better equipped to buy the freshest, tastiest local seafood available.

---

salmon croquettes

I grew up on these tasty little fried cakes, which Granny Foster used to serve for breakfast with fried eggs and biscuits, or sometimes for supper along with mashed potatoes and coleslaw. Like most Southerners, Granny used canned salmon in her croquettes. I opt instead for freshly poached or grilled salmon, a move that allows the delicate, grassy flavor of the fish to come through. Crispy and satisfying (the name *croquette* comes from the French for "to crunch"), these easy treats are an excellent way to revitalize leftovers from last night's salmon dinner, ensuring that the switch from canned to fresh fish does not necessarily sacrifice convenience.   MAKES 8 CAKES / SERVES 4 TO 6

1	tablespoon olive oil
¼	cup diced onion
1	pound grilled or poached salmon fillets, broken into large chunks
1½	cups dried bread crumbs or cracker crumbs
1	large egg, lightly beaten
	Zest and juice of 1 lemon
2	tablespoons chopped fresh parsley or basil
	Sea salt and freshly ground black pepper
	Canola oil, for sautéing

Heat the olive oil in a large nonstick skillet over medium-high heat until sizzling hot (see Know-how, page 100). Add the onion and cook, stirring occasionally, for 3 to 4 minutes, until soft and translucent.

Transfer the onion to a mixing bowl and add the salmon, ½ cup of the bread crumbs, the egg, lemon zest and juice, parsley, and salt and pepper to taste; stir gently to mix. Take care not to break the chunks of fish up too small; do not overmix.

Form the salmon mixture into 8 patties, about ½ inch thick. Place the remaining 1 cup bread crumbs in a shallow bowl, season with salt and pepper to taste, and stir to mix. Dredge the croquettes with the bread crumb mixture, coating both sides and pressing gently to adhere. Refrigerate for at least 1 hour, until firm.

In the same skillet used to cook the onions, pour enough canola oil to just cover the bottom and place over medium-high heat until sizzling hot. Place the croquettes in the hot oil, cooking in batches if necessary to avoid overcrowding, and cook until golden brown, about 4 minutes per side. Flip the croquettes only once; reduce the heat to medium if they start browning too quickly. Remove from the skillet, drain on a brown paper bag, and serve warm.

soft-shell crabs with salty tomato butter

Soft-shell crab season, which generally lasts from May through June, is short and highly anticipated. That's because soft-shell crabmeat is unbelievably tender and buttery-sweet, and the shell, which you eat along with the meat, is perfectly crunchy without being the least bit tough or chewy. True fanatics don't let a moment of soft-shell crab season go to waste, eating them for breakfast, lunch, or dinner, in sandwiches or served solo. Ask your fishmonger to clean them for you. SERVES 2 TO 4

	Canola oil, for sautéing
1/2	cup all-purpose flour
1/2	cup yellow cornmeal
	Sea salt and freshly ground black pepper
	Pinch of ground cayenne pepper
1/2	cup well-shaken buttermilk
	Dash of hot sauce
4	soft-shell crabs, cleaned
	Salty Tomato Butter (recipe follows)
1	lemon, cut into wedges

Fill a large skillet with enough canola oil to cover the bottom and place over medium-high heat until sizzling hot (see Know-how, page 100). Combine the flour and cornmeal in a shallow bowl or plastic bag, season with salt and black pepper to taste and cayenne, and stir or shake to mix. Place the buttermilk and hot sauce in a shallow bowl and stir to combine. One at a time, dust the crabs lightly on both sides with the flour mixture or shake in the bag, then dip into the buttermilk mixture and back into the flour mixture to coat evenly, shaking off any excess flour.

Place the crabs in the hot oil and sauté for 3 to 4 minutes per side, until golden brown and crispy. Line a platter with a brown paper bag.

Remove from the skillet, drain on the platter, and season with additional salt and pepper, if desired. Serve warm topped with slices of Salty Tomato Butter and lemon wedges to squeeze over the crab.

salty tomato butter

This easy butter preparation adds an unexpected flavor dimension to any dish and is equally good on steaks, steamed broccoli, roasted fingerling potatoes, or fish and rice.

MAKES ONE 4- TO 5-INCH LOG OR ABOUT 1/2 CUP

8	tablespoons (1 stick) unsalted butter, softened
2	sun-dried tomatoes, packed in oil (substitute: dried and reconstituted)
6	fresh basil leaves
1	tablespoon coarse or flaky sea salt
1/2	teaspoon freshly ground black pepper

(continued)

Place the butter, tomatoes, basil, salt, and pepper in a food processor or blender and pulse until well combined and blended, stopping to scrape down the the bowl several times as you go. Transfer the mixture to a piece of wax paper, roll it into a log 1½ to 2 inches in diameter, wrap tightly in plastic, and refrigerate until firm, about 1 hour, or for up to 1 week. Slice into thin rounds as needed.

SARA'S SWAPS For a more traditional preparation, serve the crabs with Horseradish Remoulade (page 117), Herb Tartar Sauce (page 100), or Spicy Cocktail Sauce (page 283) in place of the Salty Tomato Butter.

chew on this: *about soft-shell crabs*

Soft-shell crabs are a seasonal specialty and point of pride on the Outer Banks, and I fell in love with them. My friend Della took me to the little town of Manteo, North Carolina, to go soft-shell crabbing. It was such an adventure! We got on the boat before sunrise and headed out to sea, where the crabbers located their big metal traps and pulled up the crabs. Back on shore, they dusted the freshly caught crabs in cornmeal, sautéed them in a little oil and butter, and served them to us with lemon wedges. I was blown away by the simple preparation and amazing flavors—the brine of the seawater and the sweetness of the crabmeat were incredible together.

I think people often assume that soft-shell crabs are a separate variety; actually, they are blue crabs that are caught and eaten just after they molt their hard outer shells, so the entire crustacean, "soft shell" and all, is edible. During soft-shell season, usually May and June, "busters"—crabs that are in the process of molting—seek refuge in protected areas and begin taking in lots of water so their bodies swell up and eventually crack open their outer shells. The males are called jimmies, and the females are she-crabs, sooks, or sallies, depending on how fully developed they are. The window of time for harvesting individual soft-shell crabs is very short; there is about a four-day period between the time a blue crab sheds its outer shell and the soft shell beneath it begins to harden.

easy crab cakes

I used to make crab cakes using all kinds of herbs and vegetables for added flavor and texture, but the ultrasimple crab cakes Peter and I enjoyed on a recent trip to the Maryland shore convinced me that in this case, less is more. I don't add much more to this dressed-down version than is needed to hold the cakes together, so the only time to make them is when crab is in season and at the peak of freshness.

MAKES 6 CAKES / SERVES 3 TO 6

1   pound fresh jumbo lump crabmeat, picked over
    and shells removed
½   cup fresh bread crumbs (see Know-how, page 134)
3   tablespoons your favorite or Homemade
    Mayonnaise (page 280)
1   tablespoon whole-grain mustard
1   tablespoon fresh lemon juice
1   tablespoon chopped fresh parsley
1   teaspoon sea salt
½   teaspoon freshly ground black pepper
    Pinch of ground cayenne pepper
1   tablespoon unsalted butter
1   tablespoon olive oil
1   lemon or lime, cut into wedges

Combine the crab, bread crumbs, mayonnaise, mustard, lemon juice, parsley, salt, black pepper, and cayenne and stir just to mix, leaving the crab in large, unbroken lumps. Form the mixture into six 3-inch patties. Refrigerate for about 1 hour, until firm.

Heat the butter and olive oil in a large skillet over medium heat until sizzling hot (see Know-how, page 100). Add the crab cakes and cook for about 3 minutes per side, turning only once, until golden brown. Remove from the skillet, drain on a brown paper bag, and serve hot with lemon or lime wedges to squeeze over the cakes.

SIMPLE LUMP CRAB SALAD   Place **1 pound fresh jumbo lump crabmeat** in a medium bowl and pick through the meat to remove any remaining bits of shell, taking care not to break apart the large lumps in the process. Add the **juice of 1 lime; 2 tablespoons chopped fresh mint; 2 tablespoons your favorite or Homemade Mayonnaise (page 280) or extra-virgin olive oil; 1 cored, seeded, and minced jalapeño pepper;** and **sea salt and freshly ground black pepper to taste.** Stir gently to mix. Serve immediately or refrigerate in an airtight container until ready to serve, or for up to 2 days.

lowcountry shrimp and crab boil
with spicy cocktail sauce

With blue crabs, sausage, corn on the cob, and tender new potatoes, this lowcountry-inspired shrimp boil makes for a rustic and utterly delicious spread that is just the thing for impromptu summertime gatherings. I sometimes serve it in individual tins or buckets, but that's about as refined as I ever get with this low-key dish, which is best eaten right out of the bucket or from a big pile on the table, with a crowd of friends, and always with your fingers. SERVES 10 TO 12

2	tablespoons olive oil
1	Vidalia or other sweet onion, quartered
8	garlic cloves, smashed
2	quarts cold water
	One 12-ounce beer
2	tablespoons pickling spices (see Know-how, page 114)
2	teaspoons kosher salt, plus more to taste
1	teaspoon crushed red pepper flakes
1/2	teaspoon ground cayenne pepper
1	lemon, halved
1	pound small new potatoes, such as Yukon Gold, Rose Blossom, or fingerling
6	live blue crabs (optional)
5	pounds large shrimp, shells on
1	pound spicy link sausage, such as andouille, chorizo, or linguiça, cut into 3-inch lengths
6	ears corn, shucked and halved
2	tomatoes, cored and chopped
6	sprigs fresh thyme
6	sprigs fresh marjoram or oregano
1	cup fresh basil leaves, cut into thin strips
	Freshly ground black pepper
	Spicy Cocktail Sauce (page 283)
	Crusty Garlic Bread (recipe follows), for dipping

Heat the olive oil in a large stockpot over medium-high heat until hot. Add the onion, reduce the heat to medium, and cook and stir for about 5 minutes, until soft and golden. Add the garlic and continue to cook and stir for 1 minute longer.

Add the cold water, beer, pickling spices, salt, red pepper flakes, and cayenne. Squeeze the lemon juice into the mixture and add the squeezed halves. Raise the heat to high and bring the mixture to a boil. Reduce the heat and simmer, uncovered, for about 10 minutes. Add the potatoes and cook, covered, for 10 minutes, until they are just beginning to get tender. (Depending on the size of the potatoes, they may need to cook 2 to 5 minutes more.)

(continued)

Add the crabs, if using, and bring the mixture back up to a low boil. Cover and cook for 5 minutes more. Add the shrimp, sausage, corn, tomatoes, thyme, marjoram, and basil. Return to a low boil and cook for about 5 minutes longer, until the shrimp turn bright pink and are cooked through and the potatoes are tender.

Drain the boiled ingredients, reserving about 2 cups of the cooking liquid. To serve, cut the crabs in half and crack the shells; then pile the shrimp, crab, sausage, and vegetables on a large platter (or, if eating outside, in tin buckets or down the center of a table covered with newspaper or butcher paper). Pour the reserved liquid on top if using a platter or in dipping bowls, season with salt and black pepper, and serve with Spicy Cocktail Sauce (page 283) and Crusty Garlic Bread, for dipping.

JUDY'S BILOXI SHRIMP BOIL Bring a large pot of water to a boil and add a **handful of fresh herbs, such as parsley, dill, basil, bay leaves, or any combination of these; 1 lemon, cut in half, squeezed, and added to the water;** and **1 tablespoon each** of the following: **sea salt, whole black peppercorns, crushed red pepper flakes, yellow mustard seeds, garlic flakes, and onion flakes.** Let the mixture boil for 2 to 3 minutes; then add **5 pounds fresh shrimp, shells on and preferably with the heads on.** Give the mixture a stir and cook until it comes back to a boil and the shrimp start to rise to the top of the water and are cooked through, 3 to 5 minutes. Strain, reserving some of the cooking liquid, and serve hot with **melted butter for dipping, lemon wedges for squeezing over the shrimp,** and **Crusty Garlic Bread** for dipping in the reserved cooking liquid.

crusty garlic bread

MAKES 1 LOAF

Preheat the oven to 400°F.

Slice **1 baguette or loaf of French bread** in half lengthwise and spread both sides with **soft unsalted butter.** Smash and mince **2 garlic cloves** and sprinkle evenly over the butter.

For soft bread, wrap in foil and heat in the oven until the butter is melted and the bread is warm. For crispy bread, place open-face on a baking sheet and bake to melt the butter and lightly toast. Serve warm.

Know-how: making pickling spices

You can make your own pickling spices by combining equal parts bay leaves, yellow mustard seeds, crushed red pepper flakes, sea salt, whole black peppercorns, whole cloves, and celery seeds in a glass jar. Screw the lid on the jar and shake to mix. The spices will keep in an airtight container for up to 6 months.

---

shrimp and crawfish étouffée

Étouffée is a traditional New Orleans one-pot dish whose name literally—and appropriately—comes from the French word for "smothered." Like gumbo, étouffée is a highly seasoned stew of fish or meat and vegetables that is served over steamed rice. Also like gumbo, it has a big-hearted, homey quality that makes it one of my favorite dishes to serve to crowds (especially when they include friends who aren't from the South). Although serious purists might disapprove, I never make étouffée the same way twice, and I don't take sides when it comes to never-ending debates about the proper shade of roux or whether there's room for tomatoes in a bona fide étouffée. For me, one of the joys of Cajun and Creole stews is their variability, so feel free to experiment. SERVES 6 TO 8

6	tablespoons (³/₄ stick) unsalted butter
2	tablespoons olive oil
¹/₃	cup all-purpose flour
1	onion, chopped
3	celery stalks, diced
2	red or green bell peppers, cored, seeded, and chopped
1	large tomato, cored and chopped
2	garlic cloves, smashed and minced
4	cups Fast and Fresh Broth (page 42)
	Juice of 1 lemon
1	teaspoon sea salt, plus more to taste
¹/₂	teaspoon freshly ground black pepper, plus more to taste
	Pinch of crushed red pepper flakes
2	pounds large shrimp, peeled and deveined, shells reserved for broth
1	pound crawfish
¹/₂	cup chopped fresh cilantro
1	tablespoon fresh thyme
3	fresh basil leaves, thinly sliced
	Steamed white or Streak o' Green Dirty Rice (page 217), for serving

Heat 4 tablespoons of the butter and the olive oil in a large saucepan or Dutch oven over medium-high heat until sizzling hot (see Know-how, page 100). Reduce the heat to medium, add the flour, and cook, stirring constantly with a long-handled whisk, until the mixture changes from light to golden brown, 8 to 10 minutes. Adjust the heat to low if the flour starts browning too quickly.

Add the remaining 2 tablespoons butter and the onion, celery, and bell peppers. Cook, stirring constantly, for about 5 minutes more, until the onion is soft and golden, the celery and peppers begin to soften, and the roux turns a reddish brown. Add the tomato and garlic and cook and stir for 1 minute longer.

(continued)

Slowly add 1 cup of the broth, stirring constantly, until all is incorporated. Add the remaining 3 cups broth and stir to combine and form a creamy sauce, about 2 minutes. Add the lemon juice, salt, black pepper, and red pepper flakes, reduce the heat to low, and simmer for about 15 minutes, until the vegetables are tender and the sauce is thick.

Add the shrimp, crawfish, ¼ cup of the cilantro, the thyme, and basil. Cook, stirring occasionally, for about 5 minutes, until the shrimp are bright pink and the crawfish deep red and just cooked through. Season with additional salt and black pepper, if desired. Serve warm over steamed white or Streak o' Green Dirty Rice topped with the remaining ¼ cup cilantro.

SARA'S SWAPS You can make this étouffée with most any type of shellfish, including oysters, lobsters, and scallops. It is delicious, as well, with chicken or duck or, for a little spice, andouille sausage.

chew on this: **about crawfish**

In most other parts of the country, crawfish go by the name crayfish and are more likely to be kept as aquarium pets than served for dinner. Not in the South, and especially not in Louisiana, which supplies just shy of 100 percent of the crawfish consumed in the United States. This freshwater delicacy, which looks sort of like a miniature lobster, has the sweet, buttery flavor of its crustaceous cousins. These days, you can have live crawfish delivered right to your door, so check out Sources (page 377) for online suppliers and give it a shot.

crispy fried oysters four ways

When I was in college I had a job waiting tables at the Half Shell, a little wood-paneled restaurant in Memphis that makes the best fried oysters I have ever eaten. They serve their perfectly crisp-on-the-outside, juicy-on-the-inside oysters by the half-dozen, with lemon wedges and tartar sauce, but you can also get them layered with slaw in a creamy po' boy sandwich or sprinkled atop eggs Benedict. A few years ago the Half Shell moved across the street to a larger location, and while it's never felt quite the same since they moved, I still drop by for their fried oysters every time I visit Memphis. My Half Shell–inspired version of basic fried oysters makes a perfectly good meal on its own, but check out the four easy serving suggestions if you want to take things one step further. SERVES 2 TO 4

	Canola oil, for frying
2	dozen shucked oysters (about 1 pint)
1	cup yellow cornmeal
½	cup all-purpose flour
1	teaspoon sea salt, plus more to taste
½	teaspoon freshly ground black pepper, plus more to taste
	Pinch of ground cayenne pepper
1	cup well-shaken buttermilk
1	lemon, cut into wedges
	Horseradish Remoulade (recipe follows), for dipping

Pour about ¼ inch canola oil into a large skillet and place over medium-high heat until sizzling hot (see Know how, page 100).

Drain the oysters. Combine the cornmeal, flour, salt, black pepper, and cayenne in a shallow bowl or plastic bag and stir or shake to mix. Place the buttermilk in a separate shallow bowl and add the oysters.

One at a time, dredge or shake the oysters in the cornmeal mixture and drop into the hot oil, taking care not to overcrowd the skillet. Cook for about 1 minute per side, until golden brown and crispy all over. Using a slotted spoon, remove the oysters from the oil and drain on a brown paper bag. Season with additional salt and pepper, if desired. Serve hot with lemon wedges for squeezing on top and Horseradish Remoulade, or try one of the following variations.

FRIED OYSTER SALAD   For cool, crispy contrast, scatter the **fried oysters** over **Spring Coleslaw with Fresh Herbs and Light Honey Citrus Vinaigrette (page 258).**

OYSTERS SUNNY SIDE UP   For an out-of-the-ordinary breakfast or brunch, serve the **fried oysters** on top of **Creamy Cheese Grits (page 208)** alongside **fried eggs.**

(continued)

FRIED OYSTERS AND FRESH CORN When the sweetest summer corn is available, sprinkle the **fried oysters** over a pool of **Skillet-Fried Corn (page 230)** or **Carolina Shrimp Chowder (page 41)**.

FRIED OYSTER PO' BOY For a hearty lunchtime treat, serve them in a fried oyster po' boy. Preheat the oven to 400°F.

Split a **loaf of crusty French or Italian bread** or **Crusty Garlic Bread (page 114)** in half lengthwise. Brush both sides with **melted butter** and toast for a few minutes, until golden brown.

Spread with **Herb Tartar Sauce (page 100)** or **Homemade Mayonnaise (page 280)** and pile with **fried oysters**. Sprinkle with a few **dashes of hot sauce**, season with **sea salt and freshly ground black pepper to taste,** and top with scoops of **Roxy's Grated Coleslaw (page 260)**.

horseradish remoulade

MAKES ABOUT 1½ CUPS

½ **cup your favorite or Homemade Mayonnaise (page 280)**
½ **cup Greek yogurt**
¼ **cup prepared horseradish**
2 **scallions, trimmed and chopped**
2 **small dill pickles, chopped**
2 **small sweet pickles, chopped**
1 **hard-boiled egg, chopped**
2 **tablespoons chopped fresh parsley**
2 **tablespoons capers**
1 **tablespoon Dijon mustard**
1 **tablespoon fresh lemon juice**
  Sea salt and freshly ground black pepper
  Pinch of ground cayenne pepper

Combine the mayonnaise, yogurt, horseradish, scallions, dill pickles, sweet pickles, egg, parsley, capers, mustard, lemon juice, salt and black pepper, and cayenne in a blender or food processor and pulse to blend to a chunky sauce. Serve immediately or refrigerate in an airtight container until ready to serve, or for up to 4 days.

Destination: **NEW ORLEANS, LOUISIANA**

WORTH THE DETOUR

DOMILISE'S PO-BOY AND BAR'S

classic New Orleans po' boys

(504) 899-9126

Blink and you might miss Domilise's, home of some of the best po'
boys in all of New Orleans. This hole-in-the-wall foodie magnet is tucked in a
nondescript street corner far from the touristy French Quarter, and the only
thing alerting you to the fact that you've happened upon some of the most
sought-after sandwiches in town is a small, hand-painted placard in black,
red, and green, complete with a rough-hewn fleur-de-lis. This lack of advertising, and the enormous crowds that nevertheless descend each day at
lunchtime, are pure New Orleans: make good food and folks will come.

So many folks, in fact, that during rushes you may need to stand in line
to take a number, only to wait until your number is called to finally place an
order. But as the many regulars know, Domilise's hearty po' boys are more
than worth the wait. Airy, thin-crusted loaves of locally made Leidenheimer's
French bread—delivered fresh twice daily—are loaded up with your choice
of anything from hot smoked sausage, wieners, or roast beef to fresh-fried
catfish, shrimp, or, my favorite, oysters. Next, they are "fully dressed" with lettuce, tomatoes, ketchup, grainy mustard, or gravy, depending on your protein. All sandwiches come large or small, but in the oversize world of
Domilise's, a large is enough for two, and a small is more than enough for
one. These sandwiches aren't anything fancy, but they are big, messy, and
packed with the savory, saucy sort of flavors that make po' boys so addictively delicious. While you wait on your food, belly up to the bar, sip on a
cold beer or creamy Barq's Root Beer, and watch as po' boy after po' boy is
lovingly assembled.

Packed with the savory, saucy sort of flavors that make po' boys so addictively delicious

birds

Until I graduated from high school, almost every Sun-

day of my life was spent at my grandparents' farmhouse, where we'd gather after church for lunch. Those midday meals were a never-changing ritual, and that included what went on the table. Not a Sunday went by that Granny Foster didn't make almost the same thing: fried chicken, mashed potatoes, and creamed corn, with at least four other sides that rotated with the seasons and her whims.

Of course, Southerners' love for poultry is much larger than can be contained by fried chicken alone. Many Southerners used to keep a little flock of chickens that were allowed to scratch and peck freely about the yard in exchange for eggs and meat. Today, people think of chicken as an everyday meat—almost humdrum. But it wasn't too long ago that chicken was reserved for Sundays and special occasions, when a chicken was butchered or the hunting was plentiful, and not a bit of the bird—including the liver, gizzards, heart, marrow, and feet—went to waste.

Chicken may be the most popular poultry, but it is by no means peerless, and I knew I had to expand this chapter to include all the birds Southerners regularly eat, from turkey and guinea hens to duck and quail. From Duck Two Ways, Fast and Slow (page 146) and Carl's Deep-Fried Turkey (page 149) to Pan-Seared Guinea Hen with Roasted Tomatoes, Okra, and Butternut Squash (page 156), I've tried to build these recipes according to a more traditional approach, that is to say, in a way that Granny Foster would recognize, even when the recipes themselves aren't "by the book." That means a focus on freshness and simple preparations and, perhaps most important, an appreciation for the culinary potential of the whole bird. While most of the recipes, including Chicken Under a Skillet (page 139), Chicken and Dumplings (page 142), and Crispy Chicken Cutlets with a Heap of Spring Salad (page 133), are simple enough to become standards of your weekly routine, I hope they will also inspire you to look at chicken and its brethren with new eyes.

granny foster's sunday fried chicken

Granny Foster made the best fried chicken in the world—salty and golden brown with a crackly crust that gave way to meat as moist and tender as could be. The secret is the overnight brine of water, salt, and spices that drives extra moisture and flavor into the meat, where they are locked in during the cooking process.   SERVES 4

        One 3- to 3½-pound chicken, cut into 10 pieces
        (see Know-how, page 129)
    3   tablespoons sea salt, plus more to taste
    1   tablespoon sugar
    1   tablespoon distilled white vinegar
    2   bay leaves
    2   cups well-shaken buttermilk
    2   cups all-purpose flour
    ½   teaspoon freshly ground black pepper, plus more to taste
        Pinch of ground cayenne pepper
        Crisco vegetable shortening or canola oil, for frying
        Fried Chicken Gravy (recipe follows), for serving (optional)

Place the chicken in a large bowl and cover with cold water. Add 2 tablespoons of the salt and the sugar, vinegar, and bay leaves and stir until the salt and sugar dissolve. Cover and refrigerate overnight.

When ready to cook the chicken, place the buttermilk in a shallow bowl and transfer the chicken from the brine to the buttermilk.

Place the flour, remaining 1 tablespoon salt, the black pepper, and cayenne in a separate large, shallow bowl or plastic bag and stir or shake to mix.

Melt the shortening about ½ inch deep in a large cast-iron skillet and place over medium-high heat until the temperature reaches between 350°F and 375°F. The melted shortening should be deep enough to submerge the chicken about halfway; the level of the shortening will rise slightly when you add the chicken.

Remove the chicken from the buttermilk and dredge or shake in the flour mixture, one piece at a time, to coat evenly on all sides, beginning with the large pieces. Shake off any excess flour.

Place the chicken, skin side down, in the hot shortening, reduce the heat to medium, and fry until golden brown, about 15 minutes. Check the pieces to make sure they are not browning too quickly; if so, reduce the heat or turn the pieces. Turn the chicken and fry the other side until golden brown, about 15 minutes more. The chicken is done when the juices run clear when a thigh is pierced with the tip of a small knife and an internal thermometer inserted in the thickest part of the thigh reads about 165°F. The chicken should cook for a total of 30 to 35 minutes.

Line a platter with a brown paper bag and transfer the chicken to the platter to drain. Season with additional salt and pepper and let sit for about 10 minutes before serving warm with Fried Chicken Gravy, if desired.

fried chicken gravy

Occasionally, Granny Foster would add leftover dredging flour and water to the frying pan to make a delicious brown gravy for spooning over the fried chicken and mashed potatoes. I make it just like she did, but I usually use chicken broth rather than water for added flavor.

MAKES ABOUT 2 CUPS

When the chicken is done, pour all but about **2 tablespoons of the shortening** out of the skillet, leaving all the brown bits on the bottom. Add **3 tablespoons flour** and cook, stirring constantly, over medium heat until the flour is light brown, about 2 minutes. Slowly whisk in **2 cups low-sodium chicken broth,** season with **sea salt and freshly ground black pepper to taste,** and cook and stir until the gravy is thick, 2 to 3 minutes. Serve warm.

SARA'S SWAPS No worries if you don't have time to brine the chicken overnight. For same-day fried chicken, just soak the chicken in the buttermilk (rather than the water-and-vinegar solution) for 2 or 3 hours before continuing with the recipe.

Know-how: frying chicken like a southerner

As food writer James Villas put it, "To know about fried chicken, you have to have been weaned and reared in the South. Period." But with these quick tips, you'll be making fried chicken like a true Southerner in no time.

When frying the chicken, do your best to keep the oil at a consistent, even temperature; between 350°F and 375°F is best. (Too low, and the chicken will get soggy and leaden; too high, and the outside will burn before the meat is cooked through.) My grandmother used an electric skillet, which made perfect fried chicken every time, but there are other ways to get her results. First, use a cast-iron or other heavy-bottomed skillet, if possible; it will get you halfway there by retaining heat efficiently and evenly. Make sure the pieces of chicken are roughly uniform in size (you may need to cut the breast in half crosswise) and take care not to overcrowd the skillet, which will drag down the temperature and make the chicken soggy. You can use a clip-on thermometer to monitor the oil temperature and adjust as necessary.

Turn the chicken only once or twice; if you keep turning it the crust falls off and the chicken doesn't get crispy. Use a meat fork instead of tongs to turn the chicken; this will also help keep the crust from falling off.

Drop a few tablespoons of bacon grease in with the shortening for added flavor.

Drain the chicken on a brown paper bag; it will help keep the chicken crisp.

Know-how: cutting a chicken into ten pieces

Many of the recipes in this chapter begin with a whole chicken cut into ten pieces—breast quarters, thighs, legs, and wings. Here's everything you need to know to do it yourself.

Start with a sharp knife (or, to make it really easy, use a pair of poultry shears).

Place the chicken on a cutting board, breast side up. Pull one leg away from the body and cut through the skin between the body and the thigh to expose the hip joint. Lift the chicken, bend the thigh back to push the hip joint out of the socket, and cut through the joint. Repeat with the other leg.

Bend the drumstick back toward the thigh to push the knee joint out of the socket and cut through the skin and joint. Repeat with the other leg.

Pull one wing away from the body and cut through the skin between the body and wing to expose the shoulder joint. Cut through the joint and repeat with the other wing.

Place the chicken on its back. Starting at the tail end and working your way up to the neck, slice horizontally to separate the breast from the back. Lift and cut the breast away from the back on the other side of the shoulder; discard the back or use for broth.

Place the breast, skin side down, on the cutting board and flatten with the back of your hand to expose the breastbone. Cut the breast in half through the middle of the breastbone. Cut each half in half again crosswise, just above the rib cage, to make 4 pieces of breast rather than 2.

Destination: **MASON AND MEMPHIS, TENNESSEE**

WORTH THE DETOUR

GUS'S WORLD FAMOUS FRIED CHICKEN'S

Southern fried chicken

(901) 294-2028

LIKE ALL THE BEST SOUTHERN DINERS AND JUKE JOINTS, GUS'S OF TENNESSEE sticks to what it knows best. And what it knows best—fried chicken—it has elevated to a fine art, worthy of its claim to "world's best." In fact, apart from my Granny Foster's recipe (page 127), Gus's fried chicken is, for me, the version that sets the bar for this iconic Southern dish. It isn't that it's fancy or unusual—you won't find any exotic spices or inventive presentations here—but rather that it hews to the basics, and then perfects them.

Each piece of succulent chicken hailing from Gus's deep fryer comes cloaked in a thick, magnificently brown crust that is at once crispy and juicy, spicy hot and bursting with flavor. Orders of fried chicken—sold by the piece or in a multitude of combinations—are served in loose piles with sides of creamy slaw, rich baked beans, and slices of soft white bread. Deep-fried pickles with ranch dipping sauce and thick-crusted fried green tomatoes can be bought separately; order one of each for the table and you're set.

None of Gus's several locations is particularly atmospheric—but then again, that's not why anyone goes there. Gus's is all about fried chicken and nothing but fried chicken. Happily, chicken as good as theirs is more than reason enough.

Each piece of succulent chicken hailing from Gus's deep fryer comes cloaked in a thick, magnificently brown crust.

crispy chicken cutlets with a heap of spring salad

This dish contains all the flavor and crunch you expect from fried chicken, but with all the health benefits of using boneless, skinless chicken breast. Plus, you get bonus points for scattering the cutlets over a tender arugula salad bursting with fresh herbs and drizzled with tarragon-infused Buttermilk Green Goddess Dressing. SERVES 4 TO 6

CHICKEN
1½   **pounds boneless, skinless chicken breast, sliced into 8 thin cutlets (see Know-how, page 134)**
½   **cup well-shaken buttermilk**
2   **large eggs**
   Sea salt and freshly ground black pepper
2   **cups fresh bread crumbs (see Know-how, page 134)**
½   **cup all-purpose flour**
   Canola oil, for sautéing

SALAD
6   **handfuls arugula (about 6 cups), washed and drained**
¼   **cup fresh parsley leaves**
¼   **cup chopped fresh dill**
   Sea salt and freshly ground black pepper
1   **cup Buttermilk Green Goddess Dressing (page 284)**
¼   **cup freshly grated Parmesan cheese**

CHICKEN | Rinse the chicken and pat dry with paper towels. Whisk the buttermilk and eggs along with a pinch of salt in a shallow bowl. Place the bread crumbs and flour in two separate bowls or plastic bags, season each with salt and pepper to taste, and stir or shake to mix.

Pour canola oil about ¼-inch deep into a large cast-iron or heavy-bottomed skillet and place over medium-high heat until sizzling hot (see Know-how, page 100).

While the oil is heating, dredge or shake the chicken in the flour mixture, adding one piece at a time, to evenly coat both sides, shaking off the excess, and then in the buttermilk mixture, allowing the excess to drip off. Finally, dredge in the bread crumbs to evenly coat both sides, patting to adhere.

Working in batches if necessary to avoid overcrowding the skillet, place the chicken in the hot oil and fry for 3 to 4 minutes per side, until golden brown and cooked through. Drain on a platter lined with a brown paper bag and season with additional salt and pepper. Repeat the process with the remaining cutlets, removing any brown bits with a slotted spoon and adding more oil if needed.

SALAD | Combine the arugula, parsley, and dill in a large bowl. Season with salt and pepper to taste and toss to mix.

(continued)

| Divide the salad mixture evenly between individual serving plates and place 1 or 2 pieces of warm chicken on top of each. Drizzle with the dressing, sprinkle with the Parmesan cheese, and serve warm.

SARA'S SWAPS Feel free to play around with how you season the chicken. To the flour mixture, consider adding one or more of the following: Parmesan cheese, fresh chopped herbs, ground nuts (such as almonds, pecans, or peanuts), coarse-ground cornmeal, cornbread crumbs, or ground spices, such as curry, paprika, chili powder, or chipotle. You can also use this recipe—and any of the variations—with fish (such as catfish or tilapia) or cutlets of pork or turkey.

Know-how: cutting cutlets or paillards

Place the boneless, skinless breast on a cutting board and secure it by placing your hand flat on top. Using a sharp knife, start at the thick end of the breast and slice in half horizontally (this is much easier than pounding the chicken thin). If the breast is thick enough, slice each half in half again horizontally to make cutlets about ¼ inch thick.

Know-how: making fresh bread crumbs

Fresh bread crumbs have endless uses. To make them, tear slightly stale bread into pieces. (Most any kind of bread will do, including white sandwich bread, French baguettes, rolls, and pita bread; the only ones I stay away from for this purpose are whole-grain or dark breads.) Place the bread pieces in the food processor or blender and pulse until you achieve the desired crumb. In the South, we also use crackers and cornbread interchangeably for fresh bread crumbs. They can be made in the same way, in a blender or food processor, but the cracker crumbs are better kept in the pantry. Always prepare more bread crumbs than you immediately need; stored in the freezer in a zip-top bag, they keep for up to 2 months.

braised chicken with country ham and turnips with their greens

The two-step cooking process here yields perfectly moist and flavorful results: First, you put a nice sear on the chicken in a skillet. Next, you finish it off in the oven, slow-cooking it in a wonderful pot likker of seasonal vegetables and country ham. That's it. Once you get the hang of this basic method, you can use it to make endless variations.

SERVES 4 TO 6

	One 3- to 3½-pound chicken, cut into 10 pieces (see Know-how, page 129)
	Sea salt and freshly ground black pepper
¼	cup all-purpose flour
2	tablespoons olive oil
1	bunch baby turnips (8 to 10 turnips), scrubbed, greens removed and reserved (you should have about 5 ounces of greens), or substitute 5 ounces of spinach
2	ounces country ham, diced
2	garlic cloves, smashed
1½	cups low-sodium chicken broth
1	tablespoon fresh rosemary

Preheat the oven to 375°F.

Rinse the chicken, pat dry, and remove any excess fat. Season all over with salt and pepper to taste. Lightly dust each piece, skin side only, with the flour.

Heat the olive oil in a large ovenproof, nonstick skillet over medium-high heat until sizzling hot (see Know-how, page 100). Add the chicken and brown for about 5 minutes per side.

Remove the chicken from the skillet to a plate and set aside. Add the turnips and ham and cook and stir for about 2 minutes, until the ham is slightly crispy. Add the garlic and cook and stir for 1 minute more. Add the broth and rosemary, scrape up all the brown bits from the bottom of the pan, and bring to a low boil. Reduce the heat to a simmer and return the chicken to the skillet, skin side up, along with any juice that has collected in the bottom of the plate.

Place the skillet in the oven to roast for about 30 minutes, basting the chicken with the cooking liquid several times, until cooked through and the juices run clear when the thickest part of the thigh is pierced with the tip of a small knife.

Remove from the oven and transfer the chicken to a large serving platter, loosely covered to keep warm. Add the turnip greens to the skillet, place over medium heat, and cook and stir until just wilted and tender, 3 to 5 minutes. Arrange the turnips and greens around the chicken, spoon the broth and ham on top, and serve warm.

brown bag chicken

For as long as I can remember, my mom has been cooking chicken in oven bags, those oven-safe plastic bags. So when I recently started roasting chicken in a brown paper bag, I felt sort of like I was going back to my roots. It works great because the paper bag traps just enough steam to make the chicken supermoist and tender, while at the same time letting enough steam escape to allow the skin to get golden brown. It always amazes me that the bag doesn't catch on fire—so much so that I think of this as half recipe and half magic trick. Just make sure your broiler is turned off and the bag is not touching the top of the oven. **SERVES 4**

One 3- to 3½-pound chicken
Sea salt and freshly ground black pepper
1 **onion, cut in half**
4 **sprigs fresh rosemary**
1 **tablespoon ground hot Hungarian paprika**

Preheat the oven to 400°F.

Rinse the chicken, pat dry, and remove any excess fat. Sprinkle generously with salt and pepper to taste inside and out. Place the onion and rosemary inside the cavity and rub the outside of the chicken with the paprika.

Lay a standard-size brown paper grocery bag on its side and place the chicken inside, tying the top of the bag closed with kitchen string. Place the bagged chicken on a rimmed baking sheet in the lower third of the oven, so you have plenty of room at the top. Cook for 1½ hours, remove the chicken from the oven, and carefully open the bag to release the steam. Check for doneness by inserting an internal thermometer in the thickest part of the thigh; it should read about 165°F and the juices should run clear when the thigh is pierced with the tip of a small knife. Let rest for about 10 minutes before carving. Slice the breasts and cut the wings, legs, and thighs into pieces. Serve warm.

ON THE SIDE This succulent chicken is perfect with Skillet-fried Corn (page 230), Buttermilk Mashed Creamers (page 238) or Foster Family's Candied Sweet Potatoes (page 239), and Buttermilk-Sage Dinner Rolls (page 69).

chicken under a skillet

The inspiration for this dish came from Paula Wolfert's excellent version of "chicken under a brick," and from my brand-new, heavy-bottomed cast-iron skillet. Chicken under a brick—what Wolfert calls Italian fried chicken—is a traditional Tuscan preparation in which chicken is weighted with a clay slab over dry heat. The weight of the slab drives the juices and rendered fat back into the chicken as it cooks, resulting in succulent meat with crackly, golden-brown skin. Well, I soon put two and two together, and chicken under a skillet was born. Just think of it as Southern fried chicken's long-lost Italian cousin. Note that you'll want to let the meat marinate for several hours prior to cooking to get the big flavors that make this simple dish shine.   SERVES 4

	One 3- to 3½-pound chicken
4	garlic cloves, smashed
2	lemons, 1 halved and 1 cut into wedges
2	tablespoons olive oil
2	tablespoons fresh rosemary
	Sea salt and freshly ground black pepper

Rinse the chicken, pat dry, and remove any excess fat. Using kitchen shears, cut along both sides of the backbone and remove it. Press on the breastbone to break the bone and flatten the chicken. Place the chicken in a baking dish about the same size as a large skillet. Arrange the legs and wings so the chicken lies flat at a roughly even thickness.

Tuck the garlic cloves under the skin of each breast and in between the legs and thighs. Squeeze the lemon halves over the chicken and rub the olive oil all over to coat. Place the lemon halves, cut side down, in the pan. Sprinkle the rosemary and salt and pepper to taste over the chicken, pressing lightly so the seasonings adhere. Cover and refrigerate for several hours or overnight.

About 30 minutes before cooking, remove the chicken from the refrigerator and bring to room temperature.

Preheat the oven to 400°F.

Heat a dry cast-iron or other large ovenproof skillet or grill pan over medium-high heat to just before the smoking point (see Know-how, page 147). Place the chicken in the skillet, breast side down, arranging and flattening the wings and legs; the meat should sizzle when it hits the skillet. Reduce the heat to medium and place another, slightly smaller cast-iron skillet on top of the chicken and cook, undisturbed, for 12 to 15 minutes, until the skin is golden brown and crispy. Flip the chicken, place the skillet back on top, and cook until crispy on the other side, 15 to 20 minutes more.

Transfer the chicken to the oven and cook for 15 to 20 minutes more, until an internal thermometer inserted in the thickest part of the thigh reads about 165°F and the juices run clear when the thigh is pierced with the tip of a small knife. Remove from the oven and season with additional salt and pepper, if desired. Place the chicken on a cutting board, loosely covered, and let rest for about 10 minutes. Cut into pieces and serve warm with lemon wedges to squeeze over the chicken.

chicken country captain

This exotically spiced curry of chicken, tomatoes, peppers, dried fruit, and nuts is proof of Southern food's cosmopolitan roots. Served with steamed rice, slivered almonds, and fresh parsley, it is wonderfully bone-warming and fragrant.   SERVES 4 TO 6

	One 3- to 3½-pound chicken, cut into 10 pieces (see Know-how, page 129)
³/₄	**cup all-purpose flour**
2	**teaspoons sea salt**
½	**teaspoon freshly ground black pepper**
2	**tablespoons olive oil**
1	**onion, diced**
1	**red bell pepper, cored, seeded, and diced**
2	**celery stalks, diced**
3	**garlic cloves, smashed and minced**
2	**tablespoons hot curry powder**
1	**tablespoon grated fresh ginger**
1	**tablespoon fresh thyme**
½	**teaspoon crushed red pepper flakes**
2	**tablespoons balsamic vinegar**
1	**cup low-sodium chicken broth**
2	**tomatoes, cored and diced, or 1 cup canned diced tomatoes, with juices**
½	**cup chopped dried apricots**
	Zest and juice of 1 orange
1	**tablespoon your favorite chutney, plus more for serving**
¼	**cup slivered almonds, toasted, for garnish (optional)**
2	**tablespoons chopped fresh parsley, for garnish (optional)**

Preheat the oven to 350°F.

Rinse the chicken, pat dry, and remove any excess fat. Place the flour in a small, shallow bowl or large plastic bag, season with 1 teaspoon of the salt and ¼ teaspoon of the black pepper, and stir or shake to mix. Heat the olive oil in a large ovenproof skillet or Dutch oven over medium-high heat until sizzling hot (see Know-how, page 100).

Dredge or shake the chicken in the seasoned flour one piece at a time, shaking off any excess. Place in the hot skillet, and cook for about 8 minutes per side, turning frequently for even browning, until brown on all sides. Remove from the skillet and set aside.

Put the onion, bell pepper, and celery in the same skillet and cook over medium heat, stirring, for about 5 minutes, until the vegetables are soft. Add the garlic, curry, ginger, thyme, and red pepper flakes; cook and stir for 1 minute more.

Add the balsamic vinegar and stir, scraping up all the brown bits from the bottom of the pan.

Add the broth, tomatoes, apricots, orange zest and juice, chutney, the remaining 1 teaspoon salt, and remaining ¼ teaspoon black pepper and stir to combine.

Return the chicken to the skillet, skin side up, and place in the oven to bake for 30 to 35 minutes, until the chicken is cooked through and the juices run clear when the thickest part of the thigh is pierced with the tip of a small knife.

Remove from the oven and let rest, loosely covered, for about 10 minutes. Serve warm, sprinkled with almonds and parsley, if desired. Serve additional chutney on the side.

---

chew on this: **chicken country captain**

At first glance, Country Captain might not strike you as very Southern. In fact, I'd never heard of it until we moved to North Carolina to open Foster's. It was a specialty of one of our chefs, and I still remember the first time I tried it, with its unusual flavors and sweet perfume—I was so intrigued and taken by it that it became an immediate favorite.

Like the chutney that is usually served with it, Country Captain flies in the face of most people's expectations about Southern food. And yet, although the origins of Country Captain are much debated both within and outside the South, Southerners have been laying claim to this spice-infused dish since the eighteenth century. According to lore, the recipe came straight from Bengal to the southern spice-trading ports by way of a British sea captain who had been stationed there—and the rest, as they say, is history.

The flavors aren't like those in most other Southern dishes, but Country Captain has nonetheless found a lasting place at the Southern table. One reason, I think, is that it is so similar in spirit to the many other Southern one-pot dishes and stews, from jambalaya to Brunswick stew. The spices may have been new, but in other ways it would have been immediately familiar to the Southerners who adopted it and made it their own. That interplay among different cultures is what Southern cooking is all about, and it's what I'm reminded of every time I make Country Captain.

---

chicken and dumplings

I grew up on this velvety stew of shredded chicken and puffy dumplings. Not only is it comforting and delicious, but, because it stretches a little meat a long way using just a few ingredients, it is yet another example of Southern culinary resourcefulness.

SERVES 6 TO 8

CHICKEN
	One 3- to 3$\frac{1}{2}$-pound chicken
	10 to 12 cups cold water
2	celery stalks with leaves
2	tablespoons unsalted butter
2	sprigs fresh thyme
6	fresh sage leaves
2	teaspoons sea salt
$\frac{1}{2}$	teaspoon freshly ground black pepper

DUMPLINGS
2	cups self-rising flour (see Know-how, page 53)
1	teaspoon sea salt, plus more to taste
$\frac{1}{4}$	teaspoon baking soda
	Pinch of sugar
4	tablespoons ($\frac{1}{2}$ stick) cold unsalted butter, cut into small pieces, or $\frac{1}{4}$ cup vegetable shortening
$\frac{1}{2}$ to $\frac{3}{4}$	cup well-shaken buttermilk
	Freshly ground black pepper
$\frac{1}{4}$	cup chopped fresh parsley

CHICKEN | Rinse the chicken, pat dry, and remove any excess fat. Place the chicken in a large pot and add the cold water to cover. Add the celery, butter, thyme, sage, salt, and pepper and bring to a low boil over medium-high heat.

Reduce the heat to low and simmer for 45 minutes to 1 hour, uncovered, skimming the rising foam as needed.

Remove the chicken, reserving the cooking liquid in the pot, and set aside until cool enough to handle. Skin and bone the chicken, setting aside the meat and discarding the skin and bones. Tear the meat into bite-size pieces.

DUMPLINGS | Combine the flour, salt, baking soda, and sugar in a bowl and stir to mix. Cut the butter into the flour mixture using a pastry blender or two knives in a crosscutting motion until the mixture resembles coarse meal. Work quickly so the butter remains cool and doesn't melt into the flour. Make a well in the center of the flour mixture and add $\frac{1}{2}$ cup of the buttermilk. Stir to combine, just until the dough comes together. If the dough is dry and crumbly, add a little more buttermilk, 1 tablespoon at a time, just until the dough comes together.

Form into a flat disk, wrap tightly, and refrigerate for about 1 hour. Turn the dough onto a lightly floured surface, roll about $\frac{1}{4}$ inch thick, and cut into 2-inch squares.

Bring the reserved cooking liquid to a low boil and drop in the dumplings one at a time to keep them from sticking. The broth should continue at a low boil; increase the heat if needed. Add the chicken and bring back to a simmer. Cover and simmer, undisturbed, for 15 to 20 minutes, until the dumplings are cooked through. Test for doneness by slicing a dumpling in half. If it is light and airy throughout, you know it's done, but if it's dense in the center, it needs more time.

When the dumplings are done, remove from the heat, season with additional salt and pepper to taste, stir in the parsley, and serve warm.

SARA'S SWAPS Speaking of resourcefulness, my mother, Say, used to make her version of chicken and dumplings with flour tortillas in place of the dumplings. That way, she didn't have to go to the trouble of making the dumpling dough. To make this dish Say-style, use 4 flour tortillas, cut in half crosswise and then into 1-inch strips, in place of the dumplings. Dust the tortillas lightly with flour to keep them from sticking when cut and add the strips to the pot, one at a time, with the shredded chicken. Cover and cook for about 10 minutes, until plump and tender.

autumnal chicken pot pie

This is not your typical pea-and-carrot-laden pot pie. Inspired by fall flavors, this sophisticated version is loaded with butternut squash, oyster and chanterelle mushrooms, and fresh sage—all tucked under a layer of golden, flaky puff pastry. SERVES 6 TO 8

1	**small butternut squash, peeled, seeded, and cut into 1-inch cubes**
1	**tablespoon olive oil**
	Sea salt and freshly ground black pepper
6	**tablespoons ($^3/_4$ stick) unsalted butter, plus more if needed**
8	**ounces mixed fresh mushrooms, such as oysters, chanterelles, shiitakes, or hedgehogs, cleaned and thinly sliced ($3^1/_2$ to 4 cups)**
2	**shallots, minced**
$^1/_4$	**cup all-purpose flour**
$3^1/_2$	**cups low-sodium chicken broth**
4	**cups cooked shredded chicken**
1	**tablespoon chopped fresh sage or 1 teaspoon dried crumbled sage**
1	**sheet frozen puff pastry, such as Pepperidge Farm or Dufour Pastry Kitchens, thawed in the refrigerator**
1	**large egg, lightly beaten with 2 tablespoons milk, for egg wash**

Preheat the oven to 400°F. Lightly grease an ovenproof 9- or 10-inch skillet or a 2-quart baking or soufflé dish.

Toss the squash in a bowl with the olive oil to lightly coat. Season with salt and pepper to taste, spread evenly on a rimmed baking sheet, and bake until tender and golden brown, 25 to 30 minutes. Remove from the oven and set aside.

Melt the butter in a large skillet over medium-high heat and cook the mushrooms and shallots, stirring frequently, for 5 to 6 minutes, until light brown, adding more butter if needed. Add the flour and cook, stirring constantly, until light brown, 3 to 4 minutes longer. Slowly stir in the broth, scraping the brown bits from the bottom of the pan, and bring to a low boil, stirring constantly, until slightly thick, about 5 minutes.

Add the chicken and sage, season with salt and pepper to taste, and stir to mix. Reduce the heat to a simmer and cook, stirring frequently, until the mixture is thick and creamy, about 10 minutes. Remove from the heat, stir in the reserved squash, and allow to cool.

Meanwhile, roll the puff pastry on a lightly floured surface just to even out the lines. Cut the pastry to fit the top of the baking dish, leaving enough excess to allow the pastry to drape over the sides by about $^1/_4$ inch.

Fill the prepared skillet or baking dish with the chicken mixture, leaving about $^1/_2$ inch of space at the top, and place the pastry over the dish. Cut several slits in the crust to allow steam to escape. Decorate as desired, brush with the egg wash, and refrigerate for at least 1 hour.

Preheat the oven to 375°F. Place the pie on a rimmed baking sheet and bake until the filling is bubbling around the edges and the pastry is puffy and golden brown, 45 to 50 minutes. Remove from the oven and serve warm.

duck two ways, fast and slow

The wonderful contrast between buttery, almost confited duck legs and crispy, skillet-fried breast is worth the little bit of extra effort this dish requires. Add a bottle of Syrah or Pinot Noir and a few easy sides, like a simple green salad and Buttermilk Mashed Creamers (page 238), and you've got the makings of an elegant dinner party.

SERVES 2 TO 4

	One 4- to 5-pound duck
2	teaspoons sea salt
1	teaspoon freshly ground black pepper
1	tablespoon fresh rosemary, plus 2 or 3 sprigs
1	tablespoon fresh thyme, plus 2 or 3 sprigs
1	cup dry red wine
2	tablespoons balsamic vinegar
1	bunch small carrots
4	shallots
2	garlic cloves, smashed
1 to 2	cups low-sodium chicken broth
2	bay leaves

Rinse the duck, pat dry, and remove the thighs and legs (see Know-how, page 157). Remove the meat from the breast by cutting down the center and along the rib cage on each side of the breastbone with a sharp knife. Discard the carcass or reserve for broth. Trim the excess fat from the legs and breast. Score the skin on the legs and breast with a sharp knife, being careful not to cut through to the meat.

Place the legs and breasts in a dish and season with 1 teaspoon of the salt, ½ teaspoon of the pepper, 1½ teaspoons of the chopped rosemary, and 1½ teaspoons of the thyme.

Combine the red wine, vinegar, remaining 1½ teaspoons rosemary, and remaining 1½ teaspoons thyme in a shallow dish and stir to mix. Pour the mixture over the duck and turn several times to coat on both sides with the marinade. Cover and refrigerate for several hours or overnight.

To cook the legs, preheat the oven to 325°F.

Heat a dry cast-iron or other ovenproof skillet over medium-high heat to just before the smoking point (see Know-how, page 147). Remove the duck legs from the marinade, reserving the marinade, and sauté them, skin side down to start, for 4 to 5 minutes per side, until golden brown. Transfer to a plate and set aside.

Add the carrots and shallots to the same skillet with the duck fat, reduce the heat to medium, and cook and stir for about 5 minutes, until the vegetables are light brown around the edges. Add the garlic and cook and stir for 1 minute longer.

Set the duck legs, skin side up, on top of the vegetables in the same skillet and add ½ cup of the marinade and 1 cup of the broth, enough to submerge the legs about three-quarters of the way up, adding more broth if needed; the top part of the skin should not be covered. Add the bay leaves, cover, and roast in the oven for 2 to 2½ hours, until the legs are fork-tender (see Know-how, page 172). Remove from the oven and skim the fat from the top of the liquid.

To cook the breast, heat a separate dry cast-iron or heavy-bottomed skillet over medium heat to just before the smoking point. Season the breast with the remaining 1 teaspoon salt and ½ teaspoon pepper and sauté, skin side down, until the skin is golden brown and crispy, about 8 minutes. Flip the breast, pour off some of the fat if necessary, and continue to cook for another 5 to 6 minutes for medium doneness. Remove from the skillet and let rest, loosely covered, for about 5 minutes before slicing.

To serve, place a few slices of breast, a leg or thigh, and vegetables on each plate. Spoon the cooking liquid over and around the duck and vegetables and serve warm.

SARA'S SWAPS We often make two meals out of this dish by cooking the breast one night and letting the legs marinate overnight or for several days before cooking. Or, do all your cooking at one time, eat the breast the first night, and reheat the legs the next night.

Know-how: cooking without alcohol

Nine times out of ten, when a recipe calls for alcohol, the alcohol is there to add extra flavor—so omitting it will change the flavor profile slightly, but it certainly won't make or break the dish. If you prefer not to use alcohol in your cooking, try compensating by adding a splash of fruit juice, balsamic or white wine vinegar, or vegetable or chicken broth instead. For sweets, you can use flavorings like pure vanilla extract, lemon zest and juice, orange zest and juice, or strongly brewed coffee, depending on what will complement the other flavors in the dessert. The bottom line: don't stress, and have fun coming up with alternative seasonings.

Know-how: heating a skillet to just before the smoking point

Whenever a recipe calls for heating an unoiled skillet or pan to just before the smoking point, place the skillet over medium-high heat for about 2 minutes, just until you see the first small wisps of smoke starting to curl off the surface. Cast iron works best for this level of heat.

carl's deep-fried turkey

Every Thanksgiving, my friend Carl, who is also a pastor, makes his deep-fried turkey for some of the women in his church. Using a turkey fryer frees up the oven to make lots of sides, stuffing, and pies. Carl seasons his turkey with plenty of cayenne pepper, so much that it made me nervous the first time I saw him make it. But I shouldn't have worried—it came out perfectly browned and crisp, with just a hint of heat. Be sure to follow the manufacturer's instructions for your fryer and get a turkey that will fit easily in the fryer, no more than fourteen pounds. It is safest to cook this outside. SERVES 8 TO 10

	One 12- to 14-pound fresh turkey (preferably not previously frozen)
	Sea salt and freshly ground black pepper
8	tablespoons (1 stick) unsalted butter, softened
2	tablespoons ground cayenne pepper
2½ to 3	gallons peanut oil, for frying

Rinse the turkey inside and out and thoroughly pat dry with paper towels (for safety reasons, the turkey must be completely dry and thawed, inside and out). Trim the excess fat from the neck and remove the tail. Make a small incision in the skin between the breast and thigh (this allows the oil to cook the thighs more evenly without overcooking the breast). Season all over, inside and out, with salt and black pepper to taste. Rub the butter all over the turkey to coat evenly and sprinkle evenly with the cayenne.

Pour enough peanut oil in the turkey fryer to reach the fill line, or as directed in the user's manual for your fryer. Heat the oil to 360°F.

Place the turkey in the fry basket and slowly and carefully submerge it in the hot oil. Do not adjust the temperature at this time; it will come back up quickly. Cover the fryer with the lid and cook for 45 to 65 minutes (about 4 minutes per pound), maintaining the temperature of the oil between 350°F and 360°F, until the turkey is golden brown and an internal thermometer inserted in the thickest part of the thigh reads between 170°F and 180°F.

Line a rimmed baking sheet with brown paper bags. Lift the turkey from the fryer and gently transfer it to the baking sheet to drain. Let sit for 15 to 20 minutes, loosely covered, before carving. Serve warm.

barbecued turkey

I think people often pressure themselves to put on a big, fancy spread for the holidays—but I'm all for keeping things simple, which is no problem if you start with this sticky, tangy barbecued turkey. Turning the holidays into a cookout sets such a casual, welcoming tone that you can't help but take it easy and have a good time. I made this turkey the year Martha Stewart joined us for Thanksgiving, and it was such a big hit that we've taken to making it all year round. Be sure to plan ahead to allow for at least six hours of marinating time. SERVES 8 TO 10

One 12- to 14-pound turkey
Sea salt and freshly ground black pepper
1   cup apple cider vinegar
2   tablespoons unpacked light brown sugar
1   teaspoon crushed red pepper flakes
2   cups your favorite or West Tennessee Thick and Sticky BBQ Sauce (page 307), plus more for serving

Rinse the turkey inside and out, pat dry, and trim any excess fat. Place the turkey, breast side down, in a disposable aluminum roasting pan. Season the inside of the cavity with salt and black pepper to taste.

Combine the vinegar, brown sugar, and red pepper flakes in a bowl and stir until the sugar dissolves. Pour the sauce over the turkey and massage all over into the skin. Cover and let marinate, breast side down, refrigerated, for 6 to 8 hours or overnight.

About 1 hour before cooking, remove the turkey from the refrigerator and let come to room temperature. Prepare a hot fire in a charcoal or gas grill and let the coals burn to gray ash with a slight red glow. Keep the coals on one side of the grill to create areas of direct and indirect heat (see Know-how, page 151); if using a gas grill, heat just one side on medium.

Flip the turkey, breast side up, in the roasting pan and brush all over with the marinade in the bottom of the pan. Flip the turkey again so it is breast side down and place the pan over the indirect heat (the side without the coals), cover the grill with the lid, and cook for about 2 hours, basting the turkey every 30 minutes with the marinade on the bottom of the pan and rotating the pan a quarter turn each time.

Use a fire-starter chimney to heat new coals; replenish the coals every hour or so, as needed, to maintain an even temperature of about 350°F (see Know-how, page 151).

Flip the turkey, breast side up, in the roasting pan and continue to cook, rotate, and baste with the barbecue sauce 1 to 1½ hours longer, until the skin is crisp and an internal thermometer inserted in the thickest part of the thigh reads between 165°F and 170°F. Remove the turkey from the grill and let rest, loosely covered, for about 20 minutes before carving. Serve warm with additional barbecue sauce on the side.

Know-how: grilling basics

Start a fire using a chimney starter (available at most home improvement stores) and hardwood charcoal, if available.

Open the vents on the bottom of the grill.

When the coals are lit and glowing red, dump them from the chimney onto one side of the grill and spread evenly on one side only.

When the coals turn to gray with a red glow, they have reached their hottest point; the coals will begin to cool after that.

If using a gas grill, set the grill on high for recipes that call for gray ash with a bright red glow; on medium for those that call for gray ash with a slight red glow; and on low for gray ash.

Place the grate at least 6 inches above the coals and allow to get fully hot before grilling.

To determine how hot the coals are, hold your hand above the grate, about 6 inches above the coals, and count how many seconds you can keep it there before it becomes un-comfortable: hot: 1 to 2 seconds;   medium: 3 to 4 seconds;   low: 5 to 6 seconds.

To cook over direct heat, place the meat directly over the coals. Steak and fish are usually seared and should be placed over direct heat when the coals are at their hottest. If you are cooking something that takes longer, like chicken or pork, place it over direct, medium-hot heat to brown and crisp the skin, then move to the indirect heat until the coals die to low to finish cooking.

To cook over indirect heat, move the meat to the side of the grill without the char-coal, but maintain the fire so the grill stays hot. Cover with the lid and open the vents.

For slow-cooking dishes like Wood-Smoked Backyard Barbecued Pig (page 170), monitor the temperature using a thermometer. If your grill doesn't come with one, insert an instant-read thermometer in the grill vent to get a read on the temperature and try to maintain the temperature indicated in the recipe.

To replenish the heat, prepare extra coals in a fire-starter chimney placed over a sep-arate grill and add the hot coals to the hotter, charcoal side of the grill as needed.

For information on grilling steak, see page 190.

chicken-fried quail with creamy thyme gravy

This crispy fried quail is for anyone whose favorite part of fried chicken is the crust. Because quail are so small, you get a satisfyingly high crust-to-meat ratio—but the meat itself is flavorful enough to stand up to all that crust. I drape my version in a veil of creamy, herb-flecked pan gravy.   SERVES 4 TO 6

QUAIL
8	partially boned quail
1/2	cup well-shaken buttermilk
1	large egg
2	dashes hot sauce
1	cup dried bread crumbs
1/2	cup all-purpose flour
	Sea salt and freshly ground black pepper
	Pinch of ground cayenne pepper
	Canola oil, for frying
2	tablespoons bacon drippings (optional)

GRAVY
1	shallot, minced
3	tablespoons all-purpose flour
2	cups milk
1	tablespoon fresh thyme
	Sea salt and freshly ground black pepper

QUAIL | Preheat the oven to 200°F. Line a rimmed baking sheet with a brown paper bag.

Rinse the quail and pat dry with paper towels. Combine the buttermilk, egg, and hot sauce in a shallow bowl and whisk to mix. In a separate shallow bowl or plastic bag, combine the bread crumbs, flour, salt and black pepper to taste, and cayenne and stir or shake to mix.

Pour canola oil ¼ inch deep in a large skillet, add the bacon drippings, if using, and place over medium-high heat until sizzling hot (see Know-how, page 100).

Dip each quail into the buttermilk mixture, then into the bread crumb mixture to evenly coat. Place in the skillet 3 or 4 at a time, taking care not to overcrowd the skillet. Cook for 4 to 5 minutes per side, until golden brown and crispy and the interior is slightly pink. If the quail are browning too quickly, reduce the heat slightly. Transfer the quail to the lined baking sheet and place in the oven to keep warm. Repeat with the remaining quail, and pour off all but 3 tablespoons of the oil, reserving the pan drippings.

GRAVY | Add the shallot to the same skillet and cook and stir over medium heat for about 1 minute. Sprinkle the flour over the shallot and cook and stir for 1 minute more, scraping up all the brown bits from the bottom of the pan. Whisk in the milk, thyme, and salt and pepper to taste and cook, stirring, until the gravy is thick and creamy, 3 to 5 minutes.

Spoon the gravy over the quail and serve warm.

> ON THE SIDE   This chicken-fried quail is delicious with Summer Succotash (page 232), Spring Coleslaw with Fresh Herbs and Light Honey Citrus Vinaigrette (page 258), and Watercress Angel Biscuits (page 54). Or try them for breakfast over Country Ham and Hominy Hash (page 82) or with Buttermilk Waffles (page 91) in place of fried chicken.

chew on this: **about quail**

Southerners have long been crazy for quail, a small bird favored for eating and—perhaps especially—hunting. It was one of the few game species to flourish in the new landscape carved out by cotton farming, and the birds remain a favorite catch of hunters today.

That was certainly true in my family, and I've been eating quail for as long as I can remember. Whenever my dad and grandfather brought them home from a hunt, Granny Foster would dust them lightly with flour and fry them in a skillet for breakfast along with pan gravy and angel biscuits. Like many Southerners, my grandfather called quail "bobwhites" for their characteristic whistle, which sounds like they are singing "bobwhite! bobwhite! bobwhite!" The meat tastes sort of like chicken, but with a lovely, nutty-sweet twang, and quail can be prepared in all the ways you'd prepare chicken—but with much shorter cooking times.

Quail are so dainty that you will want to budget at least one, but more likely two, per person. Farmed quail can be bought from a number of online providers and usually come partially boned (see Sources, page 377).

grilled quail with saul's red mole

One of the things I love most about Southern food is how it is constantly evolving, and these days that change has a lot to do with the culinary traditions of recent immigrants from Mexico, Cuba, and Central and South America. I first learned how to make mole from my friend Saul, after I tried his rendition at one of my favorite Durham restaurants, Nana's, and persuaded him to teach me how to make it myself. The South's favorite game bird is smothered in this rich, spicy Mexican sauce infused with dark chocolate and spices, thickened with ground seeds and nuts, and spiked with numerous chiles, exemplifying the old-yet-new trend. The result is incredibly complex and distinctive. You will have extra mole, so give it a try on other dishes, like eggs, grilled chicken, or steak. SERVES 4 TO 6

MOLE

2	dried ancho chiles
2	dried pasilla chiles
2	dried guajillo chiles
2	dried jalapeño peppers
2	Roma (plum) tomatoes, cored
1/2	onion, sliced
1/2	apple, peeled and cored
1/2	ripe plantain, peeled and halved
1	garlic clove
3	tablespoons olive oil
2	cups low-sodium chicken broth, plus more if needed
1	tablespoon pumpkin seeds
1	tablespoon white sesame seeds
1	tablespoon peanuts
1/2	cinnamon stick, broken into pieces
2	teaspoons coriander seeds
2	teaspoons cumin seeds
1	slice white bread, cubed
1 3/4	ounces Abuelita brand chocolate, chopped
	Sea salt and freshly ground black pepper

QUAIL

8	partially boned quail
2	tablespoons olive oil
1	tablespoon fresh thyme
	Sea salt and freshly ground black pepper
2	tablespoons chopped fresh cilantro or scallions
1	lime, cut into wedges

MOLE | Preheat the oven to 400°F.

Heat a dry cast-iron skillet to just before the smoking point (see Know-how, page 147).

Remove and discard the seeds from the ancho, pasilla, guajillo, and jalapeño peppers and roast the chiles in the skillet over medium-high heat, turning regularly to avoid burning, about 3 minutes, until the chiles release a toasted scent. Transfer the chiles to a bowl of warm water to soak for 10 to 15 minutes, until soft, then drain.

While the chiles are soaking, place the tomatoes, onion, apple, plantain, and garlic in the skillet and drizzle with 1 tablespoon of the olive oil. Roast in the oven until slightly brown, about 20 minutes. Remove from the oven and cool slightly.

Place the tomatoes, onion, and garlic in a blender and reserve the apple and plantain and set aside. Add the soaked chiles and 1 cup of the broth and puree until smooth. Remove from the blender and place in a large bowl.

Place the pumpkin seeds, sesame seeds, peanuts, cinnamon stick, coriander seeds, cumin seeds, and bread in a skillet and dry roast over medium-high heat, stirring or shaking the pan constantly, until they release an aroma, about 3 minutes. Remove from the heat, cool slightly, and transfer to the same blender. Add the remaining 1 cup broth, the roasted apple and plantain, and the chocolate and puree until smooth. Place in the bowl with the chile mixture, season with salt and pepper to taste, and stir to combine. The consistency should be about the same as a pureed soup or loose sauce; if the mole is too thick, add more broth until the desired consistency is reached.

Heat the remaining 2 tablespoons oil in a large saucepan over medium heat until hot. Add the pureed chile mixture, reduce the heat to low, and cook, stirring occasionally, for about 20 minutes, until the color darkens and the flavors meld.

QUAIL | Prepare a hot fire in a charcoal or gas grill and let the coals burn to gray ash with a slight red glow; if using a gas grill, heat the grill on medium.

Rinse the quail, pat dry, and place in a shallow dish. Drizzle with the olive oil and sprinkle evenly with the thyme and salt and pepper to taste. Turn several times to coat evenly with the oil and herbs.

Grill the quail for 10 to 12 minutes, turning several times to prevent charring. The skin will be golden and crispy and the interior slightly pink.

Transfer the quail to a platter, cover loosely, and let rest for about 5 minutes before serving. Reheat half the mole, if necessary; spoon the sauce over and around the quail; and sprinkle with cilantro or scallions. Serve warm with lime wedges to squeeze over the quail.

pan-seared guinea hen with roasted tomatoes, okra, and butternut squash

Guinea hens are birds, related to pheasants, and are an excellent and highly flavorful alternative to chicken. Because they're smaller—usually two or three pounds—even whole birds cook quickly and yield just the right amount of meat for one meal. If you can't find guinea hen, a small chicken will do the trick nicely. SERVES 2 TO 4

VEGETABLES

1	small butternut squash, peeled, seeded, and cut into chunks
2	tomatoes (about 1 pound), cored and quartered
2	tablespoons olive oil
2	tablespoons sherry vinegar
	Sea salt and freshly ground black pepper
1	pound small okra, trimmed

HEN

	One 2$\frac{1}{2}$- to 3-pound partially boned guinea hen, quartered (see Know-how, page 157)
2	tablespoons fresh thyme
	Sea salt and freshly ground black pepper
1	tablespoon olive oil
1	tablespoon unsalted butter
$\frac{1}{2}$	cup dry white wine
$\frac{1}{2}$	cup low-sodium chicken broth
1	tablespoon chopped fresh chives

VEGETABLES | Preheat the oven to 400°F.

Combine the squash, tomatoes, olive oil, and vinegar in a bowl, season with salt and pepper to taste, and toss to coat. Spread in a single layer on a rimmed baking sheet and roast for about 30 minutes, stirring halfway through. Add the okra and toss to coat with the pan liquids. Roast for another 10 minutes, until the okra is tender and bright green and the edges of the squash are golden brown. Remove from the oven and set aside, loosely covered to keep warm.

HEN | While the vegetables are roasting, rinse the hen, pat dry with paper towels, and trim any excess fat. Season both sides with 1 tablespoon of the thyme and salt and pepper to taste, pressing gently to adhere.

Heat the olive oil and butter in a large, heavy-bottomed skillet over medium-high heat until sizzling hot (see Know-how, page 100). Place the hen in the skillet, skin side down. Reduce the heat to medium and cook until the skin is golden brown and crispy, about 10 minutes. Flip over and cook the other side until the flesh is firm to the touch, about 4 minutes. Remove the hen and set aside, loosely covered, to keep warm.

Pour off all but about 1 tablespoon of fat from the skillet and return the skillet to the heat. Add the wine and scrape up any brown bits from the bottom of the skillet. Cook and stir for about 1 minute, until the wine reduces by half.

Stir in the broth, remaining 1 tablespoon thyme, and the chives. Season with additional salt and pepper and cook and stir for 2 to 3 minutes more. Add the legs and vegetables to the skillet and place in the oven to roast for about 15 minutes, until the meat is cooked through and the juices run clear when the thickest part of the thigh is pierced with the tip of a small knife. Add the breast and continue to cook for another 3 to 5 minutes, just to warm through.

ASSEMBLY | Arrange the vegetables on a larger serving platter or divide evenly between individual serving plates and top with pieces of hen. Spoon the cooking liquid over and around the hen and vegetables and serve warm.

ON THE SIDE   This dish is a meal in and of itself, but I like to serve it alongside Kate's Sweet Potato Refrigerator Rolls (page 66) or Creamed Vegetable Rice (page 216), and, for more formal entertaining, after a first course of Summer Corn Relish (page 297).

Know-how: quartering and partially boning guinea hen or other birds

This technique can also be used on chicken, duck, turkey, or pheasant.

Place the hen on its back on a cutting board. Using a sharp knife and starting at the neck end of the breast, cut along one side of the breastbone to cut the breast meat away from the rib cage, cutting as close to the rib cage as possible. Repeat on the other side.

Cut off the wing tips, leaving the small drumstick (or section next to the breast) attached.

Turn the hen over, bend the thigh back to push the hip joint out of the socket, and cut through the joint. Repeat with the other leg.

Scrape the meat away from the thighbone, cut at the joint, and remove the thighbone, leaving the leg bone.

pig
a food group
all its own

When I was five years old, I had a pet pig named Pig who lived nearby on my grandparents' farm. My grandparents kept a few pigs in a pen out back, but Pig was more like a yard dog. He used to follow me around while I played outside, and he was smart—even learning to push me on the swings with his pink snout. Growing up in the South, we got to know our food and especially our pig.

Any way you slice it, pig is an icon here in the South. As with tailgating on Saturday afternoons, Southerners really do love pork that much. So it's not a stretch to say that in the South, pig is a food group all its own; how else to explain the fact that fatback-drenched collards are innocently offered up by many Southerners as vegetarian-friendly fare?

Take barbecue. From the vinegary, finely chopped hash of eastern North Carolina to dry-rubbed Memphis ribs, each region of the South boasts its own coveted version of this signature dish. The barbecue I grew up on in western Tennessee is like no other, and we locals get pretty snobby about it. Pitmasters in that little corner of the world slowly roast the whole pig over a carefully tended hickory fire in raised cinder pits. The meat is pulled—never chopped—when it's fall-off-the-bone tender, then doused with your choice of hot pepper–spiked vinegar or a sweet and spicy ketchup-based sauce.

That's how my dad, who was something of a pitmaster himself, fixed his pig. Every year on the Fourth of July and Labor Day, Dad would set up a roadside barbecue stand. He mounded the shredded, hickory-infused meat on soft white buns topped with my mom's coleslaw or dished it out in those little red and white boat-shaped paper trays. My Wood-Smoked Backyard Barbecued Pig (page 170) is the next best thing, and it's what I make when I'm feeling homesick.

I think the larger culinary world is finally starting to view pig as Southerners always have. One of the best things about the rising national interest in Southern cuisine is that it is reintroducing people to pig—the whole pig, from snout to tail. The dishes in this chapter range from tried-and-true classics to my own fresh variations on a beloved Southern theme, and I hope they will inspire you to really get to know pig, Southern-style.

crispy pork chops

see photograph on page 158

For an easy weeknight indulgence that is as crispy, crunchy, and succulent as fried chicken, make these skillet-sautéed pork chops. The key here is to pound the pork chops until they are very thin—sort of like German schnitzel—or buy them thinly sliced. (They can usually be found in the prepackaged section of your grocery's meat department; in the South, they are labeled "breakfast chops.") SERVES 4 TO 6

	Six 4-ounce bone-in pork chops
	Sea salt and freshly ground black pepper
1/2	**cup all-purpose flour**
2	**large eggs, lightly beaten**
1/4	**cup well-shaken buttermilk**
1 1/2	**cups fresh bread crumbs (see Know-how, page 134)**
1/2	**cup (1 1/2 ounces) finely grated Parmesan cheese**
2	**tablespoons fresh thyme**
2	**tablespoons canola oil**

Place the pork chops between two pieces of plastic and flatten with a mallet or the bottom of a heavy skillet until the chops are of uniform thickness, about 1/4 inch. Season both sides with salt and pepper to taste.

Place the flour on a plate and season with salt and pepper to taste. Combine the eggs and buttermilk in a separate shallow bowl and stir to combine. Combine the bread crumbs, Parmesan cheese, and thyme in a shallow bowl and stir to mix. Dust each chop with the flour on both sides, shaking off any excess, then dip it in the egg mixture and press into the bread crumb mixture to coat evenly on both sides.

Heat the canola oil in a large skillet over medium-high heat until sizzling hot (see Know-how, page 100). Add the pork chops, cooking in batches and adding more oil if needed, and sauté about 3 minutes per side, until golden brown and crispy. Transfer to a platter and serve immediately.

> *ON THE SIDE*   These crispy chops are at their best with Summer Succotash (page 232), Cucumber and Heirloom Tomato Salad (page 269), Baked Rosemary Sweet Potato Halves (page 240), or a vinegary heap of Roxy's Grated Coleslaw (page 260) and a full-bodied amber ale for sipping.

spicy pepper jelly–marinated grilled pork tenderloin

I often serve this dish when I have guests because it makes for such easy entertaining—something you'd never know from the complex combination of flavors that emerges as the red wine and orange-spiked pepper jelly melt into a sweet and spicy glaze over the heat of the grill. Don't forget to budget at least two hours of marinating time before firing up the grill. SERVES 4 TO 6

	Two 1-pound pork tenderloins
½	cup your favorite or Foster's Market Seven Pepper Jelly, plus more for serving
½	cup dry red wine
	Zest and juice of 1 orange
2	tablespoons red wine vinegar
1	tablespoon fresh rosemary
1	teaspoon crushed red pepper flakes
	Sea salt and freshly ground black pepper

Rinse the pork, pat dry, remove the silver skin (see Know-how, page 81), and trim any excess fat. Place in a shallow container or large resealable bag.

Whisk together the pepper jelly, wine, orange zest and juice, vinegar, rosemary, red pepper flakes, and salt and black pepper to taste in a small bowl. Pour the marinade over the pork and turn to coat evenly. (Or, if using a bag, pour the marinade into the bag, seal, and shake to coat the pork.) Cover and place in the refrigerator to marinate for at least 2 hours or overnight. Turn the pork several times to distribute the marinade evenly.

When ready to cook the pork, prepare a hot fire in a charcoal or gas grill and let the coals burn to gray ash with a slight red glow. Keep the coals on one side of the grill to create areas of direct and indirect heat (see Know-how, page 151); if using a gas grill, heat just one side on medium.

Remove the pork from the marinade, reserving the marinade, and season with salt and pepper. Place the pork on the hot grill directly over the coals and cook for 12 to 15 minutes, turning three times and basting often with the reserved marinade. Move the pork away from the coals, close the grill or cover the pork with foil, and cook for another 3 to 5 minutes, until an internal thermometer inserted in the tenderloin reads 145°F for medium (this is what I prefer) or 160°F for medium-well.

Remove the pork from the grill and transfer to a cutting board. Cover loosely with foil and allow to rest for 5 to 10 minutes before slicing. Cut into ¼-inch-thick slices and serve warm with additional pepper jelly on the side.

molasses-glazed grilled pork tenderloin

The assertive flavors of coffee, molasses, and balsamic vinegar meld and mellow in this sophisticated dish that is just the thing for winter entertaining. It is best served with simple sides, such as Mess o' Greens (page 245) and Sweet Potato Spoon Bread (page 214), that enhance rather than distract from the sweet, rich molasses flavor of the pork.

SERVES 4 TO 6

Two 1-pound pork tenderloins
1/4 cup strong black coffee, cold or room temperature
1/4 cup bourbon
3 tablespoons molasses
2 tablespoons balsamic vinegar
2 tablespoons olive oil
2 tablespoons fresh thyme
Sea salt and freshly ground black pepper

Rinse the pork, pat dry, remove the silver skin (see Know-how, page 81), and trim any excess fat. Place in a shallow container or large resealable bag.

Whisk together the coffee, bourbon, molasses, vinegar, olive oil, and thyme in a small bowl. Pour the marinade over the pork and turn to coat evenly. (Or, if using a bag, pour the marinade into the bag, seal, and shake to coat the pork.) Cover and place in the refrigerator to marinate for at least 2 hours or overnight. Turn the pork several times to distribute the marinade evenly.

When ready to cook the pork, prepare a hot fire in a charcoal or gas grill and let the coals burn to gray ash with a slight red glow. Keep the coals on one side of the grill to create areas of direct and indirect heat (see Know-how, page 151); if using a gas grill, heat just one side on medium.

Remove the pork from the marinade, reserving the marinade, and season with salt and pepper. Place the pork on the hot grill directly over the coals and cook for about 12 to 15 minutes, basting with the reserved marinade and turning three or four times to avoid charring.

Move the pork away from the coals, close the grill or cover the pork with foil, and cook for another 3 to 5 minutes, until an internal thermometer inserted in the tenderloin reads 145°F for medium (this is what I prefer) or 160°F for medium-well.

Remove the pork from the grill and transfer to a cutting board. Cover loosely with foil and allow to rest for 5 to 10 minutes before slicing. Slice the pork into small rounds 1/4 to 1/2 inch thick and serve warm.

memphis-style barbecued spare ribs

Memphis is known for its dry-rubbed barbecued ribs, which are all about intense spices and the unadorned texture of low-and-slow-cooked meat. The two-step cooking process I use here—the meat is first slow-cooked in the oven, then finished over a hot grill—ensures succulent, crispy-edged, tender ribs every time, rendering sauce fully optional. Even so, sauce person that I am, I usually can't help myself from cooking the meat in beer and basting it with vinegar-based barbecue sauce for a little added flavor and tang. You can try making these ribs with and without the sauce and decide for yourself. Either way, you'll need to let the ribs marinate for at least two or three hours before cooking. SERVES 4 TO 6

Two 2½-pound slabs pork spare ribs, cut St. Louis–style
1   cup Spicy Memphis Dry Rub (recipe follows)
1   onion, sliced
     One 12-ounce beer
2   cups Say's Vinegar Barbecue Sauce (page 309) (optional)

Rinse the ribs and pat dry. Massage ½ cup of the dry rub over both sides of each slab to coat evenly. Cover and let marinate, refrigerated, for 2 to 3 hours or overnight.

About 30 minutes before you're ready to cook, remove the ribs from the refrigerator, rub with the remaining ½ cup dry rub, and let come to room temperature.

Preheat the oven to 325°F.

Spread the onion in a single layer on a rimmed baking sheet and place the ribs on top; pour the beer over and around the meat. Cover tightly with foil and cook for 1½ hours, until the ribs are fork-tender (see Know-how, page 172).

About 30 minutes before you're ready to grill, prepare a hot fire in a charcoal or gas grill and let the coals burn to gray ash with a slight red glow; if using a gas grill, heat the grill on medium. Place the ribs on the grill and, if you wish, baste with Say's Vinegar Barbecue Sauce. Close the grill or cover the ribs with foil and cook, turning and basting occasionally, for about 30 minutes, or until lightly charred and smoky.

Remove the ribs from the grill and transfer to a cutting board. Slice the racks into 3- to 4-rib slabs and serve warm over the beer-basted onions with more barbecue sauce on the side.

spicy memphis dry rub

MAKES ABOUT ¾ CUP

2   tablespoons ground paprika
2   tablespoons unpacked light brown sugar
1   tablespoon dry mustard
1   tablespoon ground cayenne pepper
1   tablespoon kosher salt
1   tablespoon granulated onion
1   tablespoon crushed red pepper flakes
1   teaspoon granulated garlic
1   teaspoon freshly ground black pepper
1   teaspoon dried thyme
1   teaspoon dried oregano

Combine the paprika, brown sugar, mustard, cayenne, salt, onion, red pepper flakes, garlic, black pepper, thyme, and oregano in a small airtight container and shake to thoroughly mix. The rub will keep for up to 1 month sealed and stored in a cool, dry place.

---

chew on this: **cutting spare ribs st. louis–style**

Spare ribs are cut from the underbelly or lower rib cage of a pig, which explains why they are so fatty and succulent. But even spare ribs have their tough parts. The way to handle this is to have your spare ribs cut St. Louis–style. On ribs butchered this way, the tough, fatty-end portion of the rib tips is removed, as is the skirt, which is a tough flap of meat attached to the bony side of the ribs. This makes the ribs look more rectangular and reduces their size to about that of baby back ribs. More important, they are much more tender.

---

chew on this: **local pig**

More and more small-scale Southern farmers are embracing pigs. Even better, they are looking to heritage breeds, like Ossabaws, Red Wattles, Tamworths, and Berkshires, and sustainable growing practices to produce top-notch, humanely raised pork. Not only is the flavor a thousand times better, but it's good for the environment, the local economy, and—at least in comparison to factory farming—for the pigs themselves. Producers like these are one of the most exciting aspects of Southern food right now. I encourage you to consult Sources (page 377) or, even better, your local farmer's market, to see if you can find similar producers in your own neighborhood.

---

pork rillettes

This dish—an adaptation of an Anne Willan recipe I used to make at the Soho Charcuterie—is what my dad most often requested when I came home to visit. Rillettes are a classic French preparation similar to pâté that are made by slow-cooking fatty meat until it falls apart, packing the meat in the rendered fat, and allowing it to congeal. The resulting rough spread pairs elegantly with Rosemary Cheese Crackers (page 8) or Cornbread Toasts (page 18), grainy mustard, and pickles. The most important thing to keep in mind is that rillettes need to cook very slowly at a low, steady temperature, so make sure the cooking liquid doesn't boil once you put the dish in the oven.

SERVES 10 TO 12 AS A FIRST COURSE OR HORS D'OEUVRE

	One 3-pound bone-in pork shoulder
6	**sprigs fresh thyme**
3	**sprigs fresh rosemary**
2	**teaspoons sea salt, plus more to taste**
2	**bay leaves**
1/2	**teaspoon whole mixed peppercorns**
3	**juniper berries**
	Several grates of fresh nutmeg
3	**cups water, plus more if needed**
	Freshly ground black pepper

Preheat the oven to 325°F.

Rinse the pork, pat dry, and cut into 2-inch cubes. Place the meat, along with the bone, in a large, deep ovenproof skillet or Dutch oven. Add the thyme, rosemary, salt, bay leaves, peppercorns, juniper, and nutmeg. Add the water, place over medium-high heat, and bring to a low boil, stirring occasionally.

Cover tightly and transfer to the oven to cook for 3½ to 4 hours, until the fat is rendered and clear and the pork is fork-tender (see Know-how, page 172). You may need to add more water after 2½ to 3 hours to prevent the pork from sticking.

Remove from the oven and cool slightly. Drain the pork, reserving the fat and discarding the bone, bay leaves, and thyme and rosemary sprigs. Shred the meat with two forks and add most of the fat, reserving about ¼ cup. Mix well and season to taste with salt and pepper. Pack the pork mixture into small ramekins or glass jars, seal tightly, and refrigerate for several days before serving. To keep for up to 2 weeks, seal the containers with a layer of the remaining melted fat and store in the refrigerator. Serve cold or at room temperature with toast points or crostini (see Know-how, page 19).

wood-smoked backyard barbecued pig

This is serious, slow-cooked Southern barbecue—the kind on which pit-masters stake their reputation—in miniature. The pork shoulder, the cut used here, is the entire front leg and shoulder from a hog, meaning it's a fairly large piece of meat. It's often broken up into two cuts: the upper half of the shoulder, also called the Boston butt or pork butt, and the lower, arm-half portion, which is also (rather sweetly) called the picnic ham or shoulder. For this preparation, though, ask your butcher or farmer for the whole shoulder with the bone in and skin on. It is the best you can make at home short of going whole hog (literally), digging your own pit, and basting the thing with a rag mop. To make it, you will need access to aged hickory wood, a wood-fired grill with a hood, and, if your grill is small, a secondary grill for heating coals—or read up on digging that pit. Preparing the pig is an all-day party in itself, so set aside plenty of time for cooking and tending the fire, not to mention a cooler full of beer or (my dad's choice) a bottle of Jack Daniel's for the pitmaster.

SERVES 10 TO 12

> **One 15- to 16-pound whole pork shoulder**
> ¼ **cup unpacked light brown sugar**
> 2 **tablespoons sea salt**
> 1 **tablespoon freshly ground black pepper**
> 1 **tablespoon paprika**
> 1 **tablespoon crushed red pepper flakes**
> **Say's Vinegar Barbecue Sauce (page 309), for serving**

About 1 hour before cooking, rinse the pork, pat dry, and place in a disposable aluminum roasting pan. Combine the brown sugar, salt, black pepper, paprika, and red pepper flakes in a small bowl and stir to mix. Rub the spice mixture all over the pork and let sit until the pork comes to room temperature, about 1 hour.

Meanwhile, prepare a hot fire in a charcoal grill and split 10 to 12 pieces of hickory wood into small pieces. Place a piece of the hickory on the coals and place the grates about 12 inches above the fire. Let the coals burn to gray ash with a slight red glow and push them to one side of the grill to create areas of direct and indirect heat (see Know-how, page 151).

If the grill is large enough, stoke the fire at the end farthest from the pork, and push the cooler coals to the middle to cook the pork at the opposite end over indirect heat. If you don't have the space to do this, you may want to maintain a hotter fire in another small grill or starter chimney to ensure a steady supply of coals. The coals and wood should never flame.

Set a disposable drippings pan below the grates and beneath the pork. Place the pork, skin side up, over the drippings pan. Cover the grill and cook slowly over low heat for 7 to 8 hours, turning one-quarter turn every 30 to 40 minutes and adding more coals as needed. Cook until the meat is fork-tender (see Know-how, page 172) and falling off the bones, and an internal thermometer inserted in the thickest part of the shoulder reads 190°F.

(continued)

To maintain a low and steady temperature of 250°F to 300°F, you will need to add coals from the hickory wood and charcoal to the fire every 30 to 40 minutes. If the shoulder starts browning too quickly, the coals are too hot.

Transfer the pork from the grill to a cutting board and let rest, loosely covered, for about 30 minutes. Remove most of the skin and reserve for making cracklings (see below). Using a fork, pull off the meat in large chunks along with some of the crispy skin and fat. Discard the bone and extra-large pieces of fat and serve warm with Say's Vinegar Barbecue Sauce.

> *ON THE SIDE*   Years of tradition demand that this barbecue be served with, at the very least, Roxy's Grated Coleslaw (page 260), Mess o' Greens (page 245), Creamy Potato Salad (page 266), and Salt and Pepper Skillet Cornbread (page 57), but when it comes to pulled pork, the more sides, the merrier.

Know-how: making cracklings

Rather than discarding the skin, use it to make crunchy, salty cracklings, which are perfect for munching solo or garnishing soups and other dishes.

Before cooking, remove the skin from the pork and place on a piece of wax paper or foil. Place in the refrigerator to air-dry for 2 to 3 hours or overnight.

When ready to cook the cracklings, preheat the oven to 400°F or prepare a hot fire in a charcoal or gas grill and let the coals burn to gray ash with a slight red glow; if using a gas grill, heat the grill on medium. Or pull the skin from the cooked pork and proceed as follows.

Cut the pork skin into 1-inch strips and place on a rimmed baking sheet. Season all over with sea salt and place in the oven or on the grill until all the fat has rendered and the skin is crispy, about 30 minutes. Remove from the oven or grill and drain on a brown paper bag. Break into crispy pieces and serve over salads, rice, or grits.

Know-how: testing fork-tender meat

I test braised pork and other slow-cooked meats for doneness with a fork. When the meat pulls apart easily with just a fork—making it what I call fork-tender—it's ready to go. It's an easy way to test for doneness, but you want to catch the meat at the right time so it doesn't get overcooked, tough, and stringy. I usually check every 15 minutes after the first suggested cooking time. I find that the leaner, pastured meat I get from the farmer's market usually takes less time than the grain-fattened meat I get at the grocery or butcher.

sticky-sweet braised pork shanks

A few hours in a Dutch oven reduce pork shanks, which come from the lower part of the pig's leg, to a silky and robustly flavored delicacy. Serve on top of Creamy Cheese Grits (page 208). SERVES 2 TO 4

	Four 8-ounce, bone-in pork shanks
	Sea salt and freshly ground black pepper
4	sprigs fresh thyme, plus more for garnish
2	tablespoons olive oil
1	onion, chopped
½	fennel bulb, cored and chopped
2	garlic cloves, smashed and minced
3	cups low-sodium chicken broth
½	cup Marsala wine
1	tablespoon tomato paste
4	tablespoons molasses
2	tablespoons balsamic vinegar

Preheat the oven to 325°F.

Rinse the pork, pat dry, and season all over with salt and black pepper to taste and 2 sprigs of the thyme, pressing lightly so the seasonings adhere.

Heat the oil in a large, deep ovenproof skillet or Dutch oven over medium-high heat until sizzling hot (see Know-how, page 100). Add the pork and brown on all sides, about 10 minutes total. Transfer the pork to a plate and cover loosely to keep warm.

Add the onion and fennel to the same skillet, reduce the heat to medium, and cook and stir for about 3 minutes, until the onion and fennel are softened. Add the garlic and remaining 2 sprigs thyme and cook and stir 2 minutes longer.

Add the chicken broth, Marsala, and tomato paste. Season with salt and black pepper to taste and stir to thoroughly blend in the tomato paste. Return the pork to the skillet, cover, and place in the oven to cook for 2½ to 3 hours, until the meat is falling off the bones and fork-tender (see Know-how, page 172).

Remove from the oven, transfer the shanks to a platter, and let rest, loosely covered, for about 10 minutes. While the pork is resting, skim the fat from the top of the cooking liquid and strain. Place the liquid back in the skillet and stir in the molasses and vinegar over high heat and boil to reduce until the liquid is thick and syrupy, about 10 minutes.

Remove and discard the skin from the shanks. Place the shanks on a platter and spoon the sauce over and around the meat. Sprinkle with thyme and serve warm.

Destination: **MASON, TENNESSEE**

WORTH THE DETOUR
BOZO'S HOT PIT BAR-B-Q'S
pulled pork sandwiches

(901) 294-3405

GROWING UP IN SMALL-TOWN JACKSON, TENNESSEE, WE THOUGHT OF MEMPHIS as the Big City. As often as we could, Mom, Dad, Judy, and I would pile into the car and drive to Memphis to go shopping, run errands, and see a movie. My dad hated driving on the interstate—or at least that was his excuse for taking the back roads through Mason, Tennessee, where we'd inevitably arrive at Bozo's, his all-time favorite barbecue joint, just in time for lunch. Not that any of us ever complained—my family has been going out of its way for Bozo's barbecue for more than fifty years. Bozo's hickory-smoked pulled pork sandwiches, made with shoulder meat that's shredded just so, then doused in a piquant tomato-based sauce and finished with the cool crunch of vinegar slaw, are just that good. Period.

Bozo's has been in business since 1923, and like many Southern mom-and-pop eateries, it feels sort of frozen in time—a small, stubborn challenge to the changing world that surrounds it. With its dark wood paneling and long Formica counter with red swivel stools, I think it probably looks the same as it did when my grandfather first started taking my dad there all those years ago. It's actually a pretty typical meat-and-three diner, but don't go trying to get fancy—just stick with the barbecue sandwich and you can't go wrong. Whether you're visiting Memphis or just passing through, Bozo's is well worth the detour.

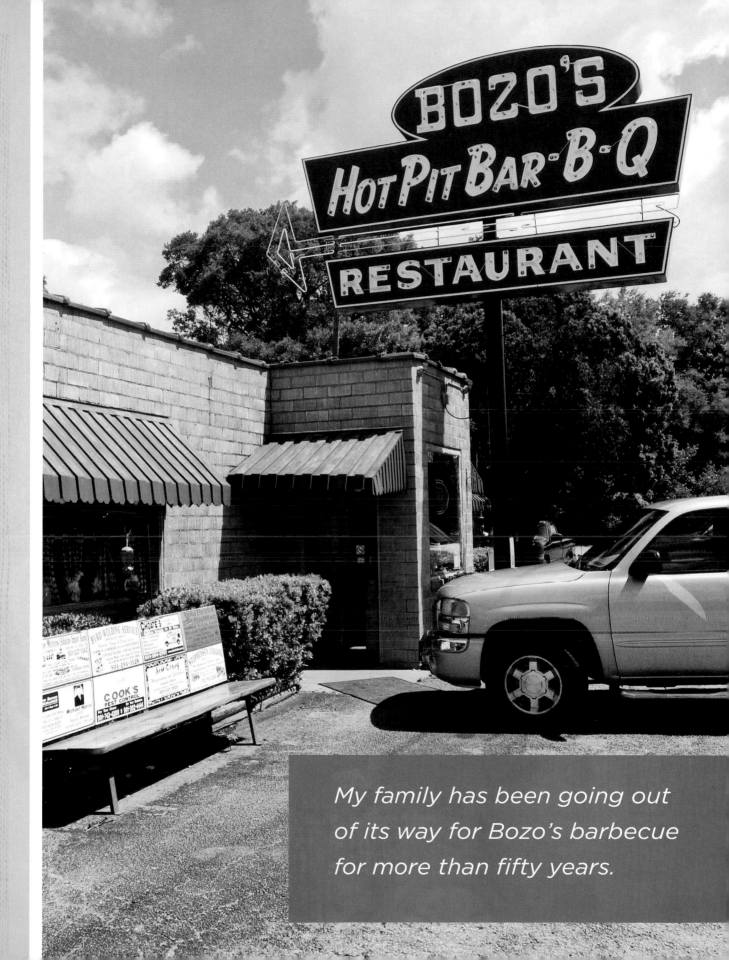

My family has been going out of its way for Bozo's barbecue for more than fifty years.

slow-roasted pulled pork butt

Here is a convenient way to duplicate succulent, hickory-smoked pork barbecue with only a fraction of the fuss. Just pop a pork butt in the oven, then finish it off quickly on the grill for smoky flavor, and voilà: a tender heap of slow-cooked, vinegar-spiked meat that you'd never know hadn't spent the whole day over the coals. SERVES 8 TO 10

	One 5-pound bone-in pork butt
2	teaspoons crushed red pepper flakes
	Sea salt and freshly ground black pepper
1/2	cup apple cider vinegar
1/2	cup water
2	cups Say's Vinegar Barbecue Sauce (page 309), plus more for serving

Preheat the oven to 325°F.

Rinse the pork, pat dry, and season with the red pepper flakes and salt and black pepper to taste, massaging the seasoning into the meat. Place the pork, fatty side up, in a large Dutch oven and add the vinegar and water to the bottom of the pan. Cover with a tight-fitting lid or foil and roast, undisturbed, for 2½ to 3 hours, until tender.

Prepare a hot fire in a charcoal or gas grill and let the coals burn to a gray ash; if using a gas grill, heat the grill on the lowest setting. Pour Say's Vinegar Barbecue Sauce over the pork and transfer the meat to the grill. Cover and cook for about 15 minutes per side, until slightly charred all over and smoky in flavor, baking with the same sauce while cooking.

Remove the pork from the grill and let rest, loosely covered, for 10 to 15 minutes before serving. Using a fork, pull the meat into large pieces, remove any extra-large chunks of fat, and serve warm with more barbecue sauce.

SARA'S SWAPS For an even easier no-fail approach to pulled pig, use my mom's go-to method. Place the pork butt in a plastic oven bag and pour the vinegar and 1 cup water over and around the meat. Season the meat by rubbing with salt and pepper and seal the bag by tying the open end tightly with kitchen string. Place in the middle of a preheated 325°F oven and roast, undisturbed, for 2½ to 3 hours, until the meat is fork-tender (see Know-how, page 172) and falling off the bone. Serve warm with West Tennessee Thick and Sticky BBQ Sauce (page 307) spooned on top.

Destination: **NEW ORLEANS, LOUISIANA**

WORTH THE DETOUR

COCHON BUTCHER'S

old-style deli food with a modern twist

(504) 588-PORK

cochonbutcher.com

SOUTHERNERS HAVE ALWAYS BEEN WILD ABOUT PORK, BUT THE PAST several years have brought something of a renaissance, with a new generation of Southern cooks ushering in a fresh, modern approach to going whole hog. Chef Donald Link's newest restaurant, Cochon Butcher, which is nestled in the heart of New Orleans's industrial warehouse district, epitomizes this trend. The small, bright shop sits adjacent to its upscale parent restaurant, Cochon, and has all the trappings of an old-school butcher shop—house-cured meats, sausages, salamis, confits, rillettes, and terrines, as well as fresh cuts of pork, beef, and lamb—reinterpreted with a thoroughly modern eye.

For example, traditional deli standards like pastrami on rye, Cuban melts, and hot dogs with all the fixings are served alongside more unusual offerings, including the pimiento cheese sliders, melt-in-your-mouth pork belly and mint sandwich on soft white bread, or the Buckboard Bacon Melt, which is layered with Swiss cheese, collard greens, and piquant pepper aioli. My favorite sandwich of all, though, is the Cochon muffaletta. It's a thick, meaty New Orleans deli classic that was first developed by the renowned Central Grocery in the early 1900s to cater to the tastes of its large Sicilian clientele. Cochon Butcher's version is true to the original, with layers of salty, tangy mortadella, sopressata, and capicola interspersed with ribbons of olive tapenade, pickled peppers, and mild provolone cheese. The big, bold flavors of Cochon's house-made meats are front and center in this and all their deli sandwiches, making them pretty much impossible to put down.

Pimiento cheese sliders, melt-in-your-mouth pork belly and mint sandwich on soft white bread

steaks, burgers, and roasts

According to Julia Reed, a writer from the Mississippi Delta who knows about such things, the most appropriate thing to do when someone dies is to pop a tenderloin into the oven. As a fellow Southerner, I know just what she means. You see, unless we're talking the cattle-ranching heartlands of Texas or good old ground chuck, beef has long been a treat in the South, something that—until recently—was usually reserved for special occasions.

That's how it was with my family. My grandparents always kept a couple of cows on their farm. So, while pork and fowl were in heavy daily rotation, and casual beef dishes like meatloaf, steaks, and hamburgers made regular guest appearances, beef remained, for the most part, something special. We all counted on my mom's Standing Rib Roast with Simple Horseradish Cream Sauce (page 202) to usher in the winter holidays, and my grandfather's and father's relentless campaigning occasionally won them Foster Family's Pot Roast with Herb-Roasted Vegetables (page 199) rather than the usual fried chicken on Sundays.

These days, beef is finding its place in everyday Southern cooking, from meat-and-threes to home kitchens. So it's no surprise that, more and more, it's getting easier to find locally raised beef throughout the South. In my parents' house, pan-fried steak was a near-weekly indulgence that was usually served with an oozing slice of melting butter, as with Pat's Skillet-Seared Steak with Herb Butter (page 185). And in our own home, Peter and I regularly rely on dishes like Pickled Jalapeño Meatloaf (page 191) or Beer-Barbecued Brisket (page 194) for homey and filling meals with lots of "leftovers" potential.

Accordingly, the dishes in this chapter will see you through just about any occasion—not just wakes and funerals—from casual suppers at home to elegant dinner parties, birthdays, holidays, and other special times.

pat's skillet-seared steak with herb butter

Forget the grill; Southerners have been pan-searing steak in cast-iron skillets since what seems like the beginning of time. That's true enough in my family, where "let's fix a steak" translates directly to "put the skillet on." According to my brother-in-law, Pat, the best way to eat said pan-seared steak is hot out of the skillet with a fat knob of butter melting away on top. He's right, of course, and this dish—embellished with a profusion of fresh green herbs—is for him. SERVES 2 TO 4

> Two 1-pound bone-in rib-eye steaks, 1 to 1½ inches thick
> 1 tablespoon olive oil
> 2 tablespoons fresh rosemary
> Sea salt and freshly ground black pepper
> Herb Butter (recipe follows)

Remove the steaks from the refrigerator and let sit for 15 to 20 minutes to come to room temperature. Drizzle the olive oil over both sides of each steak and season with the rosemary and salt and pepper to taste, rubbing the seasonings into the meat.

Heat a cast-iron skillet over medium-high heat to just before the smoking point (see Know-how, page 147). Place the steaks in the skillet and cook for 4 to 5 minutes per side (depending on the steaks' thickness) for medium-rare, 2 to 3 minutes longer for medium, or until the meat reaches the desired doneness.

Remove from the skillet and let rest, loosely covered, for about 5 minutes before serving. Top each steak with several slices of Herb Butter and cut into large pieces for serving, slicing against the grain. Season with additional salt and pepper, if desired, and serve warm.

herb butter

This recipe makes much more than you'll need for one meal, but you won't be sorry you have extra—it spruces up everything from toasted bread and steamed vegetables to grilled fish or chicken. MAKES ONE 6 X 2-INCH LOG, OR ABOUT 1 CUP

> ½ pound (2 sticks) unsalted butter, softened
> 4 roasted garlic cloves (see Know-how, page 186)
> ¼ cup fresh parsley
> 1 scallion, trimmed and chopped
> 1 tablespoon fresh thyme
> 1 tablespoon chopped fresh chives
> 1 teaspoon sea salt
> ½ teaspoon freshly ground black pepper

(continued)

Place the butter, garlic, parsley, scallion, thyme, chives, salt, and pepper in a food processor or blender and pulse until well combined and blended, stopping to scrape down the bowl several times as you go. Transfer the mixture to a piece of wax paper, roll it into a log 1½ to 2 inches in diameter, wrap tightly in plastic, and refrigerate until firm, about 1 hour, or for up to 1 week. Slice into thin rounds and use as needed.

ON THE SIDE   This herb-buttered steak is so simple and inviting that it goes with just about anything. For a quick supper, I'm most likely to serve it with Baked Rosemary Sweet Potato Halves (page 240) and Summer Succotash (page 232) or a leafy green salad drizzled with Buttermilk Green Goddess Dressing (page 284), whereas game nights call for Crispy Fried Vidalia Onion Rings (page 246) and Buttermilk Blue Cheese Dressing (page 285), for dipping.

Know-how: making roasted garlic

Using roasted garlic is a simple way to add buttery texture and deep, nutty flavor to most any dish, and making it couldn't be easier. All you do is take a whole head of unpeeled garlic, place it on a piece of aluminum foil, and drizzle liberally with olive oil. Wrap tightly in the foil and roast in a preheated 400°F oven for 30 to 35 minutes, or until the cloves are soft to the touch. Remove from the oven and cool until easy to handle. Cut the root end off the bulb and the cloves should slip easily out of their skins, so soft that they can be spread like butter (in fact, roasted garlic makes a rich-flavored, low-fat alternative to butter on toasted, crusty bread). Or, for an even faster approach, peel the desired number of individual garlic cloves, drizzle with oilve oil, wrap tightly in aluminum foil, and roast for about 15 minutes, until soft.

pimiento cheese burgers

As a kid, one of the things I looked forward to each fall was the arrival of the West Tennessee State Fair, which was held in Madison, my home county. Like all fairs, this one was chock-full of good, greasy things to eat, but I happily skipped past the corn dogs, turkey legs, and pulled pig in favor of the juicy griddle-fried hamburgers that flew like hotcakes from a booth lined with long, low benches. I top my version with tangy, creamy Pimiento Cheese for extra Southern flavor. If you don't have a griddle, a cast-iron skillet will work just fine. SERVES 4

1½	pounds ground beef or ground chuck (85% lean, 15% fat)
4	hamburger buns, split in half
1	tablespoon unsalted butter, softened
	Sea salt and freshly ground black pepper
½	cup Pimiento Cheese (page 18)
	Toppings, such as lettuce, pickles, tomatoes, onions, mustard, mayonnaise, and ketchup (optional)

Preheat the broiler.

Divide the beef into 4 parts and shape into patties, ¼ to ½ inch thick.

Split the buns in half, spread with the butter, and place, cut side up, on a baking sheet. Set aside.

Heat a griddle or cast-iron skillet over medium-high heat until just before the smoking point (see Know-how, page 147). Sprinkle both sides of each patty with salt and pepper to taste and cook for 3 to 4 minutes per side, or until cooked to the desired doneness. Place about 1 heaping tablespoon of the Pimiento Cheese on top of each patty, cover, and reduce the heat to low. Continue to cook for 1 to 2 minutes more, until the cheese melts. Remove the burgers from the skillet and place on a paper towel to drain. Let rest, loosely covered, for 3 to 4 minutes before serving.

Meanwhile, place the buns under the broiler until lightly toasted; keep an eye on them, as this happens quickly. Arrange the burgers on the buns and serve warm with a variety of toppings, if desired.

> *ON THE SIDE*   These burgers wouldn't be complete without a side of Quick Cucumber Pickles (page 287), Baked Butter Beans (page 237), and Fried Okra (page 250) or Crispy Fried Vidalia Onion Rings (page 246).

friday night steak sandwiches

My dad was the unusual male who didn't like to grill—he was a cast-iron fryer—so I became the family griller as soon as I was old enough; except for the three or four times a year when Peter makes burgers, I still am. This buttery, tangy, grilled steak sandwich—a favorite of my mother's—is supereasy, and it was one of my first specialties.

SERVES 2 TO 4

	Two 1-pound New York strip steaks, about 1½ inches thick
1/4	cup Worcestershire sauce
2	tablespoons olive oil
2	tablespoons balsamic vinegar
2	tablespoons fresh rosemary
	Sea salt and freshly ground black pepper
2	tablespoons unsalted butter
2	garlic cloves, smashed and minced
4	slices Italian or French bread, sliced in half horizontally, then in half again diagonally and crosswise
4 to 6	lettuce leaves
1	tomato, cored and sliced

Place the steaks in a shallow dish with the Worcestershire sauce, olive oil, and vinegar. Rub the marinade into the meat and sprinkle the rosemary and pepper to taste over both sides of each steak, pressing lightly so the seasonings adhere. Turn the steaks several times in the marinade to evenly coat and marinate until the meat comes to room temperature.

Prepare a hot fire in a charcoal or gas grill and let the coals burn to gray ash with a bright red glow (see Know-how, page 151). If using a gas grill, heat the grill on high.

Season the steaks with salt, place on the grill, and cook, turning only once, for 5 to 6 minutes per side for medium-rare, 2 to 3 minutes more for medium, or until they reach the desired done-ness. Remove the steaks from the grill and let rest, loosely covered, for about 5 minutes before serving.

While the steaks are cooking, heat the butter and garlic in a small saucepan over medium heat until the butter is melted and the garlic starts to release its aroma. While the steaks are resting, brush the bread slices with the garlic butter and grill for 1 to 2 minutes per side, until lightly toasted.

Cut the steaks into slices, cutting across the grain. Pile the meat on top of the toasted garlic bread, top with lettuce and tomato, and serve warm.

(continued)

Know-how: grilling steak

The key to grilling steak is to start with a scorching hot grill so the steak is quickly seared, allowing it to form a nice crust on the outside and stay good and juicy on the inside.

Test whether the grill is hot enough to sear the steak by placing your hand 6 inches above the coals; you should be able to hold your hand there for only 1 or 2 seconds.

Cook the steak on the hottest part of the grill, directly over the fire.

Do not move or flip the steak any more than necessary, as this will prevent it from searing.

Remove the meat from the grill just before it reaches the desired doneness; its temperature will continue to rise another 5 to 10 degrees once the meat is off the fire.

Rather than cutting into the steak, which causes all the flavorful juices to run out, learn to judge the steak's doneness based on the way it looks and feels when you touch it with your thumb. Rare steak is jiggly and fleshy; medium-rare is less fleshy but still a little jiggly, and well-done steak feels firm and muscular.

If you aren't yet confident in your ability to test doneness this way, insert an internal thermometer in the steak and remove the steak from the grill when it reads 110°F to 115°F for rare, 120°F to 125°F for medium-rare, and 130°F to 135°F for medium.

Always let the steak rest for at least 5 minutes, loosely covered. This seals in the juices so they don't run out when you cut into it.

For more grilling basics, see Know-how on page 151.

pickled jalapeño meatloaf

Meatloaf, like chili, is something I make when I have a dozen or so little jars of something-or-other in the fridge that need to be used up. That's how I came up with pickled jalapeño, which adds a nice kick to this otherwise traditional meatloaf. In this version, a little pork adds extra flavor to the mix. It makes for a delicious and hearty meal, but it's great for leftovers, too, which can be used to make sandwiches that are as scrumptious as they are out of the ordinary. Peter loves open-face meatloaf sandwiches topped with a fried egg. SERVES 6 TO 8

1	cup chopped fresh basil
1	small onion, diced
3	large eggs, lightly beaten
1/4	cup diced pickled jalapeño peppers, plus 6 slices for garnish
2	tablespoons Dijon mustard, plus more for serving
3	garlic cloves, smashed and minced
1	tablespoon dried basil, marjoram, or oregano
2	teaspoons sea salt
1	teaspoon freshly ground black pepper
1	cup ketchup, plus more for serving
3	tablespoons Worcestershire sauce
2	pounds lean ground beef
1	pound ground pork
1 1/2	cups cornbread or other fresh bread crumbs (see Know-how, page 134)

Preheat the oven to 375°F.

Combine the fresh basil, onion, eggs, diced jalapeño, mustard, garlic, dried basil, salt, and black pepper in a large bowl and mix well. Combine the ketchup and Worcestershire sauce in a small bowl and stir to mix. Add the beef, pork, bread crumbs, and half the ketchup mixture to the egg mixture and gently mix just until thoroughly combined; do not overmix or the mixture will become too mushy.

Place the beef mixture on a rimmed baking sheet and mold into a loaf shape, about 4 x 10 inches. Brush the remaining ketchup mixture on top of the loaf and place the jalapeño slices in a row down the center.

Bake the meatloaf for about 1 hour, until the juices run clear when the loaf is pierced with a small knife and an internal thermometer inserted in the center reads between 145°F and 150°F. Remove from the oven and let rest, loosely covered, for about 10 minutes before slicing. Serve warm with extra ketchup or spicy mustard on the side.

grilled and roasted fillet of beef with crispy roasted shallots

Roasted fillet of beef was a standard at my mom's house during the holidays, and I always crave it when the weather turns crisp. When I make it, I start the meat on the grill for extra flavor and finish it in the oven, where it cooks more evenly and comes out juicy and tender. It's a no-fail method that ensures a perfectly cooked fillet every time. SERVES 8 TO 10

One 3- to 3½-pound beef tenderloin, trimmed and tied
¼ cup olive oil
3 tablespoons fresh rosemary
2 teaspoons freshly ground black pepper, plus more to taste
2 teaspoons sea salt, plus more to taste
10 shallots, quartered

Remove the beef from the refrigerator at least 1 hour before cooking and let come to room temperature. Rub all over with 2 tablespoons of the olive oil and sprinkle with 2 tablespoons of the rosemary and the pepper, massaging the beef so the seasonings adhere.

Preheat the oven to 400°F.

Prepare a hot fire in a charcoal or gas grill and let the coals burn to gray ash with a slight red glow; if using a gas grill, heat the grill on medium.

Season the fillet all over with the salt and grill over the hot coals for 3 to 4 minutes per side, turning three times to sear on all four sides, 12 to 15 minutes total.

Remove the fillet from the grill, transfer to a rimmed baking pan, and add the shallots, remaining 2 tablespoons olive oil, and remaining 1 tablespoon rosemary. Season with salt and pepper and toss to coat the shallots evenly.

Roast in the oven for 15 to 20 minutes, until an internal thermometer inserted in the thickest part of the meat reaches 110°F for rare or 120°F for medium-rare and the shallots are crispy around the edges.

Remove from the oven, transfer the meat to a wooden cutting board, and let rest, loosely covered, for about 10 minutes before slicing. The shallots should be soft and slightly brown around the edges; if they need to be cooked a little more, put them back in the oven while the meat is resting. The temperature of the beef will continue to rise about another 5 degrees.

Slice the fillet into ½-inch-thick slices and serve warm or at room temperature with a scattering of crispy roasted shallots.

beer-barbecued brisket   *see photograph on page 180*

In the cattle-ranching heartlands of Texas, barbecue usually means beef, not pig, and brisket—which comes from the animal's lower chest—is hands down the most popular. A little patience and a few hours of smoking or braising transform this relatively tough cut into the most succulent, falling-apart-tender meat you'll ever eat. Part of the trick is marinating the meat for several hours or even overnight prior to cooking, so be sure to factor in this additional "inactive" prep time. To avoid standing over the grill for six to eight hours, I start the meat on the grill for an infusion of smoky hickory flavor and then let the oven do the rest of the work.   SERVES 6 TO 8

One 5- to 6-pound beef brisket
1/2   cup Sweet and Salty Dry Rub (recipe follows)
2   cups your favorite or West Tennessee Thick and Sticky BBQ Sauce (page 307), plus more for serving
1 1/2   cups ketchup
One 12-ounce beer
3   tablespoons Worcestershire sauce
Juice of 1/2 orange (squeezed half reserved)
1   tablespoon Dijon mustard

Season the brisket all over with the dry rub, place it in a large resealable plastic bag, and refrigerate for 4 to 6 hours or overnight.

About an hour before cooking the brisket, place 2 cups of hickory wood chips in water and let soak. Combine the barbecue sauce, ketchup, beer, Worcestershire sauce, orange juice, and mustard in a large bowl and stir to mix. Remove the brisket from the refrigerator and pour the barbecue sauce mixture over the meat. Reseal the bag, turn to coat the brisket with sauce, and let sit at room temperature for about 1 hour.

Prepare a hot fire in a charcoal or gas grill and let the coals burn to gray ash with a slight red glow. Keep the coals on one side of the grill to create areas of direct and indirect heat (see Know-how, page 151); if using a gas grill, heat just one side on medium. Drain the wood chips and add a handful to the fire.

Preheat the oven to 325°F.

Remove the brisket from the bag, reserving the marinade, and place on the hottest part of the grill, directly over the coals, to sear, about 5 minutes per side. Move the brisket to the cooler side of the grill, away from the coals. Add the remaining wood chips to the fire, cover, and cook and smoke the meat for another 30 minutes, basting with the marinade and turning several times.

Remove the brisket from the grill and transfer to a cast-iron or other ovenproof skillet with a tight-fitting lid. Pour the reserved marinade over the brisket and turn several times to coat.

Make sure the brisket is positioned fat side up and add the reserved squeezed orange half.

Cover the skillet and cook in the oven, undisturbed, for 3 to 3½ hours, until the brisket is fork-tender (see Know-how, page 172).

Remove the brisket from the oven, transfer to a platter, and let rest, loosely covered, for about 20 minutes before slicing. Serve warm with additional barbecue sauce, if desired.

sweet and salty dry rub

MAKES ABOUT 1 CUP

⅓ cup ground paprika
2 tablespoons freshly ground black pepper
2 tablespoons sea salt
2 tablespoons unpacked light brown sugar
1 tablespoon crushed red pepper flakes
1 tablespoon Colman's dry mustard

Combine the paprika, black pepper, salt, brown sugar, red pepper flakes, and mustard in a bowl or resealable plastic bag and stir or shake to thoroughly mix. Use immediately or store in an airtight container for up to 1 month.

ON THE SIDE Serve with Roxy's Grated Coleslaw (page 260) and Squash Puppies (page 65) or piled high on Kate's Sweet Potato Refrigerator Rolls (page 66) or crusty bread.

SARA'S SWAPS In the winter I bypass the grill, pan-sear the meat, and let the oven do all the heavy lifting. Season the brisket all over with the dry rub, place it in a large resealable plastic bag, and refrigerate for 4 to 6 hours or overnight. When ready to cook the brisket, preheat the oven to 325°F. Heat a large ovenproof skillet over medium-high heat and add about 2 tablespoons olive oil. Pan-sear the brisket for 4 to 5 minutes per side until brown all over, place in the oven, and proceed with the recipe.

Destination: **DURHAM, NORTH CAROLINA**

WORTH THE DETOUR

THE ORIGINAL Q SHACK'S

barbecued brisket

(919) 402-4227

theqshackoriginal.com

IF YOU KNOW ANYTHING ABOUT SOUTHERN BARBECUE, YOU KNOW THAT IT IS famously and stubbornly regional, meaning that for the most part you've got to travel to the 'cue—to Memphis for dry ribs, Kentucky for mutton, Texas for brisket, and so on. As much as I love our local style, I'm grateful that, even in the heart of eastern Carolina barbecue country, there are some exceptions. The Original Q Shack in Durham is one of them. They serve solidly good North Carolina pork barbecue, but that's not the real reason to go there. The thing you absolutely don't want to miss—and the one thing that sets it apart from the other barbecue joints in the area—is its utterly sublime Texas-style, chile-rubbed, hickory- and mesquite-smoked beef brisket. This unbelievably succulent, flavorful meat comes sliced or chopped (your choice), doused in a rich, tangy, Texas-style tomato sauce, and served with thick slices of Texas toast, thinly sliced raw onions, crispy hushpuppies, and your choice of two sides.

Jalapeño-spiked deviled eggs can be purchased for thirty-five cents a pop, sweet tea and cold beer run like water, and killer sides, like Jack cheese creamed spinach, bacon-infused stewed green beans, fried okra, and sticky BBQ beans make the prospect of ordering a veggie plate at a barbecue joint slightly less sacrilegious. Wide picnic tables and once-a-week live bluegrass make it a favorite hang-out spot, so don't be surprised if you find yourself lingering long after the food is finished. Out-of-towner advantage: bring a baseball cap from a barbecue joint not already displayed on the wall and win a free rack of ribs.

Utterly sublime Texas-style, chile-rubbed, hickory- and mesquite-smoked beef brisket

foster family's pot roast with herb-roasted vegetables

I grew up on this everyday pot roast, which each member of my family makes with his or her own special twist. My mom swears simple is best, with nothing more than meat and vegetables to flavor the dish. I, on the other hand, add wine, broth, and herbs to maximize the flavor of the meat, and I roast most of the vegetables separately so they get nice and caramelized on the outside and soft and sweet in the center.   SERVES 4 TO 6

	One 3-pound beef chuck roast
	Salt and freshly ground black pepper
2	tablespoons olive oil
1	large onion, cut into wedges
2	carrots, cut in half crosswise
1	cup dry red wine
6	sprigs fresh thyme
6	sprigs fresh rosemary
4 to 6	cups low-sodium beef broth
	Herb-Roasted Vegetables (recipe follows)

Preheat the oven to 325°F.

Generously season the roast on all sides with salt and pepper.

Heat the olive oil in a large ovenproof skillet or Dutch oven over medium-high heat until sizzling hot (see Know-how, page 100). Add the roast and sear to a rich brown color, 3 to 4 minutes per side. Place the onion and carrots around the roast in the skillet and cook and stir while the roast is searing.

Add the wine, thyme, and rosemary and cook and stir for about 1 minute, scraping up any brown bits from the bottom of the skillet. Add enough broth to cover three-quarters of the roast. Reduce the heat to medium and bring the liquid to a low boil.

Cover the pot tightly with a lid or aluminum foil and roast in the oven, undisturbed, for 2 to 2½ hours, until the meat is fork-tender (see Know-how, page 172).

Remove the roast from the oven and transfer to a serving platter. Spoon the Herb-Roasted Vegetables and onions around the meat and cover loosely to keep warm. Remove the herb stems and carrots from the skillet. Use a large spoon to skim the fat off the top of the cooking liquid. Place the skillet over high heat and reduce the liquid by half. Pour over the roast and serve warm with the roasted vegetables scattered around the platter.

(continued)

herb-roasted vegetables

Roasted vegetables are so easy and delicious—with nothing more than a drizzle of olive oil, a dash of sea salt, and a hot oven, the vegetables get all crispy and caramelized on the outside and soft in the middle. It's a great dish for company, since it can be made ahead of time and reheated or served at room temperature. But even when you don't have guests, cook enough for a crowd and use the leftovers in salads, sandwiches, quesadillas, or omelets. Most all vegetables are good for roasting, including turnips, beets, rutabagas, fennel, asparagus, corn, summer squash, tomatoes, onions, garlic, and all kinds of winter squash and pumpkins. Just make sure to wait to add quick-cooking vegetables until any slow-cooking vegetables are almost done.

SERVES 6 TO 8

1	pound small new potatoes
1	small acorn or butternut squash, cut in half, seeds removed, and cut crosswise into 1-inch slices
2	tablespoons olive oil
2	tablespoons unsalted butter, melted
4	tablespoons fresh rosemary
4	tablespoons fresh thyme
	Sea salt and freshly ground black pepper
1	red onion, quartered
5 or 6	small carrots, trimmed
2	parsnips, peeled and cut into chunks

Preheat the oven to 400°F.

Place the potatoes and squash on a rimmed baking sheet. Drizzle with 1 tablespoon of the olive oil and 1 tablespoon of the butter and toss to coat the vegetables evenly. Spread evenly in a single layer and season with 2 tablespoons of the rosemary, 2 tablespoons of the thyme, and salt and pepper to taste. Roast for 40 to 45 minutes, stirring several times while cooking, until soft when pierced with the tip of a small knife and light brown around the edges.

While the potatoes and squash are roasting, place the onion, carrots, and parsnips on a separate rimmed baking sheet with the remaining 2 tablespoons rosemary, 2 tablespoons thyme, 1 tablespoon olive oil, and 1 tablespoon butter. Season with salt and pepper to taste, stir the vegetables to coat evenly, and spread in a single layer. Roast for 25 to 30 minutes, stirring several times. Remove from the oven, arrange on a platter with the other vegetables around the pot roast, and serve warm.

standing rib roast with
simple horseradish cream sauce

Elegant and timeless, roasted prime rib is my idea of the quintessential dinner party centerpiece. The best part is that, unlike many other "fancy" dishes, it couldn't be easier—just pop the roast in the oven and let it do its thing. The meat should be allowed to marinate at least one full day or night, but if you have the time, let it dry in the refrigerator for up to two days; doing so tenderizes the meat and intensifies the flavors. Either way, ask the butcher to leave the bones attached to the meat, which ensures that the roast will be juicy and flavorful. SERVES 6 TO 8

  One 4-bone, 8½- to 9-pound standing rib beef roast,
  chine bone attached
2 tablespoons sea salt
2 tablespoons Colman's dry mustard
2 tablespoons fresh rosemary
1 tablespoon dried onion flakes
2 teaspoons freshly ground black pepper
  Simple Horseradish Cream Sauce (recipe follows)

Place the beef in a large roasting pan and season all over with salt, rubbing it into the meat and bones. Combine the mustard, rosemary, onion flakes, and pepper and stir to mix. Rub the spice mixture all over the beef to coat evenly. Cover loosely and place in the refrigerator overnight, or for up to 2 days.

About 2 hours before cooking, remove the meat from the refrigerator and let come to room temperature.

Move a rack to the lower third of the oven and preheat the oven to 450°F.

Roast the beef for 20 to 25 minutes, until it begins to brown and sizzle. Reduce the temperature to 325°F and continue to cook for about 2 hours, until an internal thermometer inserted in the middle of the roast registers 110°F to 115°F for rare, or 20 to 25 minutes more, until the thermometer reads 120°F to 125°F, for medium-rare (the temperature will continue to rise another 5 degrees while the meat rests). Remove the roast from the oven and let sit, loosely covered, for about 30 minutes before carving.

To carve, remove and discard the chine bone (see Know-how, page 203) and slice the meat to the desired thickness. Arrange on a serving platter and serve warm with the horseradish sauce on the side.

simple horseradish cream sauce

This rich sauce adds cool heat to Friday Night Steak Sandwiches (page 188), Crispy Fried Oysters Four Ways (page 117), and Foster Family's Pot Roast with Herb-Roasted Vegetables (page 199).

MAKES ABOUT 1 CUP

½	cup sour cream
¼	cup prepared horseradish
2	tablespoons heavy cream
1	teaspoon hot sauce, such as Texas Pete or Tabasco
1	teaspoon fresh rosemary
	Sea salt and freshly ground black pepper

Combine the sour cream, horseradish, heavy cream, hot sauce, and rosemary in a bowl and stir to combine. Season with salt and pepper to taste and refrigerate in an airtight container until ready to serve, or for up to 4 days.

Know-how: carving rib roast

The chine bone is the flat bone that lies just below the rib bones, and the added flavor it imparts is well worth the effort of removing the bone after roasting. (If you'd rather not deal with it, ask the butcher to remove the bone and tie it back onto the roast. If you do this, you will need to reduce the cooking time by 30 to 40 minutes.)

After the roast is done, place it on a cutting board, loosely covered, and let rest for about 15 minutes. To remove the chine bone, use a sharp boning or slicing knife to slice from the end of the bone to the back of the roast, cutting as close as possible to the bone. Place the roast on the board, rib side down, and slice into thick portions, cutting between the ribs.

For thinner portions, remove the rib bones by placing the roast on its bottom, where you removed the chine bone (with the ribs standing up), and use a sharp knife to slice between the rib bones and the meat, cutting as close to the bone as possible, to remove the roast in one piece. Place the roast on the cutting board, rib side down, and slice into portions across the grain to the desired thickness. Cut only the number of slices you want to serve immediately; this will keep the meat moist.

grits and rice

*L*ike sweet tea, fried chicken, and pulled pig, grits have long symbolized Southern food. But it wasn't until relatively recently that many non-Southerners actually *tried* grits, thus ensuring that grits remained, to many, a mystery. Thankfully, over the past ten years or so, grits—along with Southern cuisine more generally—have enjoyed something of a coming-out in the larger food world, to the point that it's no longer unheard-of to find grits in restaurants north of the Mason-Dixon Line.

It's a good thing, because as far as I'm concerned, you can't truly "get"—or more important, fully enjoy—Southern food without grits and rice. They have always been the unsung heroes, the heart of Southern cuisine. After all, what's a Southern breakfast without cheese grits? Lowcountry cooking without rice pirlou? Or a Creole or Cajun meal without beans and rice or jambalaya?

It all started because wheat, the grain favored by Europeans, didn't take to the wet, hot Southern climate of the New World. Taking a cue from Native Americans, European Southerners quickly turned their focus to corn, a native grain. Soon after came rice, which was brought to the low-lying coastal regions from Africa.

These days, Southerners and Southern companies like Anson Mills and Carolina Plantation Rice are working to preserve this culinary heritage by rehabilitating heirloom and regional varieties of the grains. We tend not to think this way about staples, but the variety and type of grain you start with can make as much difference to a finished dish as the vegetables you choose for a salad.

Southerners eat grits and rice morning, noon, and night, so it is only right that the dishes in this chapter run the gamut from simple sides, like Creamy Cheese Grits (page 208) and Creamed Vegetable Rice (page 216), to hearty suppers, including Red Beans and Rice with Andouille Sausage (page 220), Pea and Bacon Pirlou (page 218), and Roasted Tomato Grits with Country Ham and Cracklings (page 213). All of these recipes are versatile and easy, but what really unites them—what really makes them *Southern*—is how gracefully they complete meals at any time of day, quietly transforming the kitchen table to a welcome table.

creamy cheese grits

Here is the only recipe for basic cheese grits you'll ever need. Distilled to their essence, grits are tender, satisfying, and endlessly versatile. Serve them plain with eggs or meat or dress them up with anything from fresh herbs and country ham to roasted garlic and sautéed mushrooms.   SERVES 6 TO 8

3	cups water
1	teaspoon sea salt, plus more to taste
1	cup yellow stone-ground grits
1	cup milk
1	cup (4 ounces) grated sharp Cheddar cheese
4 to 6	tablespoons ($^1/_2$ to $^3/_4$ stick) unsalted butter, cut into pieces, plus more to taste
	Freshly ground black pepper

Bring the water to a boil in a large saucepan over high heat. Add the salt and whisk the grits into the boiling water in a slow, steady stream. Reduce the heat to low and cook, stirring often, for 15 to 20 minutes, until the mixture thickens and most of the liquid is absorbed. Add the milk and continue to cook and stir for another 5 minutes, until the grits are tender and reach the desired thickness.

Remove the grits from the heat and add the cheese and butter to taste, stirring until both are melted. Season with salt and pepper to taste and serve warm.

Know-how: making perfectly cooked grits

For perfectly creamy grits with just a little bite, remove the grits from the heat when they are still a bit thin and loose—just a touch less creamy than you want. They will continue to cook and thicken as they cool. If they become too thick, just stir in a little more milk.

SARA'S SWAPS   I love the simplicity of this dish, but you can easily dress it up by adding creamy goat cheese, pepper Jack, or blue cheese and stirring in mixed fresh herbs, such as parsley, dill, thyme, and rosemary, along with corn or hominy and spinach or watercress for added color and texture. Top it off with crispy bacon or country ham, chopped toasted pecans, or roasted poblano chiles.

cheesy grits casserole

Over the years, my love of stone-ground yellow grits has turned me into a certified grits snob. And, like most Southerners with a grits chip on my shoulder, I tend to blame flavorless "quick grits"—the finely milled, prepackaged variety that has been pre-steamed to be partially cooked—for unfairly maligning this Southern delicacy's reputation. So imagine my surprise when I discovered, thanks to an ingenious Craig Claiborne recipe, that this puffy, soufflé-like casserole is actually much better made with quick grits. There's just no denying texture that light and airy. You can, of course, use stone-ground grits; the casserole will be a littler grainier but equally flavorful. SERVES 6 TO 8

2	cups milk
2	cups water
1	cup quick grits
	Sea salt and freshly ground black pepper
1½	cups (6 ounces) grated sharp Cheddar cheese
1	teaspoon hot sauce
3 or 4	grates of fresh nutmeg
6	large eggs, separated
½	cup (1½ ounces) freshly grated Parmesan cheese

Preheat the oven to 425°F. Generously butter a 2-quart soufflé dish and place in the freezer.

Bring the milk and water to a boil in a large saucepan. Whisk the grits into the milk mixture in a slow, steady stream and bring the mixture back up to a low boil. Reduce the heat to a simmer and cook and stir for 3 to 5 minutes, until the grits are just tender. Season with salt and pepper to taste.

Remove from the heat and stir in the Cheddar cheese, hot sauce, and nutmeg. Transfer the mixture to a large bowl and let cool slightly.

Whisk the egg yolks into the grits until fully combined. Place the egg whites in a large bowl and beat with an electric mixer until soft peaks form, about 2 minutes. Fold in one-third of the egg whites to lighten the mixture, then gently fold in the remaining whites.

Spoon the mixture into the prepared dish, spread evenly, and sprinkle with the Parmesan cheese. Bake for about 25 minutes, until puffed and firm around the edges and still slightly soft in the center. Remove from the oven and let sit for about 5 minutes before serving warm.

creamy grits with roasted butternut squash and blue cheese

Oven-caramelized squash and tangy blue cheese make this creamy side hearty enough to double as a vegetarian entrée. It makes an excellent weeknight supper crumbled with crispy bacon or prosciutto and served with a simple green salad and a glass of crisp, sweet Sauternes or creamy Chardonnay. SERVES 4 TO 6

1	small butternut squash, peeled, seeded, and chopped or sliced
3	tablespoons olive oil
2	teaspoons sea salt, plus more to taste
	Freshly ground black pepper
3	cups water
1	cup stone-ground yellow grits
1	cup milk
1	cup (3 ounces) freshly grated Parmesan cheese
3	tablespoons unsalted butter
1	tablespoon fresh rosemary, plus more for garnish
½	cup (2 ounces) crumbled Gorgonzola or other blue cheese

Preheat the oven to 400°F.

Toss the squash with the olive oil to coat evenly and season with salt and pepper to taste. Spread in a single layer on a rimmed baking sheet and bake until golden brown around the edges, 30 to 35 minutes, stirring halfway through.

While the squash is baking, bring the water to a boil in a large saucepan. Add the 2 teaspoons salt and slowly add the grits in a steady stream, whisking constantly. Reduce the heat to low and cook and stir for 15 to 20 minutes, until the grits begin to thicken. Add the milk and continue to cook and stir for another 5 minutes, until the grains are tender and the mixture is thick.

Remove from the heat and add the Parmesan cheese, butter, and rosemary, stirring to melt Taste for seasoning and add salt and pepper, if desired.

Place the grits on a platter or divide evenly between individual serving plates and scatter the roasted squash on top. Sprinkle with the Gorgonzola, garnish with rosemary, and serve warm.

roasted tomato grits with country ham and cracklings

This is my go-to grits dish, the first one I think to make and the one to which I keep returning over the years. I love how the roasted tomatoes, flavored by the country ham, form a rich, saucy sort of gravy for the creamy cheese grits. Cracklings add big flavor. If they aren't available, substitute crispy pieces of thick-cut bacon. SERVES 4 TO 6

8   plum tomatoes, cored and halved lengthwise
3   tablespoons olive oil
2   tablespoons fresh rosemary or thyme
1   tablespoon balsamic vinegar
2   teaspoons sea salt, plus more to taste
     Freshly ground black pepper
1/2 cup crumbled cracklings (see Know-how, page 172)
     or crispy bacon
3   cups water
1   cup stone-ground yellow grits
1   cup milk
6   thin slices country ham (about 9 ounces)
1   cup (4 ounces) grated sharp Cheddar cheese
1/2 cup (1 1/2 ounces) freshly grated Parmesan cheese
3   tablespoons unsalted butter

Preheat the oven to 400°F.

Combine the tomatoes, olive oil, rosemary, and vinegar on a rimmed baking sheet. Season with salt and pepper to taste and toss to coat the tomatoes evenly. Spread the tomatoes in a single layer, cut side down, and roast for about 30 minutes, until they begin to shrivel and soften and the undersides have caramelized. Remove the tomatoes, turn off the oven, and place the cracklings in the oven to warm.

While the tomatoes are cooking, bring the water to a boil in a large saucepan. Add the 2 teaspoons salt and slowly add the grits in a steady stream, whisking constantly. Reduce the heat to low and cook and stir for 15 to 20 minutes, until the mixture begins to thicken. Add the milk and continue to cook and stir for 5 minutes more, until the grains are tender and the mixture is thick.

While the grits are cooking, sauté the ham slices in a cast-iron skillet or grill pan until warmed through and slightly brown around the edges, about 4 minutes per side. Remove from the skillet and cover loosely to keep warm.

When the grits are ready, remove from the heat and stir in the Cheddar cheese, Parmesan cheese, and butter. Taste for seasoning and stir in additional salt and pepper, if desired.

Serve warm topped with the roasted tomatoes and their juices, a few slices of the ham, and a sprinkling of the cracklings and parsley.

sweet potato spoon bread

Spoon bread is like a cross between grits and cornbread, with a lovely, dense, puddinglike texture set off by cornmeal's fine grain. I don't need an excuse to bring sweet potatoes into the mix—I've been known to add them to just about everything—but in this case they reinforce the silky texture of the spoon bread in addition to adding their characteristic orange color and mild, sweet flavor.   SERVES 8 TO 10

4	tablespoons (1/2 stick) unsalted butter, melted
2	medium sweet potatoes (about 1 pound)
2 1/2	cups milk
1	tablespoon fresh thyme
1	tablespoon unpacked light brown sugar
2	teaspoons sea salt
1/2	teaspoon freshly ground black pepper
1	cup finely ground white or yellow cornmeal
4	large eggs, separated
2	teaspoons baking powder

Preheat the oven to 400°F. Generously grease a 2-quart soufflé dish with about 1 tablespoon of the butter.

Wrap the potatoes in foil and bake for 45 to 55 minutes, until soft to the touch. Remove from the oven and discard the foil. When the potatoes are cool enough to handle, remove and discard the potato peels, transfer the potatoes to a large bowl, and mash.

Reduce the oven temperature to 350°F.

Bring the milk, thyme, brown sugar, salt, and pepper to a low boil in a saucepan over medium heat. Whisk the cornmeal into the milk mixture in a slow, steady stream. Cook, whisking constantly, for 4 to 5 minutes, until the mixture is thick and pulls away from the bottom of the pan. Remove from the heat and let cool slightly.

Add the potatoes, egg yolks, remaining 3 tablespoons butter, and the baking powder and stir to thoroughly combine.

Place the egg whites in a large bowl and beat with an electric mixer until soft peaks form. Gently fold the whites into the cornmeal-potato mixture.

Spoon the batter into the prepared dish and bake until golden brown and puffy, 35 to 40 minutes. The edges will be firm and the center will still be a little soft. Remove from the oven and let sit for about 10 minutes before serving warm.

carolina gold rice

Carolina Gold rice, a fat, golden-hued, long-grained variety native to South Carolina, is so flavorful that only simple preparations are required. It is excellent in its most basic form, cooked in water with just a little salt and pepper, but for special occasions I opt for this gently embellished preparation.   SERVES 4 TO 6

1	tablespoon olive oil
1	tablespoon unsalted butter
1	shallot, minced
2	cups Carolina Gold rice (see Sources, page 377)
	Sea salt and freshly ground black pepper
2	tablespoons fresh thyme
2½	cups low-sodium chicken or vegetable broth

Heat the olive oil and butter in a saucepan over medium-high heat until sizzling hot (see Know-how, page 100). Add the shallot and cook and stir for about 2 minutes, until soft and translucent. Add the rice, season with salt and pepper to taste, and stir to coat with oil and butter. Cook for about 2 minutes, stirring occasionally. Add the thyme and just enough broth to cover the rice by about ¼ inch, stirring just once to combine.

Cover, reduce the heat to low, and simmer for about 20 minutes, until the rice is tender and all the liquid is absorbed. Remove from the heat and let sit, covered, for about 5 minutes. Serve warm.

---

chew on this: **about carolina gold rice**

Often called the grandfather of long-grain rice in the Americas, Carolina Gold is a beautiful variety that was the star of the antebellum rice trade and a driving force in the creation of a distinct Southern culinary tradition. Despite these claims to fame, Carolina Gold fell by the wayside after the Civil War, along with the South's rice economy. It was half forgotten and nearly extinct by the time Richard Schulz, a Georgia surgeon and plantation owner, rehabilitated the grain in the 1980s. Thanks to his efforts, it is now once again commercially available from vendors like South Carolina's Carolina Plantation Rice and Anson Mills (see Sources, page 377).

---

creamed vegetable rice

Thick and saucy, this country ham and summer vegetable–strewn rice dish is my Southern version of risotto. Like risotto, it gets its full-bodied, creamy texture from the starch released by the rice as it cooks. SERVES 6 TO 8

2	tablespoons unsalted butter
1	tablespoon olive oil
1	cup long-grain white rice (preferably Carolina Gold)
2	ounces country ham, diced
	Sea salt and freshly ground black pepper
2½	cups low-sodium chicken broth
1	tablespoon fresh thyme
1	small zucchini, diced
1	carrot, diced
½	cup heavy cream
½	cup (3 ounces) sliced wild mushrooms, such as chanterelles, shiitakes, morels, or hedgehogs
½	cup (1½ ounces) freshly grated Parmesan cheese
2	tablespoons chopped fresh parsley

Heat 1 tablespoon of the butter and the olive oil in a saucepan over medium heat until the butter melts. Add the rice and country ham and cook and stir for 2 to 3 minutes, until the rice is fully coated and the ham is slightly brown around the edges. Season with salt and pepper to taste. Add 2 cups of the broth and the thyme, stir just once, cover, and simmer for about 20 minutes, until most of the liquid is absorbed.

Layer the zucchini, carrot, remaining ½ cup broth, and the heavy cream over the rice without stirring. Cover and simmer for about 8 minutes, just until the liquid is absorbed and the vegetables are tender.

While the vegetables are cooking, heat the remaining 1 tablespoon butter in a skillet over medium-high heat until sizzling hot (see Know-how, page 100). Add the mushrooms and sauté until golden brown, about 3 minutes.

Just before serving, stir the mushrooms, Parmesan cheese, and parsley into the rice and serve warm.

SARA'S SWAPS To make a lighter version of this dish that feels just as indulgent, substitute strained Greek yogurt or more chicken broth for the heavy cream.

streak o' green dirty rice

Dirty rice is a Cajun specialty so named for the brownish hue imparted by the chicken livers or giblets that also provide its rich mineral flavor. Today, we mostly think of dirty rice as a side, but because it is a cheap source of protein and calories it would have been served as a main dish in leaner times. This version—streaked with a bright green scattering of fresh herbs—is my take on Paul Prudhomme's classic recipe. SERVES 6 TO 8

1	tablespoon olive oil
1/4	pound ground country sausage
2	chicken livers, trimmed and connective tissue removed
1	onion, diced
2	celery stalks with leaves, chopped with leaves reserved
1	jalapeño pepper, cored, seeded, and diced
1 1/2	cups long-grain white rice (preferably Carolina Gold)
2	garlic cloves, smashed and minced
2	teaspoons fresh thyme
1	teaspoon chopped fresh marjoram
1	teaspoon sea salt
1	teaspoon ground cumin
1/2	teaspoon crushed red pepper flakes
1/2	teaspoon freshly ground black pepper
1/2	teaspoon ground paprika
1/2	teaspoon Colman's dry mustard
2	cups low-sodium chicken broth
1/2	cup chopped fresh parsley
8	fresh basil leaves, thinly sliced

Heat the olive oil in a saucepan over medium-high heat until sizzling hot (see Know-how, page 100). Add the sausage and chicken livers and cook and stir for 3 to 4 minutes, breaking up the sausage and livers as they cook, until golden brown. Drain off all but about 2 tablespoons of the fat. Add the onion, celery, and jalapeño and cook and stir for about 5 minutes, until the vegetables are tender. Add the rice, garlic, thyme, marjoram, salt, cumin, red pepper flakes, black pepper, paprika, and mustard and stir to coat the rice. Cook for about 2 minutes, stirring occasionally.

Add the broth, stir just once, and bring to a low boil. Reduce the heat, cover, and simmer for about 15 minutes, until most of the liquid is absorbed. Turn off the heat and let the rice sit, undisturbed, for 10 minutes, until the grains are tender and all the liquid is absorbed. Add the reserved celery leaves, parsley, and basil and fluff with two forks before serving hot.

pea and bacon pirlou

A Charleston classic, pirlou (aka purloo or pilau) is an everything-but-the-kitchen-sink rice pilaf that is the lowcountry contribution to the family of rice dishes, including jambalaya and gumbo, hailing from the rice-growing regions of the Southeast. Pirlous usually feature seafood of some kind—as you might expect, given their watery origins—but I like the way this simplified version showcases the grassy flavor of fresh field peas.

SERVES 4 TO 6

4	slices thick-cut bacon (about $1/4$ pound)
1	onion, diced
2	celery stalks, diced
1	garlic clove, smashed and minced
$1^{1}/_{2}$	cups long-grain white rice (preferably Carolina Gold)
2	tablespoons fresh thyme
$1/2$	teaspoon Colman's dry mustard
$1/4$	teaspoon hot paprika
	Pinch of ground cayenne pepper or crushed red pepper flakes
	Sea salt and freshly ground black pepper
4	cups low-sodium chicken broth
1	large tomato, cored and chopped
1	pound shelled fresh or frozen field peas, such as lady peas, pink-eyes, purple hulls, or zippers
2	tablespoons chopped fresh parsley or celery leaves, plus more for garnish
2	tablespoons unsalted butter

Cook the bacon in a saucepan over medium heat until crispy, then remove and drain on a brown paper bag. Add the onion and celery to the bacon fat and cook and stir until the vegetables are soft, about 5 minutes. Add the garlic and continue to cook and stir for 1 minute longer. Stir in the rice, thyme, mustard, paprika, cayenne, and salt and black pepper to taste and cook and stir for about 3 minutes to coat the rice.

Add the broth and tomato and stir to mix. Bring to a low boil and simmer, uncovered, stirring occasionally, until most of the liquid is absorbed and the rice is cooked, about 20 minutes. The rice will be creamy, not fluffy and dry.

While the rice is cooking, rinse and drain the peas, discarding any blemished peas or bits of pod. Place the peas in a saucepan with about 3 cups of water. Season with salt and black pepper and bring to a low boil. Simmer, stirring occasionally, skimming as needed, for 15 to 20 minutes, until the peas are tender. Drain and set aside to keep warm.

Add the parsley and butter to the rice mixture and season with additional salt and black pepper, if necessary. Spoon the peas over the pirlou, sprinkle with the reserved bacon and more parsley, and serve.

red beans and rice with andouille sausage

Long-simmering red beans practically cook themselves, a fact that didn't escape the many generations of hardworking Louisiana Creole women who supposedly made this dish every Monday, on laundry day. Even now, many Creole restaurants serve red beans and rice as a lunch special on Mondays. SERVES 8 TO 10

2	tablespoons olive oil
1	pound smoked ham, cut into 1-inch chunks
2	onions, chopped
2	red or green bell peppers, cored, seeded, and chopped
2	garlic cloves, smashed
2½	cups (about 1 pound) dried red beans, soaked in water overnight and drained
1	cup chopped fresh parsley
2	tablespoons Worcestershire sauce
4	bay leaves
1	tablespoon fresh thyme
1	teaspoon crushed red pepper flakes
1	teaspoon freshly ground black pepper, plus more to taste
3	generous dashes of hot sauce, plus more for serving
	Sea salt
1	pound andouille sausage, sliced
	Steamed long-grain white rice or Carolina Gold Rice (page 215)
4	scallions, trimmed and minced

Heat the olive oil in a large heavy-bottomed pot or Dutch oven over medium-high heat until sizzling hot (see Know-how, page 100). Add the ham and cook and stir for about 5 minutes, until it begins to brown. Reduce the heat to medium, stir in the onions and bell peppers, and cook, stirring occasionally, for about 10 minutes more, until the onions are soft and light brown and the peppers are brightly colored and tender. Add the garlic and cook for 1 minute more, stirring constantly.

Add the beans, ½ cup of the parsley, the Worcestershire sauce, bay leaves, 1½ teaspoons of the thyme, the red pepper flakes, black pepper, hot sauce, and salt to taste. Add enough water to cover the beans by about 2 inches and simmer, uncovered, for about 2 hours, stirring occasionally, until the beans are tender. Add more water if needed; the beans should always be covered by at least 1 inch of water.

When the beans are tender, remove the bay leaves, stir in the sausage and remaining 1½ tea-spoons thyme, and cook for about 30 minutes more, stirring occasionally, until the beans develop a thick, creamy gravy. Stir in the remaining ½ cup parsley and season with additional salt and black pepper, if desired.

Serve hot over a bed of steamed white rice or Carolina Gold Rice, garnished with the scallions and with extra hot sauce on the side.

anytime hoppin' john

When it comes to good luck, Southerners don't take any chances. Each year on New Year's Day, we hedge our bets by eating hoppin' John, a rustic mix of rice, black-eyed peas, bacon, and onion that is thought to bring good fortune in the year to come. (Literally—the peas in the dish represent coins, and the stewed collards that are usually served on the side are the rich green of dollar bills.) For extra good luck, serve with Mess o' Greens (page 245). SERVES 4 TO 6

2	cups fresh or frozen black-eyed peas
3 to 4	cups water
2	tablespoons olive oil
1/4	pound smoked ham, diced
1	small red onion, diced
1/2	red bell pepper, cored, seeded, and diced
1	jalapeño pepper, cored, seeded, and diced
1	cup long-grain white rice (preferably Carolina Gold)
2	teaspoons fresh thyme
1	teaspoon sea salt, plus more to taste
1 1/2	cups low-sodium chicken or vegetable broth
1	tablespoon chopped fresh parsley
1	tablespoon chopped fresh cilantro
1/4	teaspoon crushed red pepper flakes
	Freshly ground black pepper
	Heirloom Tomato Salsa (page 102), for serving
	Scallions, trimmed and chopped, for garnish

Place the peas in a saucepan with the water and bring to a low boil over medium heat. Reduce the heat and simmer for about 20 minutes, until just crisp-tender.

Meanwhile, place the olive oil in a separate large saucepan over medium-high heat until hot. Add the ham and cook and stir for 2 to 3 minutes, until the ham is light brown around the edges. Reduce the heat to medium and add the onion, bell pepper, and jalapeño and cook and stir until the vegetables are tender, 3 to 4 minutes. Add the rice, thyme, and salt and cook and stir until the rice is coated. Add the broth and stir only once to mix, reduce the heat to low, cover, and simmer for about 10 minutes.

Drain the peas and add to the pan with the rice; continue to cook, covered, for another 10 minutes, until all of the liquid is absorbed, the peas are tender, and the rice is fluffy. Remove from the heat and stir in the parsley, cilantro, and red pepper flakes. Season with salt and black pepper to taste and serve warm, topped with the salsa and garnished with scallions.

hoppin' john cakes

MAKES 6 TO 8 CAKES

Place **2 cups of the cold, leftover Hoppin' John** in a bowl and mash slightly with a potato masher. Add **1 large egg, lightly beaten, ¼ cup fresh bread crumbs (see Know-how, page 134) and 2 tablespoons all-purpose flour.** Stir to combine, then form the mixture into small cakes, about 2 inches round. Place ¼ **cup additional fresh bread crumbs** in a small low bowl and season with **sea salt and freshly ground black pepper.** Dip each cake into the bread crumbs, pressing the cakes into the bread crumbs so that they adhere on both sides. Refrigerate the cakes until firm, about 1 hour.

Heat enough **oil to cover the bottom of the skillet** over medium-high heat until sizzling hot (see Know-how, page 100). Sauté the cakes until golden brown and heated through, about 3 minutes per side, turning only once. Serve warm topped with a **poached egg** or a **handful of mixed greens** and **Heirloom Tomato Salsa (page 102).**

shrimp jambalaya

Yet another in the seemingly endless parade of hearty one-pot dishes from the Creole and Cajun traditions, jambalaya is a close cousin of Spanish paella (which comes as no surprise, given Louisiana's earlier ownership by Spain). I love jambalaya, whether it's made in the "red" Creole style, with tomatoes, or in the "brown" Cajun style, without, because even though it requires a little slicing and dicing, it's actually a fairly fast and weeknight-friendly one-dish dinner—and it really sticks to your ribs. I often make mine with shrimp (as in this recipe), but jambalaya is sort of like gumbo in that it is made with everything from chicken, sausage, pork, and oysters to alligator, boar, venison, and turtle—basically, anything that swims, crawls, grazes, or flies in the vicinity of Southerners. **SERVES 6 TO 8**

2	slices thick-cut bacon, chopped
2	tablespoons olive oil
1	onion, diced
1/4	pound tasso or other smoked spicy ham, chopped
3	celery stalks, diced
1	red bell pepper, cored, seeded, and diced
4	garlic cloves, smashed and minced
2	cups long-grain white rice (preferably Carolina Gold)
2	teaspoons sea salt, plus more to taste
1	teaspoon ground cumin
1/2	teaspoon freshly ground black pepper, plus more to taste
	Pinch of crushed red pepper flakes
3	tomatoes, cored and chopped
3 1/2	cups Fast and Fresh Broth (page 42) or low-sodium chicken broth
3	bay leaves
1	tablespoon fresh thyme
2	pounds large shrimp, peeled and deveined (reserve shells if making Fast and Fresh Broth)
3	tablespoons chopped fresh parsley
2	scallions, trimmed and minced

Cook the bacon in a large skillet or Dutch oven with a tight-fitting lid uncovered over medium heat until crispy. Remove the bacon and place on a paper towel–lined dish to drain.

Add the olive oil to the same skillet and heat over medium heat until sizzling hot (see Know-how, page 100). Add the onion and tasso and cook, stirring often, for about 5 minutes, until the onion is soft and golden and the ham is light brown around the edges. Add the celery and bell pepper and cook and stir for about 5 minutes more, until tender. Add the garlic and cook, stirring constantly, for 1 minute longer. Add the rice, salt, cumin, black pepper, and red pepper flakes and cook and stir for about 2 minutes, until the rice is thoroughly coated with the oil. Stir in the tomatoes and cook for 1 minute more.

Pour in the broth, add the bay leaves and thyme, and stir only once. Bring the mixture to a low boil, reduce the heat, and simmer, covered tightly, for about 20 minutes, until most of the broth has evaporated and the rice is plump and tender.

Scatter the shrimp over the top of the rice, increase the heat to low, and cover to steam the shrimp, 7 to 10 minutes, until bright pink and cooked through and until the rice is tender and the liquid absorbed. Divide the jambalaya evenly among individual serving plates, sprinkle with parsley and scallions, and serve hot.

farm-stand vegetables, casseroles, and salads

*T*he hardest part about putting this chapter together was taming the urge to include a whole book's worth of recipes just for sides and salads. Southerners have always had a special fondness for sides, and I think the sides, as much as anything, define Southern food. Take, for example, the ubiquity of meat-and-threes, restaurants where the main component on each plate—the meat—is frequently overshadowed in volume and popularity by the three sides that accompany it. A typical meat-and-three might have as many as twenty vegetable sides to choose from, not to mention the ever-popular "vegetable plate."

My love of vegetable sides was instilled in me at an early age, not at restaurants but at home. For my grandmother and mother, a proper Sunday dinner included no fewer than six vegetable sides, most of them inspired by their gardens and the shifting of the seasons. They might be as simple as sliced tomatoes and pickles, but the important thing was that there were a lot of choices. Such meals weren't limited to Sundays; many times, especially in summer, we would have nothing but vegetable sides for dinner—things like fried okra, stewed peas, sweet potato casserole, skillet-fried corn, and collards—along with a big skillet of cornbread. It was something we looked forward to. It doesn't matter which vegetable varieties you use, only that you use the freshest, best ones you can find.

The most exciting thing about living and eating in the South today—and one of the main things that sold me on starting a business here—is the resurgence of interest in local food and seasonal eating. Not only is there an old guard of committed farmers who've dedicated their lives to growing quality food, but there is also a new generation of young, small-scale farmers who bring energy and new ideas to the market. This means that you can now find, in addition to unusual varieties of the usual suspects, things that aren't often associated with the South, like fresh soybeans, Chinese long beans, and bok choy. It is those farmers, and those vegetables, that are at the heart of every recipe in this chapter. They are why I love, and ultimately why I *live* in, the South.

skillet-fried corn

Granny Foster used to make this buttery treat with the sweetest summer corn. I make mine with corn and squash. She would scrape or "milk" the cobs with the back of a knife to get out all the starchy liquid, thus thickening the cooking liquid without diluting the bright corn flavor. SERVES 4 TO 6

Shuck **6 ears fresh corn** and cut the kernels directly into a bowl. After removing the kernels, hold each stripped cob over the bowl and scrape with the back of a knife to release the juices. Cut **4 fresh basil leaves** into thin strips and set aside.

Heat **4 tablespoons (½ stick) unsalted butter** in a heavy skillet over medium heat until foamy. Add the kernels and their juices, rinse the bowl with ¼ **cup water,** and add the rinsing liquid to the skillet. Season with **sea salt and freshly ground black pepper to taste** and cook and stir until the kernels are tender and the liquid thickens, 3 to 4 minutes. Stir in the basil and serve warm.

stewed field peas

Unlike my mom and many Southern cooks of her generation, for whom fatback was the preferred flavoring agent, I most often make peas in a savory broth flavored by bacon, country ham, or olive oil. Either way, the cooked peas yield a rich, saucy pot likker that just begs to be soaked up with cornbread.   SERVES 4 TO 6

2	slices thick-cut bacon, chopped
1	tablespoon olive oil
1	onion, chopped
3	cups (about 1 pound) shelled fresh or frozen crowder or other field peas
3 to 4	cups water
2	tablespoons unsalted butter
1	small chile pepper
4	fresh sage leaves
2	teaspoons sea salt, plus more to taste
1/2	teaspoon freshly ground black pepper, plus more to taste

Place the bacon and olive oil in a saucepan over medium heat and cook and stir until the bacon is crisp, about 4 minutes. Add the onion and cook and stir for another 3 minutes, until soft and translucent.

Meanwhile, rinse and drain the peas, discarding any blemished peas or bits of pod. When the onion is cooked, place the peas in the pan and add the water. Add the butter, chile pepper, sage, salt, and black pepper and stir to mix. Bring to a low boil and reduce the heat to a simmer. Cover and cook until the peas are tender, 20 to 25 minutes, skimming the foam as it rises to the top of the cooking liquid. Remove from the heat, season with additional salt and black pepper, if desired, and serve warm.

---

chew on this: *about field peas*

When Southerners mention peas, nine times out of ten they are talking about fresh field peas, not the ubiquitous green peas in the frozen food aisle of the grocery store. The term *field pea* is a catchall used to refer to hundreds of varieties with names that range from journalistic (black-eyed, pink-eyed, and purple hull), to Southern gothic (Dixie Lees, lady peas, and Old Timers). Hardy and drought tolerant, they are also perfectly suited to the climate of the South. Unlike sugar snap and English peas, which can be eaten raw or cooked, pod and all, field peas must be shelled and cooked prior to serving. Field peas differ subtly in flavor from variety to variety, but they are uniformly delicious, with a robust, nutty flavor and an addictively creamy finish.

---

summer succotash

Succotash is a traditional stew of fresh butter beans and corn made velvety by the last-minute addition of butter. The basics—beans and corn—are a must, but beyond that it seems most every Southern family has its own particular version. I typically let the farmer's market determine the mix of vegetables, but this rendition, with sweet bell peppers, basil, and summer squash, is one of my all-time favorites. SERVES 8 TO 10

2	cups (about $1/2$ pound) shelled fresh or frozen butter beans
	Sea salt and freshly ground black pepper
2	tablespoons olive oil
1	Vidalia or other sweet white onion, chopped
1	red bell pepper, cored, seeded, and diced
2	summer squash (such as yellow crookneck or zucchini), diced
4	ears corn, shucked
2	tomatoes, cored and chopped, or 1 cup cherry tomatoes, halved
2	tablespoons unsalted butter
$1/4$	cup fresh basil leaves, torn into pieces

Rinse and drain the beans, discarding any blemished beans or bits of pod. Place the beans and 4 cups of water in a saucepan over medium-high heat and bring to a simmer, stirring occasionally and skimming foam from the top as needed. Add salt and black pepper to taste and simmer until the beans are crisp-tender, about 15 minutes. Rinse and drain well.

Heat the olive oil in a large skillet over medium-high heat until sizzling hot (see Know-how, page 100). Add the onion and cook and stir until tender, about 3 minutes. Add the bell pepper and continue to cook and stir for 2 to 3 minutes longer, until crisp-tender. Add the summer squash and cook until tender and golden around the edges, 5 to 6 minutes longer.

While the squash are cooking, cut the corn from the cobs into a large bowl and scrape the stripped cobs with the back of the knife to release the juices into the bowl. Add the butter beans, corn kernels and their juices, tomatoes, and butter to the skillet, season with salt and black pepper to taste, and continue to cook just until the tomatoes begin to break down and the corn is tender, about 3 minutes. Stir in the basil and serve warm or at room temperature.

ON THE SIDE Succotash's buttery flavor and texture make it hearty enough to double as a vegetarian entrée spooned over Carolina Gold Rice (page 215) or Creamy Cheese Grits (page 208), but it also makes a great side for Spicy Pepper Jelly–Marinated Grilled Pork Tenderloin (page 163) or Easy Crab Cakes (page 111).

Destination: **MEMPHIS, TENNESSEE**

WORTH THE DETOUR
CUPBOARD RESTAURANT'S
veggie sides
(901) 201-6733

THE ENTRÉE OFFERINGS AT THE CUPBOARD, A TOP-NOTCH MEAT-AND-THREE in Memphis, include everything from meatloaf, burgers, and fried chicken to baked catfish and chicken and dumplings, all of which are solidly good. But, like most meat-and-threes, it doesn't really matter either way—the real stars are the many vegetable sides that make up the majority of the menu and of each plate that emerges from the kitchen.

Having been in business more than forty years, the Cupboard is something of a Memphis institution, but it's a designation they've earned with more than just staying power; they also serve some of the freshest, most flavorful Southern sides around. The Cupboard's selection includes a mouthwatering array of less common offerings that are usually found only in the home kitchens of the most traditional Southern cooks. These include creamy corn pudding, fresh turnip greens, crowder peas, speckled butter beans, black-eyed peas, carrot and raisin salad, fresh buttered squash, eggplant casserole, spiced beets, stewed okra and tomatoes, rutabaga, and thick slices of fresh tomato of a blushing shade of deep red that can only be achieved from vine ripening.

In range and quality, it's a selection even Granny Foster, who rarely served a meal with fewer than six sides, would have approved of. And those entrées? All but forgotten.

They serve some of the freshest, most flavorful Southern sides around.

baked butter beans

My mom always made these sticky-sweet baked beans for picnics and cookouts. I make them year-round with most any type of cooked dried beans, including navy, pinto, or great Northern. In the summer, though, fresh and tender butter beans are my favorite. When entertaining, I often give this homey dish an air of sophistication by baking and serving it in individual-size ramekins or custard dishes topped with slices of pork belly in place of the bacon. SERVES 6 TO 8

4	cups (about 1 pound) shelled fresh or frozen butter beans
	Pinch of kosher salt
3	slices thick-cut bacon
1	onion, chopped
1/2	cup your favorite or West Tennessee Thick and Sticky BBQ Sauce (page 307)
1/2	cup ketchup
1/4	cup Worcestershire sauce
1/4	cup loosely packed light brown sugar
1/4	cup molasses
2	tablespoons Dijon mustard
1	teaspoon sea salt
1/2	teaspoon freshly ground black pepper
	Pinch of crushed red pepper flakes

Preheat the oven to 350°F. Lightly grease a 2-quart baking dish.

Rinse and drain the beans, discarding any blemished beans or bits of pod. Bring a pan of water to a boil and add the kosher salt. Add the beans and cook, stirring occasionally and skimming foam from the top as needed, for about 15 minutes. Drain, rinse, and drain again thoroughly.

While the beans are cooking, sauté the bacon in a large skillet over medium-high heat until just slightly cooked but not crispy, 1 to 2 minutes per side. Remove from the pan, drain on a paper towel, and set aside.

Reduce the heat to medium and add the onion to the same skillet. Cook and stir for about 5 minutes, until soft and golden.

Combine the beans, onion, barbecue sauce, ketchup, Worcestershire sauce, brown sugar, molasses, mustard, sea salt, black pepper, and red pepper flakes in a bowl and stir to mix.

Spoon the bean mixture into the prepared dish and place the bacon strips on top. Bake for 45 minutes to 1 hour, until the bacon is crispy and the beans are bubbling around the edges. Remove from the oven and serve warm.

buttermilk mashed creamers

The secret to making perfect mashed potatoes—the sort of classically creamy, fluffy mashers that are the stuff of comfort food fantasies—is starting with the right spuds. Waxy potatoes, which are high in moisture and low in starch, have full-bodied flavor that adds depth of character, and they hold up well when boiled, but they tend to get gluey when mashed. Starchy potatoes, on the other hand, are more one-dimensional in flavor but are better at absorbing moisture, which means that they whip up beautifully. I use midrange potatoes, such as Yukon Golds, russets, or round purple-skinned Caribes, which allow me to take advantage of the best of both worlds. SERVES 4 TO 6

Peel **2 pounds Yukon Gold or russet potatoes** and cut any larger potatoes in half so that all are roughly the same size. Place in a large saucepan and add cold water to cover by about 2 inches. Bring to a low boil over medium-high heat, cover, reduce the heat, and simmer for about 30 minutes, until the potatoes are tender when pierced with the tip of a small knife.

Drain the potatoes and return to the saucepan while still warm. Remove from the heat, add **6 tablespoons (¾ stick) unsalted butter,** cover, and let sit until the butter melts. Add **½ cup well-shaken buttermilk** and mash with a potato masher or whip with electric beaters until the potatoes are creamy and all the butter and buttermilk are incorporated. Season with **sea salt and freshly ground black pepper to taste** and stir to mix. Serve warm.

SARA'S SWAPS It's hard to beat the taste of classic mashed potatoes, but it can be fun to mix in new flavors and textures. Start by combining several kinds of potatoes, such as russets, Yukon Golds, and Yellow Finns, or blending in roasted winter or root vegetables, like cauliflower, sweet potatoes, celery root, or parsnips. Next, try swirling in fresh herbs, like chives or dill, crème fraîche or sour cream, Cheddar or Parmesan cheese, prepared horseradish, whole-grain mustard, roasted garlic, or chipotle chiles in adobo sauce.

foster family's candied sweet potatoes

This recipe is a Foster family standard, a permanent fixture at holidays and other large family gatherings. Along with most other Southerners, I've been a huge fan of sweet potatoes for as long as I can remember, but in my case I think this sticky-sweet preparation may be the root of my obsession. When I make it today, I add fresh orange juice and zest to brighten the flavors and cut the sweetness just a hair, yielding what I think of as a grown-up version of this childhood favorite. SERVES 4 TO 6

3	medium sweet potatoes (about 2 pounds)
1	cup water
1/2	cup granulated sugar
1/2	cup firmly packed light brown sugar
4	tablespoons (1/2 stick) unsalted butter
	Juice of 1 orange
1	cinnamon stick
	Pinch of sea salt

Peel the potatoes and cut in half lengthwise. Cut each half lengthwise into 3 or 4 wedges, depending on the size of the potato.

Place the potatoes and water in a large saucepan over medium-high heat. Add the granulated sugar, brown sugar, butter, orange juice, cinnamon stick, and salt and bring the mixture to a low boil, stirring occasionally. Reduce the heat and simmer, covered, for about 25 minutes, until the potatoes are tender when pierced with the tip of a small knife and the sauce is thick and syrupy. Serve warm with the syrup spooned over and around the potatoes.

ON THE SIDE Sweet potatoes and pork are a match made in heaven, so I especially like serving these with Memphis-Style Barbecued Spare Ribs (page 166) or Slow-Roasted Pulled Pork Butt (page 177). Of course, they also make a great side for dishes like Standing Rib Roast with Simple Horseradish Cream Sauce (page 202) or Barbecued Turkey (page 150).

baked rosemary sweet potato halves

These baked sweet potato halves couldn't be easier to throw together, but the unexpected addition of piney rosemary and fresh lime makes them anything but ordinary. SERVES 4 TO 8

Preheat the oven to 375°F.

Drizzle **2 tablespoons olive oil** and **1 tablespoon melted unsalted butter** onto a rimmed baking sheet. Sprinkle with **1 tablespoon fresh rosemary** and **sea salt and freshly ground black pepper to taste.** Cut **4 sweet potatoes** in half lengthwise. Rub the cut side of each potato half in the butter, olive oil, and seasonings and arrange, cut side down, on the baking sheet.

Bake until the potatoes are soft to the touch and the cut sides are golden brown, 30 to 35 minutes. Remove from the oven and serve warm with **sea salt** and **lime wedges** to squeeze over the potatoes.

SARA'S SWAPS Try using different sweet potato varieties, like rosy Covingtons and Beauregards, sweet orange Vardamans (named after the Mississippi town touted as the "sweet potato capital of the world"), pale O'Henrys, and purple sweet potatoes, to see which ones you like best. You also can make this dish with similar results using peeled slices of winter squash, like butternut, acorn, or delicata. For a more savory interpretation, try using Yukon Gold, Russian Banana Fingerling, or White Rose potatoes.

ON THE SIDE Because they couldn't be easier to throw together, I make these rosemary-inflected sweet potatoes all the time when they are in season, and I serve them with anything from Pat's Skillet-Seared Steak with Herb Butter (page 185) or Crispy Pork Chops (page 162) to Pickled Jalapeño Meatloaf (page 191) or Granny Foster's Sunday Fried Chicken (page 127).

farm-stand grilled vegetable skewers with pesto vinaigrette

What better way to make use of the frenzy of vegetables that bursts on the scene in midsummer than these easy grilled skewers, all dressed up in pesto vinaigrette. Keep it fun and simple by loading the skewers with whatever mix of fresh, seasonal vegetables you find at the market. **MAKES ABOUT 12 SKEWERS / SERVES 6 TO 12**

VINAIGRETTE

½   **cup olive oil**

¼   **cup basil pesto or Arugula Pesto (page 255)**

    Juice of 1 lemon

VEGETABLES

½   **pound okra, stem ends removed**

1   **red bell pepper, cored, seeded, and cut into 2-inch wedges**

1   **yellow bell pepper, cored, seeded, and cut into 2-inch wedges**

1   **red onion, cut into 2-inch wedges**

6   **small summer squash (such as yellow, zucchini, or pattypan), cut into 2-inch chunks**

1   **cup cherry or grape tomatoes**

1   **cup fresh sage leaves**

    Sea salt and freshly ground black pepper to taste

VINAIGRETTE | Combine the olive oil, pesto, and lemon juice in a small bowl and whisk to mix thoroughly.

VEGETABLES | Prepare a hot fire in a charcoal or gas grill and let the coals burn to gray ash with a slight red glow; if using a gas grill, heat the grill on medium. If using wooden skewers, soak in water while prepping the vegetables to help prevent burning.

Skewer the okra, red and yellow peppers, onion, squash, and tomatoes, alternating vegetables for varied flavor and color and adding a sage leaf every 3 or 4 vegetables. Be sure to leave some room at the dull end of each skewer free for easy handling.

Brush the skewers with the vinaigrette and season with salt and black pepper to taste. Place on the grill and cook for 3 to 4 minutes per side, until the vegetables are slightly charred but still crisp-tender. Remove from the grill and serve warm with the remaining vinaigrette on the side, for dipping.

(continued)

ON THE SIDE   These vegetable skewers are so fresh and flavorful that they're often the first thing to go, even when they're served with steak or other grilled meat. Embrace their popularity and make them the star of the show by serving over Pea and Bacon Pirlou (page 218), Creamy Cheese Grits (page 208), or Creamed Vegetable Rice (page 216) as a main dish, or serve alongside Grilled Grouper with Heirloom Tomato Salsa (page 102) or Molasses-Glazed Grilled Pork Tenderloin (page 165).

IN SEASON   I grill outside year-round, so I often modify these skewers according to whatever is in season. Here are a few of my favorite veggie combinations to get you thinking outside the summer box.

FALL

Sweet potatoes, turnips, leeks, and cauliflower florets

WINTER

Acorn squash, Brussels sprouts, celery root, and cipollini onions

SPRING

Radishes, spring onions, asparagus, and fennel

---

chew on this: *Farmer's Market Veggie Guide*

One of the greatest things about shopping at farmer's markets (and some gourmet groceries) instead of your average supermarket is the many vegetable varieties you encounter. In addition to sweet basil, for example, you're liable to find Thai, lemon, purple, and cinnamon basil, all at the same market. All that variety is exciting, but it can be overwhelming, too. I encourage you to talk with your market vendors, who are typically very knowledgeable and enthusiastic about their produce, and to try new things.

GREENS	SQUASH	TOMATOES
beet greens	butternut squash	Better Boy
bok choy	Kobochu squash	Arkansas Traveler
collard greens	pumpkin	Beefstake
kale	turban squash	Carolina Gold
turnip greens	acorn squash	Cherokee Purple
mustard greens	delicata squash	Brandywine
Swiss chard	Red Kuri	Early Girls

---

mess o' greens

My mom used to cook greens in such big batches that she would wash them on the rinse cycle in the washing machine. For her, a "mess" was a discrete unit of measurement equal to approximately one large grocery bag full. I think most Southerners operate under this assumption, at least as far as greens are concerned. It may seem like you're starting out with far more greens than you'll ever need, but keep in mind that they'll cook down quite a bit. If they don't all fit in the pan at first, start with as many as will fit and add to the pot as the greens cook down. SERVES 6 TO 8

2	tablespoons olive oil
2	ounces country ham, diced
4	bunches (about 4 pounds) mixed hardy greens, such as turnip greens, collards, mustard, and kale, washed and drained
½	teaspoon crushed red pepper flakes
	Sea salt and freshly ground black pepper
1	cup low-sodium chicken or vegetable broth
	Hot Pepper Vinegar (page 308), for serving

Heat the olive oil in a large saucepan or Dutch oven over medium-high heat until sizzling hot (see Know-how, page 100). Add the ham and cook until crispy around the edges.

Remove and discard the stems from the greens and tear the greens into large pieces. Add the greens to the ham and season with red pepper flakes and salt and black pepper to taste.

Add the broth and cover the pan. Reduce the heat to low and simmer for 25 to 30 minutes, stirring occasionally, until the greens are tender. Check to make sure the greens don't start to stick to the bottom of the pan; if they do, lower the heat and add a little more broth or water.

Taste for seasoning and add more salt and pepper, if desired. Drizzle with Hot Pepper Vinegar and serve warm.

ON THE SIDE   It should be illegal to serve Mess o' Greens without Salt and Pepper Skillet Cornbread (page 57) or Creamy Cheese Grits (page 208) for sopping up the savory pot likker.

crispy fried vidalia onion rings

Sweet Vidalia onions are the perfect foil for the salty crust on these beer-battered onion rings, which make great party food along with Pimiento Cheese Burgers (page 187). Serve them in high street-food style by piling individual servings in handheld cones rolled from newspaper, brown paper bags, or butcher paper. Let the batter sit for the full three hours; this will allow deep, yeasty flavors to develop.   SERVES 4 TO 6

Combine **1 cup beer** and **1 cup all-purpose flour** in a shallow bowl and stir to mix. Season with **sea salt and freshly ground black pepper to taste** and allow the mixture to sit, undisturbed, for 3 hours at room temperature.

When ready to cook the onion rings, cut **1 large Vidalia or Bermuda onion** into ¼-inch-thick slices. Separate the slices into rings.

Preheat the oven to 200°F. Line a rimmed baking sheet with a brown paper bag.

Pour **4 to 5 inches of canola oil** into a large saucepan and place over medium-high heat until the oil reaches 350°F to 375°F.

Dredge the onion rings a few at a time in the beer batter. Allow the excess batter to drip off and carefully place the battered rings, one at a time, in the hot oil, taking care not to overcrowd the pan. Fry until golden brown, 2 to 3 minutes.

Using tongs or a slotted spoon, transfer the onion rings to the prepared baking sheet to drain. Place in the oven to keep warm while frying the remaining rings.

Sprinkle with **sea salt to taste** and serve hot with **ketchup** for dipping or sprinkled with **Hot Pepper Vinegar (page 308)**, English pub–style.

fried green tomatoes with buttermilk green goddess dressing

I've shared recipes for fried green tomatoes before, but each time I've tried to gussy them up by adding herbs or layering them with other ingredients. I like those dishes, of course, but the fact is there is something wonderful about making fried green tomatoes the way my mother and grandmother made them—that is, simply. Stripped of nonessentials, the warm tartness of green tomatoes, tempered by a hint of sugar, and the toasted crunch of cornmeal crust shine through in perfect balance. SERVES 6 TO 8

1/2	cup well-shaken buttermilk
1	large egg
1/2	cup all-purpose flour
1/2	cup yellow cornmeal
2	tablespoons sugar
1	teaspoon sea salt, plus more to taste
1/2	teaspoon freshly ground black pepper, plus more to taste
	Canola oil, for frying
4	large green tomatoes, cored and sliced into 1/2-inch-thick rounds
1/2	cup Buttermilk Green Goddess Dressing (page 284)

Preheat the oven to 200°F. Line a rimmed baking sheet with a brown paper bag.

Place the buttermilk and egg in a shallow bowl and whisk to combine. Combine the flour, cornmeal, sugar, salt, and pepper in a separate shallow bowl and stir to mix.

Pour canola oil into a large skillet to just barely cover the bottom and place over medium-high heat until sizzling hot (see Know-how, page 100).

One at a time, dip the tomato slices first in the buttermilk mixture and then in the flour mixture to coat both sides, shaking off any excess. Working in batches to avoid overcrowding the skillet, carefully place 4 to 6 tomato slices in the hot oil and fry until the undersides are golden brown, about 2 minutes. Flip and fry until the other sides are golden brown, about 2 minutes. (Wait until the slices get nice and crispy before flipping them over only once; if you flip them any more, the coating will fall off.)

Use tongs or a slotted spatula to transfer the fried tomatoes to the prepared baking sheet to drain. Place in the oven to keep warm and repeat the process with the remaining tomato slices.

Season with additional salt and pepper and serve warm with the dressing drizzled over the top or on the side.

fried okra

We had fried okra almost nightly at my grandmother's house during the summer. It's my mom's idea of a green vegetable, how can you fault her? It *is* green, underneath the golden, deep-fried crust. SERVES 4 TO 6

2	**pounds small, firm okra**
½	**cup well-shaken buttermilk**
1	**large egg**
	Dash of hot sauce
½	**cup yellow cornmeal**
½	**cup all-purpose flour**
	Sea salt and freshly ground black pepper
	Canola oil, for frying

Preheat the oven to 200°F. Line a rimmed baking sheet with a brown paper bag.

Rinse and drain the okra, trim the stem ends, and cut the pods crosswise into ½-inch rounds.

Place the buttermilk, egg, and hot sauce in a shallow bowl and whisk to combine. Combine the cornmeal, flour, and salt and pepper to taste in a separate shallow bowl and stir to mix.

Pour about ½ inch of canola oil into a large skillet and place over medium-high heat until sizzling hot (see Know-how, page 100). Working in batches, dip the okra into the buttermilk mixture, shake off any excess, and toss in the cornmeal mixture to coat. Separate the pieces to prevent clumping.

Carefully place the okra in the oil and fry, turning once or twice, until golden brown all over, 3 to 4 minutes. Use a slotted spoon to transfer the fried okra to the prepared baking sheet to drain. Place in the oven to keep warm and repeat the process with the remaining okra. Sprinkle with additional salt, if desired, and serve hot.

fried eggplant with sugared tabasco sauce

Anytime I go to Galotoire's, in New Orleans, I start by ordering a round of their legendary fried eggplant. The thing that makes it special—and so distinctly New Orleansian—is the strange but delicious mix of confectioners' sugar and Tabasco sauce that is served on the side, for dipping. SERVES 4 TO 6

1	large eggplant (about 2 pounds)
	Pinch of kosher salt
	Canola oil, for frying
1/2	cup well-shaken buttermilk
2	large eggs
1/2	teaspoon sea salt
1/2	teaspoon freshly ground black pepper
1/2	cup all-purpose flour
1/2	cup dried bread crumbs
1/2	cup fresh bread crumbs (see Know-how, page 134)
1/4	cup grated Parmesan cheese
	Sugared Tabasco Sauce (recipe follows), for serving

Preheat the oven to 200°F. Line a rimmed baking sheet with a brown paper bag.

Peel and cut the eggplant in half crosswise, then cut each half lengthwise into 1/2-inch-thick wedges (like French fries). Place the wedges in cold water with the kosher salt and soak for about 20 minutes; rinse and drain well.

Pour about 1/2 inch of canola oil into a large skillet and place over medium-high heat until sizzling hot (see Know-how, page 100).

Place the buttermilk, eggs, 1/4 teaspoon of the sea salt, and 1/4 teaspoon of the pepper in a shallow bowl and whisk to combine. Combine the flour, dried bread crumbs, fresh bread crumbs, Parmesan cheese, remaining 1/4 teaspoon sea salt, and remaining 1/4 teaspoon pepper in a separate shallow bowl and stir to mix.

Dip each eggplant wedge into the buttermilk mixture and dredge in the bread crumb mixture to coat evenly, shaking off any excess. Working in batches if necessary to avoid overcrowding the skillet, place the wedges in the hot oil and fry for about 3 minutes per side, until golden brown and crispy around the edges.

Use tongs or a slotted spatula to transfer the fried eggplant to the prepared baking sheet to drain. Place in the oven to keep warm and repeat the process with the remaining eggplant. Serve hot with Sugared Tabasco Sauce.

sugared tabasco sauce

MAKES ABOUT 1/3 CUP

Place about 1/4 **cup confectioners' sugar** on a small plate or bowl. Add **6 to 8 dashes of Tabasco sauce** and stir to mix and form a thick sauce. Add more hot sauce as needed or to taste.

braised cabbage

This is my standard winter vegetable side, which is so simple, comforting, and savory-sweet that I make it at least once a week during the cold months.

SERVES 4 TO 6

2	tablespoons unsalted butter
1	tablespoon olive oil
1/2	head green cabbage (about 1 1/2 pounds), cored and cut into 4 to 6 wedges
1/2	cup low-sodium chicken or vegetable broth
1	teaspoon sea salt
	Freshly ground black pepper
	Pinch of crushed red pepper flakes

Heat the butter and olive oil in a large saucepan or Dutch oven over medium-high heat until sizzling hot (see Know-how, page 100). Place the cabbage in the saucepan, cut side down, and cook for 3 to 4 minutes, until golden brown.

Pour the broth over the cabbage and sprinkle with the salt, black pepper to taste, and red pepper flakes. Cover and bring the liquid to a low boil over medium heat. Reduce the heat to a simmer and cook for about 15 minutes, until the cabbage is tender and most of the broth has evaporated. Remove from the heat and serve warm.

ON THE SIDE Braised Cabbage's mild sweetness makes it a natural partner for chicken and beef dishes, such as Brown Bag Chicken (page 136), Grilled and Roasted Fillet of Beef with Crispy Roasted Shallots (page 193), and Beer-Barbecued Brisket (page 194).

SARA'S SWAPS With the addition of carrots, potatoes, and onions, this simple dish becomes a meal in and of itself—a sort of vegetable pot-au-feu. For this variation, sauté the onions, carrots, and cabbage until tender before adding the potatoes and broth. You may need to add a little more broth. Cook until the potatoes are just tender and serve warm over Carolina Gold Rice (page 215) or, for a heartier supper, in place of the roasted vegetables with Foster Family's Pot Roast (page 199).

sweet potato casserole

This is a refined version of those marshmallow-topped sweet potato casseroles that are popular around the holidays. The crunchy, buttery streusel topping and unexpected addition of orange zest and black and cayenne peppers make for a wonderfully fragrant and complexly flavored twist on a comfort-food classic. SERVES 8 TO 10

FILLING
6	medium sweet potatoes (about 4 pounds)
1/2	cup half-and-half
1/4	cup maple syrup
2	large eggs
3	tablespoons unsalted butter
	Zest and juice of 1 orange
1	teaspoon sea salt
1/2	teaspoon freshly ground black pepper

TOPPING
1	cup chopped pecans
1/2	cup all-purpose flour
1/4	cup packed light brown sugar
5	tablespoons cold unsalted butter, cut into small pieces
	Pinch of sea salt
	Pinch of ground cayenne pepper

FILLING | Preheat the oven to 400°F.

Wrap the potatoes in foil and bake until soft to the touch, 45 to 55 minutes. Remove the foil. When cool enough to handle, slip off and discard the skins and place the potatoes in a large bowl.

Reduce the oven temperature to 350°F. Lightly grease a 2-quart casserole dish.

Add the half-and-half, maple syrup, eggs, butter, orange zest and juice, salt, and black pepper and mash with a potato masher to blend well. Spoon the mixture into the prepared baking dish.

TOPPING | Place the pecans, flour, brown sugar, butter, salt, and cayenne in a large bowl and stir to mix. Cut the butter into the flour mixture using your fingers until the mixture is crumbly and moist.

ASSEMBLY | Sprinkle the topping evenly over the potatoes and bake for about 40 minutes, until the topping is golden brown and the potatoes are bubbling around the edges. Remove from the oven and serve warm.

arugula pesto snap beans

The quick blanching process used in this superfresh salad unlocks the beans' flavors without boiling away their satisfyingly snappy crispness. As with most salads, using few, minimally processed ingredients means that the quality of each ingredient—from the oil to the greens and even the salt—plays a significant role in the quality of the finished product. Using high-quality seasonal ingredients makes this salad positively shine.

SERVES 6 TO 8

	Pinch of kosher salt
2	pounds snap beans, stem ends removed
½	cup Arugula Pesto (recipe follows) or basil pesto
¼	cup extra-virgin olive oil
4	handfuls baby arugula (about 6 cups), washed and drained
1	cup (3 ounces) freshly grated or shredded Parmesan cheese
	Sea salt and freshly ground black pepper

Bring a large saucepan of water to a boil and add the kosher salt. Prepare a large bowl of ice water and set aside.

Blanch the beans (see Know-how, page 261), cool in the ice water, and drain thoroughly (I usually blot with a paper towel to remove excess water). Chill in the refrigerator.

Whisk together the pesto and olive oil until thoroughly combined. Toss the beans in a large bowl with the arugula and ½ cup of the cheese; season with sea salt and pepper to taste. Gently mix just once to coat the beans with the pesto–olive oil mixture. Sprinkle with the remaining ½ cup cheese and serve at room temperature or refrigerate in an airtight container until ready to serve.

arugula pesto

MAKES ABOUT 1½ CUPS

4	cups firmly packed arugula, washed and drained
1	cup (3 ounces) freshly grated Parmesan cheese
½	cup slivered almonds
4	garlic cloves, smashed
1	teaspoon sea salt
½	teaspoon freshly ground black pepper
	Juice of 1 lemon
½	cup extra-virgin olive oil

Place the arugula, Parmesan cheese, almonds, garlic, salt, and pepper in a blender or food processor and pulse several times to chop. Add the lemon juice and pulse to puree. With the motor running, add the olive oil and puree until smooth. Refrigerate in an airtight container until ready to use, or for up to 1 week.

summer squash casserole

I defy you to find a covered dish supper in the South that doesn't include at least one of these golden-brown, gratinlike squash casseroles. Unassuming as it may appear, this cheesy, egg-puffed dish is possessed of a mild, sweet squash flavor and wonderfully creamy texture that wins the hearts of even the pickiest eaters. SERVES 8 TO 10

4	slices thick-cut bacon
2	tablespoons unsalted butter
3	pounds yellow summer squash, chopped
1	onion, chopped
1	cup your favorite or Homemade Mayonnaise (page 280)
1	cup (3 ounces) freshly grated Parmesan cheese
3	large eggs
3/4	cup fresh bread crumbs or cornbread crumbs (see Know-how, page 134)
6	fresh basil leaves, thinly sliced
	Sea salt and freshly ground black pepper

Preheat the oven to 350°F. Lightly grease a 2-quart casserole dish.

Fry the bacon in a large skillet over medium heat until crispy. Remove from the skillet and place on a paper towel to drain. Add the butter to the same skillet and melt over medium heat. Add the squash and onion and cook and stir for about 10 minutes, until soft and lightly brown. Remove from the heat and let cool slightly.

Combine the mayonnaise, Parmesan cheese, eggs, and ½ cup of the bread crumbs in a large bowl and whisk to combine. Add the squash mixture and basil, season with salt and pepper to taste, and stir to mix.

Spoon the casserole mixture into the prepared dish, sprinkle with the remaining ¼ cup bread crumbs, and crumble the reserved bacon on top. Bake for about 40 minutes, until bubbling around the edges, puffy, and slightly soft in the center. Remove from the oven and let sit for about 5 minutes before serving warm.

> *ON THE SIDE*   This creamy, comforting squash casserole is the vegetable equivalent of mac and cheese, and it's great with all the same things, like Beer-Barbecued Brisket (page 194), Crispy Pork Chops (page 162), and Granny Foster's Sunday Fried Chicken (page 127).

spring coleslaw with fresh herbs and light honey citrus vinaigrette

I created this delicate slaw to showcase the vegetables—curlicue pea shoots, tender carrots, spicy arugula, and fresh herbs—that mark the arrival of spring.

SERVES 8 TO 10

SLAW

1/2	**head green cabbage (about 1 1/2 pounds), cored and very thinly sliced**
2	**cups arugula, washed and drained**
2	**cups pea shoots, washed and drained**
1	**bunch small multicolored carrots or 2 large carrots, julienned**

VINAIGRETTE

1/2	**cup extra-virgin olive oil**
1/4	**cup chopped mixed fresh spring herbs, such as chives, mint, cilantro, parsley, and dill**
	Zest and juice of 1 lime
	Zest and juice of 1 lemon
1	**shallot, minced**
2	**tablespoons sherry vinegar**
1	**tablespoon honey**
	Sea salt and freshly ground black pepper

SLAW | Combine the cabbage, arugula, pea shoots, and carrots in a large bowl and toss gently to mix.

VINAIGRETTE | Combine the olive oil, herbs, lime zest and juice, lemon zest and juice, shallot, vinegar, and honey in a bowl and whisk to mix.

Pour the vinaigrette over the cabbage mixture, season with salt and pepper to taste, and toss gently to mix. Serve at room temperature or refrigerate in an airtight container until ready to serve. (If making ahead of time, wait to add the pea shoots until just before serving.)

ON THE SIDE   The bright mixture of honey and citrus in the vinaigrette makes this slaw the perfect accompaniment for mild fish, like Grilled Grouper with Heirloom Tomato Salsa (page 102) or Chicken Under a Skillet (page 139).

roxy's grated coleslaw

My friend Roxy makes this zingy coleslaw, which I love for its sweet and tangy flavors. It's as close as I come to making that classic, creamy Southern slaw that goes with everything from pulled pork or fried fish to burgers and fries. It also makes a great topping for grilled hot dogs or chicken sausages served in grilled pita bread. SERVES 6 TO 8

1	cup distilled white vinegar
1	tablespoon honey
1/2	head green cabbage (about 1 1/2 pounds), cored and grated
2	carrots, grated
2	scallions, trimmed and minced
	Sea salt and freshly ground black pepper
3/4	cup your favorite or Homemade Mayonnaise (page 280)
2	tablespoons Dijon mustard
	Pinch of ground cayenne pepper
1/4	cup chopped fresh parsley

Place the vinegar in a small saucepan over medium-high heat and boil, uncovered, until reduced by half, 3 to 4 minutes. Stir in the honey and set the mixture aside to cool.

Combine the cabbage, carrots, and scallions in a large bowl. Pour the vinegar mixture on top and toss to coat evenly. Season with salt and black pepper to taste and toss again. Refrigerate for about 20 minutes.

In a small bowl, combine the mayonnaise, mustard, and cayenne. Stir to blend, then add the parsley. Toss the mayonnaise mixture with the cabbage mixture. Taste for seasonings and adjust, if necessary. Serve chilled or refrigerate in an airtight container for up to 2 days until ready to serve.

---

chew on this: **about pole beans**

When I was growing up, my grandmother called pole beans (as well as green beans and wax beans) "snap beans" for the sound they made when you snapped them in half or crunched into one raw. I can remember many evenings spent on Granny Foster's porch trimming and halving a large colander of pole beans. As much as the flavor of the beans, that snapping sound takes me right back to my childhood.

Pole beans, which are named for their habit of climbing poles, trellises, and fences like peas, are like long, broad versions of green beans. They are tender enough to eat raw, but because they have thick, tough skin and house larger beans, require a little extra cooking. There are many varieties of pole bean, ranging from curved yellow Annelinos and curlicue Ram's Heads to big green Musicas and long Purple Peacocks, but my favorites are the full-flavored, flat Italian Romanos. Before preparing this salad, find a seat on a porch or in a yard with a bowl of rinsed beans and get snapping.

picnic-style carrot and beet salad

Southerners just love beets—perhaps because beets are one of the rare vegetables that will grow in the South straight through spring and summer and all the way into the fall. But I like to make this jewel-toned salad best in the spring, when you can get multicolor carrots, like Yellowstones, Purple Dragons, Atomic Reds, and Yayas, and beets, like Boros, Bulls' Bloods, and Candy Stripes. SERVES 4 TO 6

Combine the **zest and juice of ½ orange** with the **zest and juice of 1 lime** in a large bowl. Whisk in **½ cup extra-virgin olive oil** and season with **sea salt and freshly ground black pepper to taste.**

Add **1 pound trimmed and julienned or grated mixed beets, 2 large julienned or grated carrots,** and **1 cup flat Italian parsley or cilantro leaves.** Toss gently to mix, season with **additional salt and pepper,** and refrigerate until ready to serve.

Know-how: blanching vegetables

Blanching crispy vegetables like beans, carrots, and cauliflower is a way of flash-cooking them just long enough to unlock some of the flavor, enhance the color, and give the vegetables a nice, tender-crisp texture. It's how you make crudités, but the technique is perfect for salads, too. All you do is plunge the vegetables in boiling water, taking care not to overcrowd the pot and cool the water, just until they are bright in color and barely tender, 30 seconds to 2 minutes (the time will vary depending on the vegetable). Then, using a strainer, transfer the vegetables immediately to a large bowl of ice water to stop the cooking and lock in the bright color and crisp texture. Cool completely before straining and continuing with your recipe.

---

mixed bean salad with herb vinaigrette

Allowing the farmer's market to determine the mix of beans in this filling salad gives new meaning to the traditional "three-bean salad." Fresh beans are always a
treat, but I make this dish year-round by using canned navy, garbanzo, or cannellini beans
when fresh ones aren't available. If using canned beans, just skip the blanching step and toss
the beans with the herb vinaigrette.   SERVES 6 TO 8

SALAD

½	**pound green, Roma, or pole beans**
½	**pound French green beans**
½	**pound wax beans**
½	**pound Tongue of Fire beans**
	Pinch of kosher salt
2	**tablespoons chopped fresh parsley**
2	**tablespoons chopped fresh oregano, marjoram, or basil**

VINAIGRETTE

	Zest and juice of 1 lemon
2	**tablespoons sherry vinegar**
1	**teaspoon Dijon mustard**
1	**garlic clove, smashed and minced**
¼	**cup extra-virgin olive oil**
1	**tablespoon chopped fresh parsley**
1	**tablespoon chopped fresh chives**
	Sea salt and freshly ground black pepper

SALAD | Snap off and discard the stem ends of all the beans. Bring a large pot of water to
a boil and add the kosher salt. Prepare a large bowl of ice water and set aside.

Working with one variety at a time, blanch the beans (see Know-how, page 261), cool in the
ice water, and drain thoroughly (I usually blot with a paper towel to remove excess water). Chill in
the refrigerator. (You may need to add more ice between batches.)

Place the beans in a large bowl and add the parsley and oregano.

VINAIGRETTE | Stir together the lemon zest and juice, vinegar, mustard, and garlic in a
small bowl. Slowly whisk in the olive oil until well incorporated. Add the parsley and chives and season with salt and pepper to taste.

Pour the vinaigrette over the beans and serve at room temperature or refrigerate until ready
to serve.

pink-eyed pea and
roasted sweet potato salad

With their grassy flavor and creamy texture, pink-eyed peas subtly re-inforce the sweet earthiness of roasted sweet potatoes. As always, fresh peas are best, but in the winter you can make this dish with frozen field peas or dried or canned navy beans.

SERVES 4 TO 6

SALAD
- 3 **medium sweet potatoes (about 2 pounds), peeled and cut into 1-inch-thick wedges**
- 3 **tablespoons extra-virgin olive oil**
- 1 **tablespoon fresh thyme**
  Sea salt and freshly ground black pepper
- 2 **cups shelled fresh or frozen pink-eyed peas**
- 1 **roasted red pepper, peeled, cored, seeded, and diced (see Know-how for jalapeño peppers, page 281)**
- 1/4 **cup chopped fresh cilantro**

VINAIGRETTE
- 1/4 **cup sherry vinegar**
  Zest and juice of 1 lime
- 1 **shallot, minced**
- 1 **teaspoon sugar**
- 1/2 **cup extra-virgin olive oil**
  Sea salt and freshly ground black pepper

SALAD | Preheat the oven to 400°F.

Toss the potatoes with the olive oil, thyme, and salt and black pepper to taste. Spread in a single layer on a rimmed baking sheet and roast for 25 to 30 minutes, stirring halfway through, until tender and golden brown around the edges.

While the potatoes are roasting, bring a saucepan of water to a boil and add salt. Rinse and drain the peas, discarding any blemished peas or bits of pod. Add the peas and cook until just tender, 8 to 10 minutes. Drain, rinse until cooled completely, and drain again.

Remove the potatoes from the oven and let cool to room temperature.

Place the potatoes and peas in a large bowl, add the red pepper and cilantro, and mix.

VINAIGRETTE | Combine the vinegar, lime zest and juice, shallot, and sugar in a small bowl and stir to combine. Add the olive oil in a slow, steady stream, whisking constantly, until incorporated. Season with salt and pepper to taste.

Pour half the vinaigrette over the potato mixture and toss. Taste for seasoning, adding more vinaigrette, if desired. Serve or refrigerate in an airtight container until ready to serve.

creamy potato salad

I use buttery Yukon Gold potatoes and a sprinkling of fresh dill in my version of my mom's classic picnic-style potato salad. It's best before being refrigerated, when it's still slightly warm and extra creamy, so try to make it just before serving, if time allows. SERVES 6 TO 8

10 to 12	small Yukon Gold potatoes (about 3 pounds), halved
	Pinch of kosher salt
3	large eggs
1	cup your favorite or Homemade Mayonnaise (page 280)
2	large dill pickles or Jimmy's Dills (page 288), diced (about 1 cup)
4	celery stalks, diced
2	scallions, trimmed and diced
3	tablespoons your favorite or Sweet Pickle Relish (page 299)
2	tablespoons chopped fresh dill
1	tablespoon Worcestershire sauce
	Dash of hot sauce
	Sea salt and freshly ground black pepper

Place the potatoes in a large saucepan with enough water to cover by about 2 inches. Bring the water to a boil and add the kosher salt. Reduce the heat to a low boil and simmer for 15 to 17 minutes, until the potatoes are just tender.

Add the eggs, cover, and steam for 10 minutes more, until the potatoes are tender when pierced with the tip of a small knife. Drain the potatoes and eggs and set aside to cool slightly. Crack and peel the eggs under cold running water, then chop and place in a large bowl with the potatoes.

Add the mayonnaise, dill pickles, celery, scallions, pickle relish, dill, Worcestershire sauce, and hot sauce and season with salt and pepper to taste. Stir to combine all the ingredients, mashing some of the potatoes with a wooden spoon.

Serve slightly warm or at room temperature or refrigerate in an airtight container until ready to serve, for up to 2 days.

SARA'S SWAPS For Pesto Potato Salad, make this recipe as directed, but in place of the mayonnaise add ½ cup Arugula Pesto (page 255).

cucumber and heirloom tomato salad

This simple and refreshing salad is what I crave on especially hot summer days in North Carolina, when even the trees begin to droop and I can't bear the thought of turning on the oven. That's the only time to make it, since it's also when the tomatoes and cucumbers are at their peak and growing like weeds. Have fun mixing and matching colors and shapes using the many varieties—both familiar and strange—that you're apt to find at your local farmer's market.   SERVES 4 TO 6

6	small Kirby cucumbers (about 1 pound), sliced into ¼-inch rounds
4	heirloom tomatoes (about 2 pounds), cored and cut into a mix of wedges and chunks
	Handful fresh basil leaves (about 1 cup), torn into pieces
¼	cup white wine vinegar
¼	cup avocado oil or extra-virgin olive oil
	Juice of 1 lime
1	teaspoon sugar
	Sea salt and freshly ground black pepper

Combine the cucumbers, tomatoes, basil, vinegar, avocado oil, lime juice, sugar, and salt and pepper to taste in a large bowl and toss gently to mix. Mix only once so the tomatoes don't start to break down.

Let sit at room temperature for 10 to 20 minutes before serving so the flavors can marry. Serve at room temperature. If you want to make it ahead of time, refrigerate until ready to serve and add the tomatoes just before serving.

SARA'S SWAPS   Dress up this summer salad with a scoop of Simple Lump Crab Salad (page 111) or Deviled Ham Salad (page 11), which blend in perfectly. Or use the salad to make a great sandwich by stuffing it in toasted pita bread along with slices of shaved feta or fresh mozzarella.

watermelon-tomato salad with shaved feta and handfuls of mint

I first tried this when Bill Smith, chef of the famed Crook's Corner restaurant in Chapel Hill, North Carolina, made a similar salad for a magazine feature. I know what you're probably thinking—strange combination, right? But let me tell you, it really works. As much as I trust Bill's palate, even I was surprised by how well the mild-sweet melon and acid-sweet tomato went together. I have since made many variations using different kinds of melons, tomatoes, herbs, and cheese, but this one is my all-time favorite. SERVES 6 TO 8

3	large heirloom tomatoes (about 1½ pounds), cored and cut into chunks, or 2 cups cherry tomatoes, halved
4	cups cubed watermelon
½	cup fresh mint, roughly chopped
½	cup fresh basil, roughly chopped
2	tablespoons extra-virgin olive oil
2	tablespoons sherry vinegar
	Juice of 1 lime
	Sea salt and freshly ground black pepper
½	cup (about 2 ounces) shaved fresh feta (preferably French)
1	lime, cut into wedges

Combine the tomatoes, watermelon, mint, basil, olive oil, vinegar, lime juice, and salt and pepper to taste in a large bowl and toss to mix. Cover and refrigerate for several hours. Just before serving, sprinkle the feta over the salad and serve with lime wedges and sea salt for squeezing and sprinkling on top.

ON THE SIDE   For a tasty summer lunch or supper, pair this refreshing salad with Carolina Shrimp Chowder (page 41), Fried Oyster Po' Boy (page 118), or Beer-Barbecued Brisket (page 194).

grilled peach salad with
shaved country ham and summer herbs

Salted watermelon, cornbread, and molasses. You don't have to look far to see how much Southerners like to mix their sweet with their salty. This summery salad, featuring balsamic-glazed grilled peaches and shaved country ham tossed with fresh herbs and creamy goat cheese, is an elegant tribute to this unendingly popular flavor combination. For real Southern flavor, use sticky-sweet Georgia peaches. SERVES 4 TO 6

¼	cup plus 2 tablespoons extra-virgin olive oil
1	tablespoon balsamic vinegar
4	peaches, halved and pitted
2	ounces country ham, thinly sliced
6	cups baby arugula, washed and drained
½	cup chopped mixed fresh mint, parsley, and basil
	Juice of 1 lime
	Sea salt and freshly ground black pepper
½	cup (2 ounces) crumbled soft goat cheese

Prepare a hot fire in a charcoal or gas grill and let the coals burn to gray ash with a slight red glow; if using a gas grill, heat the grill on medium.

Combine 2 tablespoons of the olive oil with the vinegar, stir to combine, and brush the mixture on the cut sides of the peaches. Grill the peaches, cut side down, until golden-brown grill marks appear and the skins start to loosen, about 3 minutes. Remove from the grill. When cool enough to handle, peel and discard the skins, which should slip off easily.

Heat 1 tablespoon of the remaining olive oil in a cast-iron skillet over medium-high heat until sizzling hot (see Know-how, page 100). Add the ham and cook until crispy, about 2 minutes per side. Remove and drain on a paper towel or brown paper bag.

Place the arugula, herbs, remaining 3 tablespoons oil, the lime juice, and salt and pepper to taste in a large bowl and toss to mix. Chop the peaches into large chunks or quarters and add to the salad, tossing to mix. Transfer the salad to a large serving platter or individual serving plates. Break the ham into large pieces and scatter on top. Sprinkle evenly with the goat cheese and serve at room temperature.

Know-how: cooking with cast iron on the grill

Given that you'll already be firing up the grill to cook the peaches, there's no need to go inside to cook the ham. Just treat the grill like a cooktop. For high heat, place a cast-iron skillet directly over the hot coals; for a slightly cooler cooking temperature, move it off to the side, away from the coals.

---

tomato aspic

Delicate and shimmering red, molded tomato aspics are the stuff of ladies' luncheons and afternoon teas, circa 1950. But when fresh tomatoes, garlic, and herbs step in for canned tomato juice, this old-school dish is transformed into a modern summertime must. Serve topped with a creamy dollop of Homemade Mayonnaise (page 280) or Buttermilk Green Goddess Dressing (page 284). MAKES EIGHT TO TEN 8-OUNCE SERVINGS

4	pounds tomatoes (about 8), cored and quartered
1	onion, chopped
4	celery stalks, chopped
4	bay leaves
4	garlic cloves, smashed
5	whole cloves
3/4	cup water
	Zest and juice of 1 lemon
1	tablespoon sugar
1	tablespoon balsamic vinegar
1	sprig fresh basil
	Sea salt and freshly ground black pepper
2	tablespoons unflavored gelatin

Lightly grease eight to ten 8-ounce individual molds or custard cups.

Place the tomatoes, onion, celery, bay leaves, garlic, and cloves in a large saucepan with ½ cup of the water and stir to mix. Bring to a low boil and simmer for about 30 minutes, stirring occasionally and skimming the rising foam as needed. Remove from the heat and strain, discarding the bay leaves and cloves, then pushing the pulp through a sieve to make 4 to 5 cups of juice. Add the lemon zest and juice, sugar, vinegar, basil, and salt and pepper to taste and stir to combine.

Return the juice to the saucepan, bring to a boil, and reduce by about 2 cups, about 10 minutes. Reduce heat to a low boil. Fill a large bowl with ice water. Combine the gelatin with the remaining ¼ cup water in a large bowl and stir to mix. Pour the hot juice over the gelatin mixture and stir until the gelatin dissolves. Remove the basil and place the pan of juice in the water bath to fully cool, stirring regularly for even coloring and texture.

Divide the mixture evenly between the prepared molds, cover, and refrigerate for at least 4 hours or overnight, until the aspic sets up and is firm.

To unmold the aspics, run a knife around the outside edge of the molds and set in a pan of warm water for 15 to 20 seconds to loosen. Invert onto a plate or platter and serve or refrigerate until ready to serve.

dressings, pickles, and condiments

In the South, there are really just two kinds of foods:

condiments, and the edible vessels on which they are served. After all, hickory-smoked pig isn't complete without barbecue sauce, just as stewed greens need hot pepper vinegar, biscuits call out for butter and jam, deviled eggs require sweet pickle relish, and a fried egg sandwich demands a healthy dose of mayonnaise or chili sauce. And those are just the basics.

Piquant relishes, sweet and savory jams, hot and tangy pickles—these are what elevate a simple dish of beans and rice or grilled chicken from a potentially dreary weeknight meal to something bursting with bright, zippy flavor, lots of punchy color, and perhaps a bit of whimsy. Condiments, dressings, and pickles are what truly make the plate.

The Southern fixation with "fixin's" has a lot to do with the region's agrarian background and the seasonal rhythms that go along with it. The various methods of pickling, preserving, and canning allowed Southerners to essentially capture summer and all its plenty in a jar, to be opened again in the lean winter months. Of course, this sort of food preservation is now a hobby rather than a necessity, but you wouldn't know it by the way Southerners continue to adorn their food.

This preference for condiments was certainly true in my family. In fact, the largest source of inspiration for this chapter was my grandmother's recipe book and its many recipe cards scrawled in her hand and those of her friends and family. What amazes me is how many of the recipes in her book, which contains a lifetime of cooking, are devoted to sauces, condiments, flavorful "extras," and finishing touches.

No doubt about it, homemade pickles and preserves are possessed of a homey sort of magic. Unfortunately, that mysterious quality sometimes misleads folks into believing they are difficult to make; thankfully nothing could be further from the truth. In fact, for many of these recipes, canning is optional, thus making them even faster and easier. Taken together, these recipes prove that if you've got a little time, condiments, dressings, and pickles are as simple as can be—and the payoff is huge.

homemade mayonnaise

I take a cue from Granny Foster and make it a practice always to keep a jar of homemade mayonnaise in the fridge. Once you realize how easy it is to make—and how much richer the flavor—you'll never go back. After you've made this basic mayo, you can use it to create a plethora of easy dipping sauces and spreads simply by blending in flavorful herbs, spices, and relishes. MAKES ABOUT 2 CUPS

2	large egg yolks
2	cups canola oil
	Juice and zest of 1 lemon
2	teaspoons distilled white vinegar
1	teaspoon Colman's dry mustard
	Pinch of ground cayenne pepper
	Pinch of ground paprika
	Sea salt and freshly ground black pepper
1	teaspoon hot water

Place the yolks in a large bowl and slowly whisk in 1 tablespoon of the canola oil. Slowly drizzle 1 cup of the remaining oil into the eggs, about 1 tablespoon at a time, whisking constantly.

Continue to whisk, alternating additions of the lemon juice and vinegar with the remaining oil, until all the oil has been added. Add the lemon zest, mustard, cayenne, paprika, and salt and black pepper to taste and continue to whisk until the mayonnaise is thick. This can also be done in a food processor or blender. Whisk in the hot water and refrigerate in an airtight container until ready to use, or for up to 1 week.

quick basil mayo

This simple, basil-spiked mayo is one of my favorite variations on the basic recipe. It's an easy way to add creamy pesto flavor to sandwiches and dips. MAKES ABOUT 1 CUP

Place **1 cup your favorite or Homemade Mayonnaise (recipe above)** in a blender or food processor. Add **8 to 10 fresh basil leaves, sea salt and freshly ground black pepper to taste,** and a **squeeze of fresh lemon juice** and puree until smooth. Refrigerate in an airtight container until ready to use, or for up to 1 week.

roasted jalapeño mayonnaise

In this variation, the smoky spice of roasted jalapeño combines with the brightness of fresh herbs to form a creamy spread that adds new dimension to dishes like Fried Oyster Po' Boys (page 118) and Squash Puppies (page 65). MAKES ABOUT 2 CUPS

Place **1 cup your favorite or Homemade Mayonnaise (page 280)** in a blender or food processor. Add **3 roasted jalapeño peppers (see Know-how, below), ½ cup fresh cilantro, 1 trimmed and chopped scallion, 2 smashed garlic cloves, juice of 1 lime, 6 fresh basil leaves,** and **sea salt and freshly ground black pepper to taste** and puree until smooth. Refrigerate in an airtight container until ready to use, or for up to 1 week.

SARA'S SWAPS Homemade Mayonnaise adds rich flavor to everything from fried egg sandwiches to Simple Lump Crab Salad (page 111). But you can easily create your own variations by matching mayo mix-ins to whatever you are preparing. For example, Fried Green Tomato BLTs (page 79) and basic deli-meat sandwiches come alive with a layer of Arugula Pesto (page 255), roasted garlic (see Know-how, page 186), or chipotle-infused mayonnaise, and a swirl of chili sauce makes a creamy-hot dip that plays well with everything from Fried Okra (page 250) to Crispy Fried Oysters Four Ways (page 117).

Know-how: *roasting jalapeño peppers*

When roasted, jalapeño peppers acquire a deep smoky flavor that can't be beat. Arrange whole jalapeño peppers in a cast-iron skillet or rimmed baking sheet and drizzle with olive oil (about 1 tablespoon for every 3 peppers). Roast in a preheated 400°F oven for about 20 minutes, until the skin is blistered and slightly brown. Remove from the oven and set aside. When the peppers are cool enough to handle, peel them, discard the skin, seeds, and core, and proceed with the recipe.

phyllis's comeback sauce

This creamy, tangy descendant of Thousand Island and remoulade origi-
nated in the Greek restaurants of Jackson, Mississippi. From there it spread like wildfire to
every salad, burger, fried fish, and French fry in the surrounding five counties and beyond.
Most anything edible makes an acceptable receptacle for my friend Phyllis's version.   MAKES
ABOUT 2 CUPS

1	cup your favorite or Homemade Mayonnaise (page 280)
1/2	cup ketchup
1/2	cup chili sauce
2	tablespoons grated onion
2	tablespoons Worcestershire sauce
	Juice of 1 lemon
1	tablespoon white wine vinegar
1	tablespoon ground sweet paprika
2	garlic cloves, smashed and minced
2	teaspoons Colman's dry mustard
	Sea salt and freshly ground black pepper

Combine the mayonnaise, ketchup, chili sauce, onion, Worcestershire sauce, lemon juice, vinegar, paprika, garlic, and mustard in a bowl and whisk to mix well. Season with salt and pepper to
taste and refrigerate in an airtight container until ready to use, or for up to 4 days.

everyday mustard vinaigrette

I grew up eating most salads with Italian dressing or plain old oil and vinegar, which was the closest I came to vinaigrette. But now I can't live without vinaigrettes; they're so easy and flavorful. Here is one of my favorites, which I often make with the dregs from a jar of mustard that would otherwise have been thrown away.   MAKES ABOUT 1 CUP

Place **3 tablespoons red wine vinegar,** the **juice of 1 lemon, 2 teaspoons Dijon mustard,** and **1 smashed and minced garlic clove** in a jar with a tight-fitting lid and shake to mix. Add about **½ cup extra-virgin olive oil, plus more to taste,** season with **sea salt and freshly ground black pepper to taste,** and shake to combine the ingredients. Season with **fresh herbs to your liking** and drizzle over salad or grilled chicken or fish. Refrigerate in an airtight container until ready to use, or for up to 1 week.

Know-how: mixing dressing in a jar

I often mix vinaigrettes like this one in a glass jar with a tight-fitting lid. Dump in all the ingredients, screw on the lid, and shake to mix. That way, your vinaigrette is ready in a flash and already in the perfect storage container.

---

spicy cocktail sauce

MAKES ABOUT 2¼ CUPS

2	**cups ketchup**
¼	**cup prepared horseradish**
	Juice of 1 lemon
2	**tablespoons Worcestershire sauce**
	Pinch of ground cayenne pepper
	Sea salt and freshly ground black pepper

Stir together the ketchup, horseradish, lemon juice, Worcestershire sauce, and cayenne in a small bowl. Season to taste with salt and black pepper and serve or refrigerate in an airtight container for up to 1 week.

buttermilk green goddess dressing

A classic of the West Coast, this dressing was created in the 1920s by San Francisco's Palace Hotel in honor of a play by the same name. With buttermilk standing in for sour cream, my "Southern" version is light, tangy, and chock-full of green herbs. It's the quintessential spring and summer dressing, and because it's all about using the freshest herbs—whether dill, chervil, sorrel, or cilantro—I almost never make it the same way twice.

MAKES ABOUT 1 CUP

½	cup well-shaken buttermilk
¼	cup your favorite or Homemade Mayonnaise (page 280)
1	small Kirby cucumber, peeled and chopped
2	tablespoons chopped fresh chives
2	tablespoons chopped fresh tarragon
2	teaspoons Dijon mustard
	Juice of ½ lime
4 or 5	fresh basil or celery leaves
	Sea salt and freshly ground black pepper

Place the buttermilk, mayonnaise, cucumber, chives, tarragon, mustard, lime juice, and basil in a blender and puree until smooth. Season with salt and pepper to taste. Refrigerate in an airtight container until ready to use, or for up to 1 week.

SARA'S SWAPS Think of this dressing as a backdrop for whatever herbs and light greens are in season. Herbs like dill, oregano, marjoram, thyme, and parsley add personality and flavor while spinach adds a pop of green; peppery arugula and watercress add delicate heat; and lemony sorrel is refreshingly tart. To make an even lighter version, substitute plain low-fat yogurt for the mayonnaise.

buttermilk blue cheese dressing

On a recent visit to South Carolina, I was lucky enough to visit Clemson University to try some of its famous blue cheese. The university first started making its tangy, marbled cheese in the 1940s, when a dairy professor realized that the cool, dank tunnel of an unfinished local railway line would make the perfect curing environment. Although the operations have since moved indoors, Clemson continues to make its Roquefort-style cheese in small batches using the same artisanal methods (see Sources, page 377). At the campus cafes, you can try everything from blue cheese pizza to blue cheese milkshakes. This rich, creamy dressing was inspired by the flavor of Clemson blue cheese—but in a pinch, any Roquefort-style cheese will do.   MAKES ABOUT 2 CUPS

1	cup (4 ounces) crumbled blue cheese
3	tablespoons sherry vinegar
1	small shallot, minced
3/4	cup well-shaken buttermilk
1/4	cup your favorite or Homemade Mayonnaise (page 280)
1/4	cup Greek yogurt
1	tablespoon chopped fresh chives
1	teaspoon dried marjoram or basil
	Sea salt and freshly ground black pepper

Place the blue cheese, vinegar, and shallot in a small bowl and mash the cheese into the vinegar with the back of a fork to blend. Whisk in the buttermilk, mayonnaise, yogurt, chives, and marjoram until well combined. Season with salt and pepper to taste and refrigerate in an airtight container until ready to use, or for up to 1 week.

ON THE SIDE Re-create classic sports bar flavors by serving this thick, piquant dressing as a cooling dipping sauce for barbecued chicken and fresh celery, cucumber, and carrot sticks. It's also great drizzled over a wedge of crisp iceberg or Bibb lettuce.

quick cucumber pickles

Many Southerners keep a steady supply of no-fuss cucumber pickles like these in the fridge all through the summer. They're great because you don't even have to turn on the stove: just toss everything together, let it all marinate for a few hours, and you're good to go. Mild and crunchy, they are sort of a cross between cucumber salad and dill pickles, meaning they're perfect scattered over a simple green salad with Buttermilk Green Goddess Dressing (page 284), layered in Pimiento Cheese Burgers (page 187) or Pickled Jalapeño Meatloaf (page 191) sandwiches, or placed in a little dish and added to a relish tray.

MAKES ABOUT 1 PINT

1/3	cup distilled white vinegar
1/2	cup water
	Zest and juice of 1 lemon
3 or 4	sprigs fresh dill
2	tablespoons sugar
1	1-inch piece julienned fresh ginger
1	teaspoon yellow mustard seeds
1	teaspoon coriander seeds
1	teaspoon kosher salt
1/2	teaspoon freshly ground black pepper
	Pinch of crushed red pepper flakes
3 or 4	Kirby or other small cucumbers (about 1/2 pound), partially peeled to create a striped pattern and sliced into thin rounds
1	thin slice red onion

Combine the vinegar, water, lemon zest and juice, dill, sugar, ginger, mustard seeds, coriander seeds, salt, black pepper, and red pepper flakes in a bowl or glass jar and stir to mix until the sugar dissolves. Add the cucumbers and onion and toss or shake to mix and submerge the cucumbers in the liquid.

Cover and refrigerate for 4 hours or overnight to allow the flavors to develop before serving. The pickles will keep in the refrigerator for up to 1 month.

SARA'S SWAPS You can use this basic recipe to make all kinds of fast and fresh refrigerator pickles using anything from summer squash, peppers, beets, and turnips to radishes, carrots, and onions.

jimmy's dills

My dad's crunchy, garlicky dills accompanied the majority of the sandwiches I ate as a child. They were perfectly crisp every time—that satisfying snapping sound accompanying each bite was one of the best things about them—a feat my dad achieved simply by using small, firm, freshly picked cucumbers. Try to pick cucumbers that are already short enough to fit easily in the jar, about 4 inches long for pint jars. Or, for unexpected shape, taste, and color, make them using round yellow lemon cucumbers cut into wedges.

MAKES 6 PINTS

20 to 22	small Kirby cucumbers (about 3½ pounds)
12	sprigs fresh dill
12	small chile peppers
12	garlic cloves
4	cups distilled white vinegar
2	cups water
⅓	cup kosher salt
2	tablespoons sugar
2	teaspoons dill seeds
3	bay leaves
10	whole black peppercorns
10	whole cloves

Rinse the cucumbers, drain, and trim and slice each lengthwise into 4 wedges. If preserving the pickles, sterilize six 1-pint heat-tempered canning jars (see Know-how, page 291).

To each jar, add 2 dill sprigs, 2 chile peppers, and 2 garlic cloves. Tightly pack the cucumber wedges in the hot jars, leaving about ½ inch of headspace to ensure a proper seal.

Combine the vinegar, water, salt, sugar, dill seeds, bay leaves, peppercorns, and cloves in a large pot and bring to a boil, stirring until the sugar dissolves, about 1 minute.

Pour the hot liquid over the cucumbers, maintaining the ½-inch headspace.

For refrigerator pickles, seal the jars tightly and cool to room temperature. Refrigerate for 2 weeks to allow the flavors to develop before serving. Store in the refrigerator until ready to serve, or for up to 1 month.

For preserved pickles, process in a hot water bath for about 20 minutes to vacuum-seal (see Know-how, page 291). Let cool to room temperature, check the seal, and store in a cool, dark place for at least 2 weeks to allow the flavors to develop before serving, or for up to 6 months. Refrigerate after opening.

granny foster's bread and butter pickles

The perfect combination of sweet and tart, thinly sliced bread and butter pickles are the quintessential all-purpose sandwich toppers, delivering lots of big, punchy flavor in a small package. They make such a satisfyingly crunchy snack that—if you're anything like me—you'll soon graduate from layering them in sandwiches to munching them straight from the jar. MAKES ABOUT 6 PINTS

20 to 22	small Kirby cucumbers (about 3½ pounds), cut into ¼-inch slices
1	onion, thinly sliced
¼	cup kosher salt
2	garlic cloves
4	cups apple cider vinegar
3½	cups sugar
2	tablespoons mustard seeds
2	teaspoons celery seeds
1½	teaspoons ground turmeric

Place the cucumbers and onion in a large bowl with the salt and garlic. Cover with ice and toss to mix. Let stand for 3 hours to crisp, then drain well, removing any ice that has not yet melted. Do not rinse.

If preserving the pickles, sterilize six 1-pint heat-tempered canning jars (see Know-how, page 291).

Combine the vinegar, sugar, mustard seeds, celery seeds, and turmeric in a large pot and bring to a boil over medium-high heat. Cook and stir until the sugar dissolves. Add the cucumbers, onion, and garlic, bring back to a boil, and remove immediately from the heat.

For refrigerator pickles, refrigerate in airtight containers for two weeks to allow flavors to develop, or for up to 1 month.

For preserved pickles, pack in the sterilized jars, leaving ½ inch of headspace, and process in a hot water bath for about 10 minutes to vacuum-seal (see Know-how, page 291). Let cool to room temperature, check the seal, and store in a cool, dark place for 2 weeks to allow flavors to develop before serving, or for up to 6 months. Refrigerate after opening.

---

chew on this: *about pickling cucumbers*

Pickling cucumbers are firm-fleshed, small-seeded varieties that hold up especially well to pickling, meaning they keep their crunch, and they are the ones I recommend using; some of the most common varieties are Kirbys and gherkins. When selecting the cucumbers, make sure they are no longer than the jars you are putting them in; for pint jars they should be 4½ to 5 inches or less. If your cucumbers are larger, use quart jars or trim the ends.

Know-how: putting up the summer

There is something so rewarding about opening up a jar of Sour Cherry Preserves (page 304) or Green Tomato Chow-Chow (page 300) long after the berries and tomatoes of summer have given way to winter. Happily, making your own preserves is really very easy. All you need to get started are a few inexpensive pieces of equipment and an understanding of a few basic techniques. Here's everything you need to know:

EQUIPMENT

- 1 or 2 large, heavy nonreactive metal pots

- Sterile, heat-tempered glass canning jars, such as Ball or Kerr brand, plus an equal number of lids and rings.

- Tongs, for lifting the jars out of the water bath

- Funnel, for cleanly filling jars

- Canning rack, for loading jars securely in the water bath

- Magnetic lid lifter, to lift sterilized lids without touching them

Scald or sterilize the jars

The first step in canning is always to sterilize or scald the jars (including the lids and rings) in which the food will be stored. This ensures a safe, clean environment and minimizes the risk of spoilage or bacterial growth. This step is especially important if the recipe calls for processing in a water bath for less than 10 minutes. To sterilize, place the jars, lids, and rings in a large pot, cover with water, and boil for 10 to 15 minutes. Turn off the heat and leave the jars in the pot, covered, until ready to fill.

Pack the jars

- Drain and carefully fill the hot jars according to the recipe, taking care not to touch the rims or interiors with your bare hands. Use a funnel if possible.

- When filling the jars with raw vegetables, such as cucumbers, to make pickles, pack the vegetables as tightly as possible, pressing down with your fingers as you fill the jars.

- If making pickles in a brine, be sure the vegetables are completely covered with the pickling liquid.

- Make sure to leave the headspace recommended in the recipe (typically ¼ to ½ inch, depending on the acidity of the food); this ensures the jars seal properly.

- Remove any air bubbles before sealing by tapping each jar on the counter a few times or stirring with a sterilized spoon or chopstick.

- Wipe the rims using a clean cloth, place the lids on the jars, and screw on the rings until secure but not fully tightened.

(continued)

Process using the "hot pack" method

This is the method I use when making jams, fruit preserves, and chutneys.

- Pack the jars as noted above.

- The jam, preserves, or chutney should be boiling when packed in the hot, sterilized jars. This is key to ensuring that the jars seal correctly.

- Place the sterilized lids on the jars and screw on the rings until secure but not fully tightened.

- Invert the closed jars for about 2 minutes and then turn them upright (this allows the hot liquid to soften the rubber on the lid, thus ensuring a tight seal).

Process in a water bath

This is the method I use to preserve pickles and relishes.

- Always bring the water bath to a good rolling boil before you begin. Reduce the heat and keep it at a simmer after the filled jars have been added; rapidly boiling water may cause water to leak into the jars.

- Using tongs or a canning rack, carefully lower the jars into the boiling water until fully submerged, making sure they are not touching. Cover and simmer according to the recipe (typically 10 to 20 minutes, depending on what you are processing).

- You may need to adjust the cooking time for altitude. For altitudes between 1,000 and 6,000 feet, add 5 minutes; between 6,000 and 12,000 feet, add 10 minutes.

- When you are done processing, turn off the heat and let the jars sit in the water for another 5 minutes.

- Remove the jars from the water and let sit undisturbed until completely cool, about 5 hours or overnight. As the jars cool down you should be able to hear the lids popping, a sign that they are sealing correctly.

- When the jars have cooled completely, tighten the rings all the way.

Check the seal

- Check the seal on each lid. If sealed properly, the center will be slightly depressed and will not "pop" when pressed.

- If any of the lids haven't sealed, store those jars in the refrigerator for up to 1 to 2 months and use first.

Store

- Using labels or a permanent marker, clearly mark the jars with the packing date.

- Store in a cool, dark place until ready to use. Most perserves will keep for 6 months to 1 year. Refrigerate after opening and use within 1 to 2 months.

---

dilly snap beans

My dad used to make these crisp and vinegary dilly beans every summer, in those fleeting moments between the time the bean bushes bear fruit and the grazing deer eat their fill. My sister has since taken over this tradition, and the few precious jars she gives us each year are worth their weight in gold. MAKES ABOUT 6 PINTS

12	small chile peppers
12	sprigs fresh dill
12	garlic cloves, smashed
12	whole cloves
1/4	cup dill seeds
1/4	cup mustard seeds
1/4	cup kosher salt
3	pounds green beans or mixed beans, such as wax beans, haricots verts, and pole beans, stem ends trimmed to fit the jars
5	cups apple cider vinegar
5	cups water

If preserving the beans, sterilize six 1-pint heat-tempered canning jars (see Know-how, page 291).

To each jar, add 2 chile peppers, 2 dill sprigs, 2 garlic cloves, 2 whole cloves, and 2 teaspoons each of the dill seeds, mustard seeds, and salt.

Tightly pack the beans in the hot jars, leaving about ½ inch of headspace to ensure a proper seal.

Combine the vinegar and water in a large saucepan over high heat and bring to a boil. Pour the hot liquid over the beans, maintaining the ½-inch headspace.

For refrigerator pickles, seal the jars tightly and refrigerate for 2 weeks to allow the flavors to develop before serving. Store in the refrigerator until ready to serve, or for up to 1 month.

For preserved pickles, process in a hot water bath for about 15 minutes to vacuum-seal (see Know-how, page 291). Let cool to room temperature, check the seal, and store in a cool, dark place for at least 2 weeks to allow the flavors to develop before serving, or for up to 6 months. Refrigerate after opening.

judy's pickled squash

Once you start making them, you begin to see pickle potential in just about everything. That—and an overabundance of fast-growing yellow squash—is what inspired my sister, Judy, to make these unusually gratifying sweet squash pickles. I call for yellow squash here, but you can use any kind of summer squash, from Sundrops and pattypans to zucchini.

MAKES ABOUT 4 PINTS

2	pounds small yellow or other summer squash, sliced into ¼-inch rounds
1	onion, thinly sliced
2	red or green bell peppers, cored, seeded and chopped
2	tablespoons kosher salt
3	cups sugar
2½	cups apple cider vinegar
2	teaspoons mustard seeds
2	teaspoons celery seeds

Place the squash, onion, and bell peppers in a colander, sprinkle with salt, and let drain, covered, for about 1 hour at room temperature. Do not rinse.

If preserving the pickles, sterilize four 1-pint heat-tempered canning jars (see Know-how, page 291).

Tightly pack the squash, onion, and peppers, alternating layers of vegetables, in the hot jars, leaving about ½ inch of headspace to ensure a proper seal.

Combine the sugar, vinegar, mustard seeds, and celery seeds in a large pot over high heat and bring to a boil, stirring until the sugar dissolves, for about 1 minute. Pour the hot liquid over the vegetables, maintaining the ½-inch headspace.

For refrigerator pickles, seal the jars tightly and refrigerate for 2 weeks to allow the flavors to develop before serving. Store in the refrigerator until ready to serve, or for up to 1 month.

For preserved pickles, process in a hot water bath for about 15 minutes to vacuum-seal (see Know-how, page 291). Let cool to room temperature, check the seal, and store in a cool, dark place until ready to serve, or for up to 6 months. Refrigerate after opening.

summer corn relish

This tangy relish, which packs enough flavor to play a starring role on any plate, showcases the sugary sweetness of fresh summer corn. For a light and easy supper, spoon it over Chicken Under a Skillet (page 139) or Grilled Grouper with Heirloom Tomato Salsa (page 102). MAKES ABOUT 2½ PINTS

8	ears corn, shucked
1	red bell pepper, cored, seeded, and diced
½	small red onion, minced
½	cup apple cider vinegar
¼	cup sugar
6	sprigs fresh thyme
1	tablespoon minced fresh ginger
2	garlic cloves, smashed and minced
2	bay leaves
2	teaspoons kosher salt
1	teaspoon yellow mustard seeds
¼	teaspoon mixed whole peppercorns

Cut the corn from the cobs into a large bowl using a sharp knife and scrape the stripped cobs with the back of the knife to release the juices.

Place the corn, bell pepper, onion, vinegar, sugar, thyme, ginger, garlic, bay leaves, salt, mustard seeds, and peppercorns in a saucepan, stir to mix, and bring to a simmer over medium-high heat. Cook and stir for about 3 minutes, until the corn is just lightly cooked but still a little crunchy. Remove from the heat and let cool slightly.

Refrigerate in airtight containers until ready to serve, or for up to 1 week. Remove and discard bay leaves before serving.

ON THE SIDE   For fun and easy entertaining, use the many pickles and relishes in this chapter to put together the ultimate Southern relish tray, complete with cheese and crackers (like a sort of Southern antipasto). Here is a suggested menu to get you started:
• Judy's Pickled Squash (page 394) • Pickled Okra (page 298) or Dilly Snap Beans (page 293) • Quick Cucumber Pickles (page 287), Jimmy's Dills (page 288), or Granny Foster's Bread and Butter Pickles (page 290) • A scoop of Pimiento Cheese (page 18) with Rosemary Cheese Crackers (page 8) • Herb Deviled Eggs (page 10).

pickled okra

Crunchy, juicy, and vinegary, pickled okra is good enough to eat all by itself, but it also makes a handsome garnish for Wendy's Bloody Marys (page 28), Herb Deviled Eggs (page 10), or antipasto platters. MAKES ABOUT 6 PINTS

12	small chile peppers
12	sprigs fresh dill
12	garlic cloves
2	carrots, halved crosswise and quartered lengthwise (for a total of 16 wedges)
1	tablespoon dill seeds
4½	pounds small okra, stems trimmed to fit the jars
6	cups distilled white vinegar
3	cups water
½	cup kosher salt

If preserving the okra, sterilize six 1-pint heat-tempered canning jars (see Know-how, page 291).

To each jar, add 2 chile peppers, 2 dill sprigs, 2 garlic cloves, 2 or 3 carrot sticks, and ½ teaspoon of the dill seeds. Tightly pack the okra in the hot jars, leaving about ½ inch of headspace to ensure a proper seal.

Combine the vinegar, water, and salt in a large saucepan and bring to a boil, stirring to dissolve the salt. Pour the hot liquid over the okra, maintaining the ½-inch headspace.

For refrigerator pickles, seal the jars tightly and refrigerate for 2 weeks to allow the flavors to develop before serving. Store in the refrigerator until ready to serve, or for up to 1 month.

For preserved pickles, process in a hot water bath for about 20 minutes to vacuum-seal (see Know-how, page 291). Let cool to room temperature, check the seal, and store in a cool, dark place for at least 2 weeks to allow the flavors to develop before serving, or for up to 6 months. Refrigerate after opening.

SARA'S SWAPS Give vodka or gin dirty martinis (shaken, not stirred) a Southern twang by adding a splash of pickled okra brine in place of olive brine and garnishing each with 1 or 2 spears of pickled okra.

sweet pickle relish

I give my version of classic pickle relish a twist by using green tomatoes and cabbage rather than the usual cucumbers.   MAKES ABOUT 6 PINTS

5	pounds green tomatoes, cored
2	onions (about 1 pound)
1/2	head cabbage, cored
3 1/4	cups sugar
1/4	cup kosher salt
4	cups distilled white vinegar
1	tablespoon pickling spices
1	teaspoon whole black peppercorns
1	teaspoon dry mustard
1	teaspoon whole cloves

Grate the tomatoes, onions, and cabbage on a box grater or in a food processor using the grating disk. Place the vegetables in a colander over a large bowl and mix in 1/4 cup of the sugar and the salt. Cover, refrigerate, and let drain overnight.

If preserving the relish, sterilize six 1-pint heat-tempered canning jars (see Know-how, page 291).

Transfer the grated vegetables to a large pot and add the vinegar, remaining 3 cups sugar, the pickling spices, peppercorns, mustard, and cloves. Stir to mix and bring to a boil. Reduce the heat to low and simmer for 20 minutes. Remove from the heat.

For refrigerator relish, let cool slightly and refrigerate in airtight containers until ready to serve, or for up to 1 month.

For preserved relish, pack the hot relish in the sterilized jars, leaving about 1/2 inch of headspace to ensure a proper seal, and process in a hot water bath for about 20 minutes to vacuum-seal (see Know-how, page 291). Let cool to room temperature, check the seal, and store in a cool, dark place until ready to serve, or for up to 6 months. Refrigerate after opening.

green tomato chow-chow

This traditional mixed-vegetable relish, which usually features some combination of cabbage, tomatoes, peppers, and onion, is like a Southern version of sauerkraut or Korean kimchi. It has its origins in Appalachia, where big, crisp heads of cabbage thrive in the cooler mountain climate. It's typically served on stewed beans and rice, but it is excellent, too, on hot dogs and barbecue sandwiches. This version, which features the bright, tart flavor of green tomatoes, comes from an old recipe in my grandmother's collection—so old that it called for "5 cents' worth of celery seeds." MAKES ABOUT 4 PINTS

5	pounds green tomatoes, cored and roughly chopped
2	yellow onions, quartered
2	green bell peppers, cored, seeded, and quartered
2	cups sugar
1	cup apple cider vinegar
2	small chile peppers, cored and seeded
2	tablespoons kosher salt
2	tablespoons yellow mustard seeds
1	tablespoon celery seeds
1	tablespoon pickling spices
1	tablespoon whole cloves

Grate the tomatoes, onions, and bell peppers on a box grater or in a food processor using the grating disk.

Transfer the grated vegetables to a large nonreactive saucepan and add the sugar, vinegar, chile peppers, salt, mustard seeds, celery seeds, pickling spices, and cloves and stir to mix. Bring to a low boil over medium heat, skimming the rising foam as needed. Cook, stirring often, until thick, about 45 minutes. Remove from the heat. If preserving the relish, sterilize four 1-pint heat-tempered canning jars (see Know-how, page 291).

For refrigerator relish, let cool slightly and refrigerate in airtight containers until ready to serve, or for up to 2 months.

For preserved relish, pack the hot relish in the sterilized jars, leaving about ½ inch of headspace to ensure a proper seal, and process in a hot water bath for 20 minutes to vacuum-seal (see Know-how, page 291). Let cool to room temperature, check the seal, and store in a cool, dark place until ready to serve, or for up to 6 months. Refrigerate after opening.

brandied figs

In the summer, I like nothing better than to stand in the shade of my big, old fig tree and pluck the ripe fruit to a humming chorus of bees and scavenging birds. Figs are so short-lived—in terms of both season and shelf life—that you have to act quickly to enjoy them at all, so I always feel like I've done well when I come away with a jar or two of jam. A nip or three of brandy gives this version a smoky, complex flavor.   MAKES 4 PINTS

If preserving the figs, sterilize four 1-pint heat-tempered canning jars (see Know-how, page 291).

Rinse and drain **2 pounds firm ripe fresh figs** and trim the stem ends.

Place **2 cups sugar, 2 cups brandy, 1 cup water, ¼ cup balsamic vinegar, 1 tablespoon whole cloves,** a **pinch of kosher salt,** and the **juice of 1 lemon** in a large pot over medium heat and bring to a boil. Boil for about 5 minutes, stirring occasionally, until the sugar dissolves and the mixture begins to get syrupy.

Add the figs, reduce the heat to a simmer, and continue to cook for 5 minutes longer.

For refrigerator figs, pack in airtight containers and refrigerate until ready to serve, or for up to 1 month.

For preserved figs, pack the hot figs and their syrup in the sterilized jars and seal using the hot-pack method (see Know-how, page 291). Let cool to room temperature, check the seal, and store in a cool, dark place until ready to serve, or for up to 6 months. Refrigerate after opening.

ON THE SIDE   Brandied figs make a sophisticated topper for everything from vanilla ice cream, to Buttermilk Panna Cotta (page 358), to Granny Foster's Simple Pound Cake (page 314), to Carolina Rice Pudding Brûlée (page 357), to Buttermilk Waffles (page 91).

tomato jam

Whenever I'm at the market during tomato season, I keep my eyes peeled for what the farmers call "ugly tomatoes." You can buy them for a song because they're bruised, misshapen, or ripe to the point of bursting, but that makes them perfect for canning or cooking. This sweet and savory tomato jam, which is equally at home on toast for breakfast or on a baguette with fresh mozzarella and baby greens for lunch, is one of my standards.

MAKES ABOUT 2 PINTS

2	tablespoons olive oil
1	onion, chopped
2	garlic cloves, smashed and minced
3	pounds tomatoes, cored and chopped
2/3	cup unpacked light brown sugar
1/4	cup apple cider vinegar
	Zest and juice of 1 orange
2	tablespoons grated fresh ginger
1	tablespoon fresh thyme
1	small chile pepper, cored and minced
2	teaspoons crushed red pepper flakes
2	teaspoons sea salt
1/2	teaspoon freshly ground black pepper
4	whole cloves

Heat the olive oil in a nonreactive saucepan over medium heat until hot. Add the onion and cook and stir for about 5 minutes, until soft and golden. Add the garlic and cook and stir for 1 minute more. Add the tomatoes, brown sugar, vinegar, orange zest and juice, ginger, thyme, chile pepper, red pepper flakes, salt, black pepper, and cloves and stir to mix.

Bring the mixture to a boil, reduce the heat to a low boil, and simmer until thick, stirring occasionally, about 30 minutes. Using a potato masher, mash the jam to a chunky-smooth consistency. Remove from the heat and let cool slightly.

Refrigerate in an airtight container until ready to serve, or for up to 1 month.

sour cherry preserves

The Southern climate is inhospitable to all but the bravest sour cherry trees, whose exact locations are often as closely guarded as those of choice swimming holes and wild berry patches. These sour cherry preserves, which are wildly good on Favorite Buttermilk Biscuits (page 51), are what I often make when I'm lucky enough to get my hands on some sour cherries.   MAKES ABOUT 4 PINTS

5	**pounds sour cherries, pitted**
3	**cups sugar**
1	**apple, peeled, cored, and grated**
	Juice of 2 lemons
1	**teaspoon kosher salt**

Place the cherries, sugar, apple, lemon juice, and salt in a large pot over medium heat, stir to mix, and bring to a boil. Reduce the heat to a low boil and simmer for about 1 hour, stirring occasionally, until the mixture is thick and syrupy and reaches the setting point (see Know-how, below).

If preserving the jam, sterilize four 1-pint heat-tempered canning jars (see Know-how, page 291).

For refrigerator jam, let cool slightly and refrigerate in airtight containers until ready to serve, or for up to 1 month.

For preserved jam, pack the hot fruit in the sterilized jars and seal using the hot-pack method (see Know-how, page 291). Let cool to room temperature, check the seal, and store in a cool, dark place until ready to serve, or for up to 6 months. Refrigerate after opening.

Know-how: testing the setting point

When making fruit jam, the "setting point" is the temperature (usually around 220°F) at which the jam thickens sufficiently to "set up" rather than turn to liquid upon cooling. To test, either measure the temperature with a candy thermometer or spoon a small amount of jam onto a plate and let cool slightly. Run your finger through the middle of the jam; if the two halves remain separate, it has reached the setting point. If not, boil for another 3 to 5 minutes and test again.

---

quick fruit jam for all seasons

Homemade fruit jam is one of life's great pleasures, so thank goodness it's also one of life's easiest. Although many people think of the summer months as canning season, excellent fruit jam can be made any time of year. But, while doing so is always fun, it makes good economic sense only when you have access to large quantities of fruit at relatively low prices. Assuming you aren't working from your own garden, you can save money *and* make it a fun family outing by visiting your local farmer's market or picking your own fruit at one of the "pick-your-own" farms in your area. The prices can't be beat, and you'll have the satisfaction of knowing exactly where the fruit came from. Keep in mind that you may need to adjust the sugar depending on the sweetness of the fruit.   MAKES 3 PINTS

3	pounds (about 8 cups) whole berries or chopped fruit
3	cups sugar
	Juice of 2 lemons
1	teaspoon kosher salt
1	teaspoon unsalted butter

Place the fruit, sugar, lemon juice, and salt in a large pot and stir to mix. Bring to a boil over medium heat, stirring constantly until the fruit starts to release juice and the sugar dissolves, 2 to 3 minutes. Add the butter and stir to mix.

Turn the heat to low and simmer for about 40 minutes, stirring occasionally, skimming the foam as needed, until the jam thickens slightly (it will still be fairly loose) and reaches the setting point (see Know-how, page 304).

If preserving the jam, sterilize three 1-pint heat-tempered canning jars (see Know-how, page 291).

For refrigerator jam, let cool slightly and refrigerate in airtight containers until ready to serve, or for up to 1 month.

For preserved jam, pack the hot fruit in the sterilized jars and seal using the hot-pack method (see Know-how, page 291). Let cool to room temperature, check the seal, and store in a cool, dark place until ready to serve, or for up to 6 months. Refrigerate after opening.

The following are some of my favorite seasonal combinations.

IN SEASON

SPRING	Strawberry and rhubarb
SUMMER	Mixed berry (any combination of blueberries, raspberries, blackberries, cherries, and strawberries), peach
FALL	Plum, pear, or apple
WINTER	Pumpkin marmalade, orange or tangerine marmalade

A little bit of butter is often added to berry jams, but not for the reason you might expect. More than adding a hint of richness, the butter helps keep the jam from foaming, thus reducing the need to skim the jam as it cooks.

SARA'S SWAPS I love the straightforward taste of simple fruit jam, but when I'm feeling more adventurous I like to play off of the fruits' sweetness by adding less run-of-the-mill seasonings. A ¼-cup splash of balsamic vinegar deepens the flavor of strawberry or mixed berry jam, while a sprig or two of fresh thyme or rosemary imparts an elegant grassy endnote to blackberry or plum jam. Jams like these have complex flavor profiles that make them better suited for cheese and crackers than PB&Js.

Know-how: *making low-sugar jam*

More than just sweetening the pot, the sugar in jams helps preserve the fruit and enables the mixture to set up properly. Therefore, it is important to maintain a recipe's ratio of sugar to fruit if you want the finished jam to have the recipe's intended consistency. (Of course, if you are more interested in flavor than texture, by all means reduce the sugar to taste; the jam will just be a bit runnier.) Another way to get nice, thick preserves with less sugar is to use fruit pectin of some kind, which, like the sugar, also causes the preserves to set, but without adding any sweet flavor. If enough pectin is present, the sugar can be reduced to taste. Apples, pears, and quinces are good sources of natural pectin, but if you want to take a more precise approach or avoid introducing those flavors, you can use store-bought natural pectin, such as the Pomona brand. This fruit-derived powdered pectin is added to the fruit while it cooks, allowing you to reduce the amount of sugar.

west tennessee thick and sticky bbq sauce

Any recipe for barbecue sauce is bound to be contentious, no matter the formula. That's because there are as many versions of this master sauce as there are Southerners willing to defend them as definitive. Whether thick or runny, tomato-based or vinegar, all Southern barbecue sauces get their complex flavor by playing on the contrasts between spicy and sweet, tangy and smoky. I'm nonpartisan enough to appreciate them all, but of course I'm partial to the western Tennessee strains—one sharp and vinegary, the other sweet and tomato-thick—I grew up on. With tomato, vinegar, and a dash of mustard, this all-purpose hybrid version offers the best of all worlds. MAKES ABOUT 3 PINTS

1	tablespoon olive oil
1/2	onion, diced
2	garlic cloves, smashed and minced
4	cups ketchup
1/2	cup water
2	cups distilled white vinegar
1/2	cup Worcestershire sauce
1/2	cup packed light brown sugar
1	tablespoon Colman's dry mustard
1	tablespoon crushed red pepper flakes
2	teaspoons sea salt
1/2	teaspoon freshly ground black pepper
1/2	lemon, cut in half

Heat the olive oil in a large saucepan over medium heat. Add the onion and cook and stir for about 5 minutes, until soft and golden. Add the garlic and cook and stir for 1 minute more. Pour in the ketchup; then rinse the bottle with the water to capture the remaining ketchup and add it to the pan, stirring to mix. Add the vinegar, Worcestershire sauce, brown sugar, mustard, red pepper flakes, salt, and black pepper and stir to mix. Squeeze the lemon juice into the sauce, add the squeezed halves, and stir.

Bring the sauce to a low boil, reduce the heat to a simmer, and cook for about 45 minutes, stirring occasionally, until the sauce thickens and reduces slightly. Remove from the heat, let cool slightly, and remove and discard the lemon halves. Refrigerate in an airtight container until ready to use, or for up to 3 weeks.

hot pepper vinegar

A staple of barbecue and "meat-and-three" joints everywhere, hot pepper vinegar is one of the most ubiquitous of all the Southern condiments. It's doused liberally over greens, pulled pig, field peas, gumbo, beans and rice—you name it.   MAKES ABOUT 1 PINT

Wash and drain **1 pound fresh chile peppers, such as cayenne, jalapeño, or serrano.** Pack the whole peppers tightly into sterilized jars or bottles (see Know-how, page 291). If the neck of the bottle is narrow, you may need to use chopsticks to help tightly pack the peppers.

Place **2 cups apple cider or distilled white vinegar** and **1 teaspoon kosher salt** in a nonreactive saucepan over high heat and bring to a boil.

Remove from the heat and pour the liquid over the peppers to cover, using a funnel if needed. Secure with a cap or lid and store in a cool, dark place for at least a week to allow the flavors to develop. The vinegar will keep for up to 6 months at room temperature or in the refrigerator.

say's vinegar barbecue sauce

My mom's vinegar-based barbecue sauce, which she made to go along with my dad's pulled pig, is utterly addictive. Sprinkle it over Wood-Smoked Backyard Barbecued Pig (page 170) or Slow-Roasted Pulled Pork Butt (page 177).

MAKES ABOUT 2 CUPS

2	cups apple cider vinegar
1/2	cup unpacked light brown sugar
1/4	cup Worcestershire sauce
1	tablespoon sea salt
1	tablespoon freshly ground black pepper
1	tablespoon crushed red pepper flakes
1	lemon, cut in half

Combine the vinegar, brown sugar, Worcestershire sauce, salt, black pepper, and red pepper flakes in a saucepan and bring to a boil over medium-high heat. Squeeze the lemon juice into the pan and add the squeezed halves. Reduce the heat to a low boil and cook for about 20 minutes. Remove from the heat, let cool slightly, and remove and discard the lemon halves. Refrigerate in an airtight container until ready to use, or for up to 1 month.

stay awhile longer

sweets

We Southerners are famous for the strength and tenacity of our sweet tooth, it's true—how else to explain the enamel-dissolving levels of sugar we regularly put in our sweet tea? But the craving is about more than just a special affinity for all things sugared.

Southerners use sweets to mark special occasions, bestow love on family and friends, demonstrate gracious hospitality, indulge personal nostalgia, or even just to put a sweet and tidy period at the end of a meal's sentence. Perhaps because we put them to so many different uses, Southern sweets run the gamut from many-layered cakes draped in fluffy icing—and perhaps studded with fruit or nuts—to gelatinous molded jellies with canned fruit trapped inside.

I've always considered myself more of a cook than a baker—I tend not to have the patience or precision required for pastries—and yet I find myself with a seemingly endless repertoire of Southern cakes, pies, cobblers, custards, puddings and cookies, most of which have been passed down from one generation to the next. As if by osmosis, the sweets of my childhood have found their way into my recipe box and kitchen—from Granny Foster, from my mother and sister, and from my aunts Ginny and Ann, and for that I'm glad.

The desserts in this chapter, from Buttermilk–Strawberry Jam Cake (page 319) to Red Velvet Cupcakes (page 366), are culled from that repertoire. Some, like Granny Foster's Simple Pound Cake (page 314), are offered straight up, while others, like the Grilled Pound Cake and Caramel Sandwiches (page 314) made from it, are served with a modern twist. But one thing is certain: each of these sweets is guaranteed to set a gracious tone, encouraging friends and family alike to linger awhile longer.

granny foster's simple pound cake

True pound cake doesn't include leavening, meaning that it gets all its lift from eggs and the air that is incorporated into the batter when creaming the butter and sugar. For best results, bring the ingredients to room temperature before you begin. Granny's old-fashioned pound cake is true to its name, calling for a pound each of butter, eggs, flour, and sugar. Proof that "plain" can be a beautiful thing.

MAKES ONE 10-INCH BUNDT OR TUBE CAKE / SERVES 10 TO 12

2½	cups sugar (about 1 pound)
1	pound (4 sticks) unsalted butter, softened
½	teaspoon kosher salt
7	large eggs (about 1 pound)
3½	cups all-purpose flour (about 1 pound)
¾	cup heavy cream
1	tablespoon pure vanilla extract
¼	teaspoon freshly grated nutmeg

Preheat the oven to 325°F. Lightly grease and flour a 10-inch Bundt or tube pan. Have all the ingredients at room temperature before you begin.

Cream the sugar, butter, and salt in a large bowl with an electric mixer until light and fluffy, about 3 minutes (see Know-how, page 315). Add the eggs one at a time, beating well and scraping down the sides of the bowl after each addition.

Add the flour to the butter mixture in thirds, alternating with the cream and beginning and ending with the flour, stopping to scrape down the bowl several times and stirring just until all is incorporated. Do not overmix. Add the vanilla and nutmeg and stir to combine.

Spoon the batter into the prepared pan and spread evenly. Give the pan a rap on the counter to settle the batter and get rid of any air bubbles. Place the pan on the center rack of the oven and bake for 1 hour, undisturbed. Check the cake, rotate the pan, and bake for another 15 to 20 minutes, or until the cake is golden brown and a wooden skewer inserted in the center comes out clean.

Remove the cake from the oven and cool in the pan for 15 to 20 minutes. Run a small knife around the outer and inner edges of the pan before turning the cake out onto a baking rack to cool. Slice and serve warm or at room temperature.

GRILLED POUND CAKE AND CARAMEL SANDWICHES   This sticky-sweet treat brings out the kid in everyone, especially when served with a cool, tall glass of milk.

Makes 1 sandwich

Take **2 thin slices of Granny Foster's Simple Pound Cake (recipe above)** and spread 1 slice with **your favorite creamy caramel sauce.** Sandwich the slices together and lightly coat the exterior of each with **soft unsalted butter.**

Place the sandwich in a hot skillet and cook until the cake is toasted and light golden on both sides and the caramel is gooey and warm in the center. Serve warm topped with **soft vanilla or dulce de leche ice cream.**

Know-how: creaming sugar and butter

The first step in making most butter-based cakes, quick breads, and cookies is to cream butter and sugar until light and fluffy before beating in the eggs. This deceptively easy process—in which, essentially, lots of air is mixed into the batter—actually plays an important role in giving baked goods lots of lift and a nice, soft crumb. This is especially important in recipes like this pound cake, where eggs and air are the only leavening agents and must do all the "heavy lifting" on their own. Here's the idea: cream the butter and sugar on high speed until the texture turns from creamy and grainy to fluffy and smooth and the color lightens by a shade or two. This takes a good 3 minutes or more, so don't rush this part of the process. A general rule of thumb is that the more you beat the sugar, butter, and eggs, the better—but as soon as you add the flour, it's a completely different story. Once the flour is in the picture, the batter should be mixed as little as possible so it doesn't toughen.

IN SEASON   Granny Foster's pound cake is a simple pleasure on its own, but because it is so basic, it lends itself to all manner of toppings, from fresh or stewed berries and lemon curd to warm chocolate sauce or Sour Cherry Preserves (page 304). Here are a few easy ideas for any time of year.

SUMMER
Fresh berries and Farm Stand Peach Ice Cream (page 363)

FALL
Sour Cherry Preserves (page 304) with lightly sweetened whipped cream

WINTER
Brandied Figs (page 301) or Grilled Pineapple (page 328)

SPRING
Balsamic Strawberries (page 358) or Quick Fruit Jam for
All Seasons (page 305) and vanilla ice cream

buttermilk pound cake with tangy buttermilk glaze

Buttermilk is used all the time in Southern baking to create a soft, fluffy texture and add a little tang, but it's not often placed front and center. That's a shame, because this creamy beverage, which tastes sort of like a cross between cow's milk and plain, unsweetened yogurt, has a lovely tart quality that deserves to be tasted on its own. This delicate-crumbed cake is just sweet enough to balance the buttermilk's zippiness without overwhelming it.

MAKES ONE 10-INCH BUNDT OR TUBE CAKE / SERVES 10 TO 12

CAKE

3	cups sugar
3/4	pound (3 sticks) unsalted butter, softened
6	large eggs
3	cups all-purpose flour
1	teaspoon baking powder
1/2	teaspoon baking soda
1/2	teaspoon kosher salt
1	cup well-shaken buttermilk
1	tablespoon pure vanilla extract

GLAZE

1	cup sugar
1/4	cup heavy cream
3	tablespoons unsalted butter
1	tablespoon light corn syrup
1/2	cup well-shaken buttermilk
1	teaspoon pure vanilla extract

Buttermilk Crème Fraîche (page 320), for serving (optional)

CAKE | Preheat the oven to 325°F. Lightly grease and flour a 10-inch Bundt or tube pan. Have all the ingredients at room temperature before you begin.

Cream the sugar and butter in a large bowl with an electric mixer until light and fluffy, about 3 minutes (see Know-how, page 315). Add the eggs, one at a time, beating well and scraping down the sides of the bowl after each addition.

Combine the flour, baking powder, baking soda, and salt in a separate bowl and stir to mix. Stir the buttermilk and vanilla together in a small bowl.

Add the flour mixture to the butter mixture in thirds, alternating with the buttermilk mixture and beginning and ending with the flour mixture, stopping to scrape down the bowl several times and stirring just until all is incorporated. Do not overmix.

Spoon the batter into the prepared pan and spread evenly. Give the pan a rap on the counter to settle the batter and get rid of any air bubbles. Place the pan on the center rack of the oven and bake for 1 hour, undisturbed. Check the cake, rotate the pan, and bake for another 15 to 20 minutes, or until the cake is golden brown and a wooden skewer inserted in the center comes out clean.

Remove the cake from the oven and cool in the pan for 15 to 20 minutes. Run a small knife around the outer and inner edges of the pan before turning the cake out onto a baking rack set over a baking sheet to cool.

GLAZE | Stir together the sugar, cream, butter, and corn syrup in a small saucepan and bring to a low boil over medium heat. Reduce the heat to low and simmer for about 3 minutes, stirring occasionally. Remove the saucepan from the heat and stir in the buttermilk and vanilla. Let the glaze cool for 5 to 10 minutes before pouring over the warm cake. Slice and serve warm or completely cooled with a dollop of Buttermilk Crème Fraîche, if desired.

MEYER LEMON COCONUT POUND CAKE   With just a few quick additions to the basic Buttermilk Pound Cake recipe, you can make a refreshingly sweet-tart variation featuring rich, moist coconut and zippy Meyer lemons. These relatively sweet lemons have an orangelike flavor that really makes this cake stand out, but you can use regular lemons—or any other kind of citrus, for that matter—with equally pleasing results.

Makes one 10-inch Bundt or tube cake / Serves 10 to 12

Follow the recipe for the **Buttermilk Pound Cake with Tangy Buttermilk Glaze (page 316),** with the following changes: Cut the buttermilk by ¼ cup and add the **zest and juice of 3 Meyer or other lemons** when adding the buttermilk. After adding the flour and buttermilk mixtures to the butter mixture, fold in **2 cups sweetened flaked coconut** and proceed as for the main recipe. To the glaze, add the **zest and juice of 3 Meyer or other lemons** and proceed with the recipe.

Know-how: making buttermilk substitute

If you don't have access to or don't regularly buy buttermilk, you can make an easy substitute with milk and white vinegar or lemon juice. For every cup of buttermilk needed, start with 1 tablespoon of vinegar or lemon juice and add enough milk to equal a level cup. Stir to combine and let sit at room temperature for about 5 minutes, until the mixture curdles, before using.

---

mississippi mud cake

Fans of rocky road ice cream will rejoice in this unabashedly retro chocolate cake. It's a great make-ahead treat for picnics, tailgating, and kids' parties.

MAKES ONE 11 X 7-INCH CAKE / SERVES 10 TO 12

CAKE

1½	**cups sugar**
1½	**cups all-purpose flour**
	Pinch of kosher salt
½	**pound (2 sticks) unsalted butter, cut into chunks**
½	**cup unsweetened cocoa**
4	**large eggs, beaten**
1	**tablespoon pure vanilla extract**
1	**cup chopped pecans**

FROSTING

½	**cup unsweetened cocoa**
⅓	**cup confectioners' sugar, sifted**
12	**tablespoons (1½ sticks) unsalted butter, melted**
½	**cup milk**
2	**teaspoons pure vanilla extract**
3	**cups mini marshmallows**
1	**cup chopped pecans, lightly toasted**

CAKE | Preheat the oven to 350°F. Lightly grease and flour an 11 x 7-inch pan.

Combine the sugar, flour, and salt in a large bowl and stir to mix.

Melt the butter in a small saucepan and stir in the cocoa until well blended. Remove from the heat, let cool slightly, and stir in the eggs and vanilla. Pour the butter mixture into the flour mixture and stir until well combined. Add the pecans and stir to mix.

Spoon the batter into the prepared pan and spread evenly. Bake for 25 to 30 minutes, or until a wooden skewer inserted in the center comes out clean. Remove the cake from the oven, but do not turn the oven off.

FROSTING | While the cake is baking, combine the cocoa and confectioners' sugar in a large bowl and stir to mix. Add the melted butter, milk, and vanilla and stir until combined.

ASSEMBLY | Scatter the marshmallows and pecans over the cake and return to the oven for about 4 minutes, just until the marshmallows are softened and puffy. Remove from the oven and pour the frosting over the marshmallows and pecans to cover, while the cake is warm. Cool completely, cut into squares, and serve.

buttermilk–strawberry jam cake

This pretty cake was inspired by a jar of brown sugar–strawberry jam from Blackberry Farm (see Sources, page 377), a wonderful inn in the Tennessee mountains, and my grandmother's old jam cake recipe. The combination of sweet fruit preserves, soft cream, and tender yellow cake makes me think of it as one part strawberry shortcake and two parts English trifle, in sliceable form. When we make it at Foster's, we leave the sides unfrosted because it looks so homey when the frosting oozes from between the layers and down the sides of the cake. Note that the Buttermilk Crème Fraîche must be made at least two days ahead; if necessary, you can always substitute sour cream or store-bought crème fraîche.

MAKES ONE 8- OR 9-INCH 3-LAYER CAKE / SERVES 10 TO 12

CAKE

2	cups sugar
1/2	pound (2 sticks) unsalted butter, softened
4	large eggs
3	cups all-purpose flour
2	teaspoons baking powder
1/2	teaspoon baking soda
1/2	teaspoon kosher salt
1/4	teaspoon freshly grated nutmeg
1 1/4	cups well-shaken buttermilk
2	teaspoons pure vanilla extract

FROSTING

1 1/2	cups heavy cream
1 1/2	cups Buttermilk Crème Fraîche (recipe follows) or store-bought crème fraîche
1/2	cup sugar
1 1/2	cups strawberry jam or preserves
1	pint (2 cups) ripe strawberries, hulled and halved lengthwise

CAKE | Preheat the oven to 350°F. Lightly grease and flour three 8- or 9-inch cake pans. Have all the ingredients at room temperature before you begin.

Cream the sugar and butter in a large bowl with an electric mixer until light and fluffy, about 3 minutes (see Know-how, page 315). Add the eggs one at a time, beating well and scraping down the sides of the bowl after each addition.

Combine the flour, baking powder, baking soda, salt, and nutmeg in a separate bowl and stir to mix.

Add the flour mixture to the butter mixture in thirds, alternating with the buttermilk and beginning and ending with the flour mixture, stopping to scrape down the bowl several times and stirring just until all is incorporated. Do not overmix. Add the vanilla and stir to combine.

(continued)

Divide the batter evenly between the prepared pans and bake for 25 to 30 minutes, or until the cakes are golden brown and a wooden skewer inserted in the center comes out clean.

Remove the cakes from the oven and let cool in the pans for about 10 minutes. Run a small knife around the edges of the pans before turning the cakes out onto baking racks to cool completely before frosting.

FROSTING | Do not start the frosting until the cakes are completely cooled. Place the cream in a large bowl and beat to soft peaks with an electric mixer. Add the Buttermilk Crème Fraîche and sugar and continue to whip until the mixture forms stiff peaks.

ASSEMBLY | Once the cakes have cooled completely, use a long serrated knife to slice off the rounded top portion of each cake to make a flat, even surface. Discard the trimmings.

Place one layer, cut side down, on a large plate or cake stand and spread evenly with a third of the jam. Top with a third of the frosting and spread evenly. Repeat with the second and third layers. Arrange the strawberries on top, slice, and serve.

If not serving within 2 hours, store in the refrigerator; then remove the cake about 1 hour before serving and let come to room temperature.

buttermilk crème fraîche

MAKES ABOUT 2 CUPS

$1^1/_2$ **cups heavy cream**
$^1/_2$ **cup well-shaken buttermilk**
2   **tablespoons sour cream**

Combine the heavy cream, buttermilk, and sour cream in a pint glass jar. Screw the lid on the jar and shake to mix. Let sit in a cool, dark place for 2 days before refrigerating; the mixture will become thick. Crème fraîche will keep, refrigerated, for up to 2 weeks.

say's coconut layer cake with seven-minute frosting

Nothing finishes a meal quite so regally as layer cake; for Southerners, at least, it is the epitome of fine entertaining. This towering confection, draped in glossy white frosting and scattered with coconut, was one of my mother's signature dinner party desserts. You can make the cake layers two days in advance, but make the frosting no more than two or three hours before serving; it doesn't keep its silky-smooth texture very long.

MAKES ONE 8- OR 9-INCH 3-LAYER CAKE / SERVES 10 TO 12

CAKE
1½	cups canola oil
3	cups sugar
6	large eggs
2	teaspoons pure vanilla extract
3¾	cups all-purpose flour
1	tablespoon baking powder
½	teaspoon kosher salt
1½	cups milk

FROSTING
2¼	cups sugar
4	large egg whites
¼	cup light corn syrup
¼	cup water
¼	teaspoon kosher salt
¼	teaspoon cream of tartar
1	teaspoon pure vanilla extract
4	cups sweetened flaked coconut

CAKE | Preheat the oven to 350°F. Lightly grease and flour three 8- or 9-inch cake pans. Have all the ingredients at room temperature before you begin.

Place the canola oil in a large bowl and beat with an electric mixer on high speed; add the sugar and beat until light and fluffy. Add the eggs one at a time, beating well and scraping down the sides of the bowl after each addition. Add the vanilla and stir to combine.

Combine the flour, baking powder, and salt in a separate bowl and stir to mix.

Add the flour mixture to the oil mixture in thirds, alternating with the milk and beginning and ending with the flour mixture, stopping to scrape down the bowl several times and stirring just until all is incorporated. Do not overmix.

Divide the batter evenly between the prepared pans, filling each about halfway, and bake for 30 to 35 minutes, or until the cakes are springy to the touch and a wooden skewer inserted in the center comes out clean.

(continued)

Remove the cakes from the oven and let cool in the pans for about 15 minutes. Run a small knife around the edges of the pans before turning the cakes out onto baking racks to cool completely before frosting.

FROSTING | Do not start the frosting until the cakes are completely cooled. Place the sugar, egg whites, corn syrup, water, salt, and cream of tartar in a double boiler set over simmering water over low heat and beat with a handheld electric mixer on low speed for about 1 minute, until the mixture is frothy.

Increase the speed to high and beat for 5 to 7 minutes more, until the mixture becomes glossy, triples in volume, and forms soft peaks.

Remove from the heat, add the vanilla, and continue to beat for about 2 minutes longer, until the mixture becomes thick.

ASSEMBLY | Once the cakes have cooled completely, use a long serrated knife to slice off the rounded top portion of each cake to make a flat, even surface. Discard the trimmings.

Place one layer, cut side down, on a large plate or cake stand. Spread evenly with a quarter of the frosting and sprinkle with about 1 cup of the coconut. Repeat with the second and third layers. Spread the top and sides of the cake with the remaining frosting and sprinkle with the remaining coconut. Slice and serve.

SARA'S SWAPS Give this tropical cake a piña colada twist by brushing each layer with a mix of equal parts pineapple juice and rum or coconut milk before frosting and sprinkling ¼ cup crushed pineapple along with the coconut between each layer and on top of the cake. For a really delicious pineapple cake, use pineapple in place of the coconut.

Know-how: making homemade baking powder

In a pinch, you can make your own baking powder with just a few simple pantry items. For every teaspoon of baking powder needed, just mix ½ teaspoon cream of tartar, ¼ teaspoon baking soda, and ¼ teaspoon cornstarch. Because the baking soda will begin to react upon mixing, plan to use your homemade baking powder right away; it will not keep.

Destination: **ATHENS, GEORGIA**

WORTH THE DETOUR

THE GRIT'S

Southern layer cakes

(706) 543-6593

thegrit.com

Southern layer cakes are a true art, one that is often left to the capable hands of grannies, great-aunts, and old-school Southern bakeries that haven't yet abandoned ship for cupcakes' trendier waters. So imagine my surprise when I discovered that some of the best cakes to be had anywhere in the region are found at the Grit, a hip, multiethnic vegetarian diner in Athens, Georgia, where a hearty meal of curried Indian dal and brown rice or tofu teriyaki can be rounded out with thick wedges of perfectly moist, traditional Southern layer cake.

The pretty cakes lining the pastry case are made fresh in-house every day, which means the selection changes based on what's in season or what the bakers feel like throwing together. The lemon poppy seed, a delicate balance of sweet and tart that is so creamy you won't believe it's vegan, and the triple-layered, triple-chocolate Chocolate Death cake are longtime standards, but there's always something new and different to keep you coming back. Their rendition of hummingbird cake is so nutty and sticky you can almost detect the last traces of the oven's warmth; the caramel brown sugar cake is a soulful take on classic Southern caramel cake; and the strawberries and cream cake, complete with fresh strawberries and soft swirls of whipped cream, is sweet summertime perfection. It is a testament to the power of Southern layer cakes that the fusion-happy Grit doesn't mess around when it comes to dessert—and neither should you when it comes time to order.

The pretty cakes lining the pastry case are made fresh in-house every day.

hummingbird cake

Surely, this moist, pecan- and fruit-flecked cake must get its name from the sugary nectar upon which fluttering hummingbirds lunch. This namesake sweet is at least as popular among the birds' Southern human counterparts. Indeed, it is *Southern Living*'s all-time most requested recipe. This is my adaptation of the magazine's classic version.

MAKES ONE 8- OR 9-INCH 3-LAYER CAKE / SERVES 10 TO 12

CAKE

3½	cups all-purpose flour
2	cups sugar
2	teaspoons baking powder
1	teaspoon kosher salt
1	teaspoon ground cinnamon
½	teaspoon baking soda
½	teaspoon freshly grated nutmeg
1	cup canola or other vegetable oil
3	large eggs, beaten
2	cups ripe mashed bananas (about 4)
	One 8-ounce can (1 cup) crushed pineapple with juice
1	tablespoon pure vanilla extract
1	cup chopped pecans

FROSTING

1	pound cream cheese, softened
½	pound (2 sticks) unsalted butter, softened
6	cups confectioners' sugar, sifted
1	tablespoon bourbon
2	teaspoons pure vanilla extract
1	cup chopped pecans, lightly toasted

CAKE | Preheat the oven to 350°F. Lightly grease and flour three 8- or 9-inch cake pans.

Combine the flour, sugar, baking powder, salt, cinnamon, baking soda, and nutmeg in a large bowl and stir to mix. In a separate bowl, whisk together the canola oil and eggs until combined. Add the bananas and crushed pineapple with juice and stir to mix.

Stir the egg mixture into the flour mixture with a wooden spoon or spatula just to combine. Stir in the vanilla and pecans.

Divide the batter evenly between the prepared pans and bake on the center rack of the oven for 25 to 30 minutes, or until a wooden skewer inserted in the center comes out clean.

Remove the cakes from the oven and let cool in the pans for about 10 minutes. Run a small knife around the edges of the pans before turning the cakes out onto baking racks to cool completely before frosting.

FROSTING | Cream the cream cheese and butter in a large bowl with an electric mixer until light and fluffy. Slowly add the confectioners' sugar and beat until all is incorporated. Beat in the bourbon and vanilla to combine.

ASSEMBLY | Once the cakes have cooled completely, use a long serrated knife to slice off the rounded top portion of each cake to make a flat, even surface. Discard the trimmings.

Place one layer, cut side down, on a large plate or cake stand. Spread evenly with about one-third of the frosting and sprinkle with about one-third of the pecans. Repeat with the remaining layers.

If not serving within 2 hours, store in the refrigerator; then remove the cake about 1 hour before serving and let come to room temperature.

grilled pineapple upside-down cake

When pineapple caramelizes, whether on the grill or in the oven, its bright, tart flavor mellows to something warm and sweet—a neat trick that has long been the calling card of traditional pineapple upside-down cake. My grandmother's version, with its canned pineapple rings, was one of my dad's all-time favorite sweets. It's one of mine, too, but when I make it, I start with freshly grilled pineapple to double the caramelization effect and add a splash of bourbon to drive the point home.

MAKES ONE 10-INCH CAKE / SERVES 8 TO 10

TOPPING
6	**fresh pineapple rings (see Know-how, page 329)**
6	**tablespoons (3/4 stick) butter**
1	**cup unpacked light brown sugar**
1	**tablespoon bourbon**
1/2	**teaspoon kosher salt**

CAKE
1	**cup sugar**
8	**tablespoons (1 stick) unsalted butter, softened**
2	**large eggs, beaten**
2	**cups all-purpose flour**
2	**teaspoons baking powder**
1/2	**teaspoon kosher salt**
2/3	**cup milk**
2	**teaspoons pure vanilla extract**

TOPPING | Preheat the oven to 350°F.

Heat a grill pan or cast-iron skillet over medium heat until hot. Place the pineapple rings in the pan 4 or 5 at a time and cook for about 2 minutes per side, until golden brown and slightly caramelized. Remove from the heat and set aside.

Melt the butter in a 10-inch cast-iron skillet over medium heat. Sprinkle evenly with the brown sugar, bourbon, and salt and cook until the sugar dissolves, about 2 minutes. Arrange the grilled pineapple rings in a slightly overlapping layer over the butter and sugar. Remove from the heat while you mix the batter.

CAKE | Have all the ingredients at room temperature before you begin.

Cream the sugar and butter in a large bowl with an electric mixer until light and fluffy, about 3 minutes (see Know-how, page 315). Add the eggs one at a time, beating well and scraping down the sides of the bowl after each addition.

Combine the flour, baking powder, and salt in a large bowl and stir to mix.

Add the flour mixture to the butter mixture in thirds, alternating with the milk and beginning and ending with the flour mixture, stopping to scrape down the bowl several times and stirring just until all is incorporated. Do not overmix. Add the vanilla and stir to mix.

Carefully pour the batter over the pineapple in the skillet and spread evenly. Bake for 30 to 35 minutes, or until the cake is golden brown and a wooden skewer inserted in the center comes out clean.

Remove the cake from the oven and let cool in the skillet for about 5 minutes. Run a small knife around the edge of the skillet and place a large serving plate upside down over the top. Invert the skillet to release the cake and topping onto the plate. Serve warm or completely cooled.

SARA'S SWAPS When summer peaches, apricots, or plums are at their juiciest, make this a peach, apricot, or plum upside-down cake. Just substitute peeled, sliced ripe peaches, apricots, or plums for the pineapple and omit the grilling step. If using peaches, give a double whammy of sweet peach flavor by serving with Farm-Stand Peach Ice Cream (page 363).

Know-how: cutting fresh pineapple rings

Trim the top and bottom of the pineapple to form flat surfaces. Set the pineapple right side up and peel from top to bottom in long strips, slicing along the contours of the fruit. Place the peeled pineapple on its side and slice into rounds about ½ inch thick. Cut the core from the center of each round using a 1-inch cookie cutter to make a ring.

Know-how: making homemade brown sugar

If you don't have brown sugar on hand, use a mix of granulated sugar and molasses. The ratio for light brown sugar is 1 tablespoon molasses for every 1 cup of sugar; double the molasses for dark brown sugar. Just stir the sugar and molasses together thoroughly and use as needed.

lemon rub pie

It's no wonder that this intensely lemony custard pie, which is a close relative of chess pie, is a favorite of Southern seafood restaurants like the Catfish Hotel in Shiloh, Tennessee—it's got just the sort of pucker-inducing, palate-cleansing properties you need to set you straight after a heavy meal of fried catfish and hushpuppies. In this version, I use Cornmeal Crust to play off the cornmeal in the custard.

MAKES ONE 9-INCH PIE / SERVES 8 TO 10

1¼	**cups sugar**
8	**tablespoons (1 stick) unsalted butter, softened**
3	**large eggs, separated**
	Zest and juice of 2 lemons
1	**tablespoon water**
1	**tablespoon cornmeal**
½	**teaspoon kosher salt**
1	**unbaked 9-inch Cornmeal Crust (recipe follows)**

Preheat the oven to 400°F. Have all the ingredients at room temperature before you begin.

Cream the sugar and butter in a large bowl with an electric mixer until light and fluffy, about 3 minutes (see Know-how, page 315). Add the egg yolks one at a time, beating well and scraping down the sides of the bowl after each addition. Add the lemon zest and juice, water, cornmeal, and salt and stir to mix.

Place the egg whites in a separate large bowl and beat with an electric mixer on medium speed until light and frothy. Increase the speed to high and beat to soft peaks, about 2 minutes more. Gently fold the whites into the yolk mixture.

Pour the filling into the unbaked pie shell, place the pie on a rimmed baking sheet, and bake for 10 minutes.

Reduce the temperature to 300°F and bake for another 30 to 35 minutes, until the filling sets around the edges but still jiggles in the center when lightly shaken.

Remove pie from the oven and let cool for at least 1 hour before serving; the pie will firm up completely, or "set," as it cools. Serve at room temperature.

cornmeal crust

The addition of cornmeal gives this piecrust an extra-crispy bite and lots of toasty corn flavor. For even more crunch, try using coarsely ground cornmeal.

MAKES ONE 9- OR 10-INCH PIE OR TART CRUST

1¼	cups all-purpose flour
¼	cup fine yellow cornmeal
¼	cup sugar
1	tablespoon freshly grated lemon zest
	Pinch of freshly grated nutmeg
	Pinch of kosher salt
1	large egg yolk, chilled
2	tablespoons heavy cream, chilled
1	teaspoon pure vanilla extract
6	tablespoons (¾ stick) cold unsalted butter, cut into small pieces

Stir together the flour, cornmeal, sugar, lemon zest, nutmeg, and salt in a large bowl. In a separate bowl, whisk together the egg yolk, cream, and vanilla.

Cut the butter into the flour mixture using a pastry blender or two knives in a crosscutting motion until the mixture resembles coarse meal. Work quickly so the butter remains cool and doesn't melt into the flour. Add the egg mixture to the flour mixture and stir with a fork just until the dough clumps together and is moist enough to pat together. Do not mix any more than necessary.

Turn the dough onto a lightly floured work surface and, with lightly floured hands, form into a flat disk. Wrap in plastic and refrigerate for at least 1 hour, or for up to 3 days, until firm.

Check the pie recipe for special rolling instructions. To prepare a basic pie shell, remove the dough from the refrigerator and let sit for about 10 minutes. Place on a lightly floured work surface. Dust a rolling pin with flour and roll the dough between ⅛ and ¼ inch thick. Fold the dough in half or gently roll it onto the rolling pin and lift it over the pie pan. Press the dough lightly into the bottom and up the sides of the pan. Trim the excess dough, leaving about 1½ inches of dough draped over the pan. Roll the extra dough under itself to form a rim around the edge of the pan. Crimp the rim of dough with your fingers or press with the tines of a fork. Prick the bottom of the crust two or three times with a fork to create small holes.

Cover the crust with plastic wrap and refrigerate for at least 1 hour, or up to 3 days, before proceeding with a recipe or partially or fully prebaking the crust (see Know-how, page 345).

FREESTYLE LEMON BLACKBERRY TART Prepare 1 recipe **Cornmeal Crust (preceding recipe)**, prebake (see Know-how, page 345), and let cool. Cut the crust into slices or wedges and, just before serving, top each with a **dollop of lemon curd**, a **sprinkling of blackberries and blueberries,** and a **spoonful of soft lightly sweetened whipped cream or Buttermilk Crème Fraîche (page 320).**

Destination: McCLELLANVILLE, SOUTH CAROLINA

WORTH THE DETOUR

T. W. GRAHAM & CO. SEAFOOD RESTAURANT'S

homemade desserts

(843) 887-4342

twgrahamandco.com

A S I DID WITH MANY OF THE LITTLE-KNOWN SOUTHERN GEMS INCLUDED in these Sidetracked features, I first learned of T. W. Graham & Co.'s almost by accident. Peter and I were traveling north of Charleston and had just made our third culinary pit stop of the day along Route 17, all before one o'clock (what can I say—we're suckers for the many excellent mom-and-pop eateries in that part of the world). The owner asked us where we were headed next and, despite our full bellies, told us we'd be crazy not to check out T. W. Graham & Co. Of course, it ended up being the highlight of our day, and not only because of the clams, oysters, shrimp, and crabs that tasted of the marshes, streams, and seabeds where they had been harvested earlier that day, literally minutes from the restaurant's kitchen.

I knew right away that we'd hit on something special, but it wasn't until *after* lunch that I discovered T. W. Graham & Co.'s true specialty: dessert. As chef Pete Kornack explained, each of the seasonally inspired sweets, from peach cobbler and mixed berry bread pudding to key lime pie and Pawley's Island pie (a pecan- and chocolate-flecked confection that's like a cross between chocolate chip cookies and chess pie), is made from scratch by his wife, Claudia, a seventh-generation Southern cook who was born and raised in McClellanville. Claudia's desserts are simple, casual, unfussy classics of the sort Granny Foster would have relished, but the thing that makes them so special is the love and careful attention—the hallmark of all the best Southern sweets—that comes through in each sugary, flaky, creamy, crumbly, comforting, too-good-to-stop-till-the-last bite.

Claudia's desserts are simple, casual, unfussy classics.

black bottom coconut cream pie

With its dense, vanilla bean—speckled coconut custard, Oreo-cookie crust, and billowy cream, this Southern diner treat makes a strong case for skipping dinner.

MAKES ONE 9-INCH PIE / SERVES 8 TO 10

CRUST

1   prebaked 9-inch Black Bottom Cookie Crust
    (recipe follows)

FILLING

2½   cups half-and-half
3   tablespoons cornstarch
4   large eggs
¾   cup sugar
1   vanilla bean, split lengthwise, seeds scraped
     and reserved
¼   teaspoon kosher salt
2⅓   cups sweetened flaked coconut
1   tablespoon unsalted butter

TOPPING

1   cup heavy cream
¼   cup sugar
⅓   cup sweetened flaked coconut, toasted

FILLING | Combine ½ cup of the half-and-half and the cornstarch in a large bowl and whisk to blend. Add the eggs and mix thoroughly.

Place the remaining 2 cups half-and-half, the sugar, vanilla bean and reserved seeds, and salt in a heavy-bottomed saucepan and bring to a low boil, stirring occasionally, until the sugar dissolves. Remove and discard the vanilla bean and reduce the heat to low.

Whisk 1 cup of the half-and-half mixture into the egg mixture to temper the eggs. Whisking constantly, pour the egg mixture back into the saucepan with the half-and-half mixture and cook, continuing to whisk constantly, until thick, about 3 minutes. Remove from the heat and stir in the coconut and the butter. Let cool slightly.

Pour the filling into the cookie crust and refrigerate for about 4 hours, until firm.

TOPPING | When the filling is completely firm, place the cream in a large bowl and whip with an electric mixer to soft peaks. Add the sugar and whip to incorporate.

Using a spatula or pastry bag, spread or pipe the whipped cream evenly over the pie. Sprinkle with the toasted coconut and refrigerate until ready to serve.

black bottom cookie crust

This supereasy crumb-and-butter crust is what I make when I want a crispy, crumbly crust, especially for custard pies. The kind of cookie crumbs determines the flavor of the crust—this one is chocolate, but the variations are limitless. For example, a gingersnap crust would pair well with Lemon Rub Pie (page 330), while graham crackers would work nicely with Apple Sour Cream Pie (page 351). MAKES ONE 9-INCH PIECRUST

1½   cups Oreo cookie crumbs (from 6 ounces cookies) (see Know-how, below)
2   tablespoons sugar
    Pinch of kosher salt
4   tablespoons (½ stick) unsalted butter, melted

Preheat the oven to 350°F.

Combine the cookie crumbs, sugar, and salt in a large bowl and stir to mix. Pour in the butter and stir to combine and moisten all the crumbs. Spread the mixture in a pie pan, evenly pressing it over the bottom and up the sides of the pan to create a crust.

Bake for 8 to 10 minutes, until golden brown and slightly firm. Remove from the oven and let cool; the crust will firm as it cools.

Know-how: making cookie crumbs

Place cookies in a food processor and pulse eight or ten times; then leave the motor running for about 10 seconds, until the crumbs are finely ground.

SARA'S SWAPS   If you like, you can add new flavors and extra texture to the crust by adding ¼ cup ground nuts, such as walnuts, pecans, almonds, or peanuts. You can also top this pie with airy meringue rather than whipped cream; just follow the instructions for preparing the topping in Bittersweet Chocolate Tarts with Pecan Crusts (page 347). If using meringue, top the pie while the custard is still hot rather than waiting for it to cool.

bourbon apricot and sweet potato hand pies

These rustic half-moon pastries travel beautifully, making them one of my favorite picnic treats. Just wrap them in wax paper and you're off!

MAKES EIGHT 4- TO 5-INCH HAND PIES

1	cup dried apricots, chopped
1/4	cup bourbon
2	medium sweet potatoes (about 1 pound)
1/2	cup sugar, plus more for sprinkling on top
2	tablespoons unsalted butter
1/2	teaspoon ground cinnamon
1/2	teaspoon freshly grated nutmeg
1/2	teaspoon cardamom
1/2	teaspoon kosher salt
	Hand Pie Dough (recipe follows)
2	tablespoons heavy cream
1	large egg, lightly beaten

Place the apricots in a small bowl with the bourbon and soak for about 1 hour, until the fruit is soft and most of the liquid is absorbed.

Meanwhile, preheat the oven to 400°F. Lightly grease 2 rimmed baking sheets.

Wrap the sweet potatoes in foil and bake until soft, 45 to 55 minutes. Remove from the oven and discard the foil. Allow the potatoes to cool enough to handle before removing and discarding the skin.

Reduce the oven to 375°F.

Place the potato flesh in a bowl with the apricots and bourbon, the sugar, butter, cinnamon, nutmeg, cardamom, and salt and mash with a potato masher to the consistency of mashed potatoes.

On a lightly floured surface, roll the Hand Pie Dough about 1/4 inch thick. Cut eight 4- to 5-inch rounds with a cookie cutter or small knife. Place about 2 tablespoons of the sweet potato filling on the right side of each round, leaving a 1/2-inch border.

Combine the cream and egg in a small bowl and stir to mix. Brush the borders of the rounds with the egg wash and fold the left side of the dough over the filling so the edges meet and enclose the filling. Crimp the edges with a fork to seal. Cut small vents into the top of each hand pie with a paring knife.

Arrange the pies on the prepared baking sheets, brush the tops with the remaining egg wash, and sprinkle with sugar. Bake for 10 to 12 minutes, rotating the sheets halfway through, until golden brown.

Remove from the oven and let cool slightly before serving warm or completely cooled.

(continued)

hand pie dough

This dough is a pleasure to work with. It comes together beautifully and is so forgiving that if it breaks or cracks, you can simply press it back together. It is also great for making crostatas or free-form tarts. MAKES EIGHT 4- TO 5-INCH HAND PIES

2	cups all-purpose flour
3	tablespoons sugar
1/4	teaspoon kosher salt
1/2	pound (2 sticks) cold unsalted butter, cut into small pieces
1	large egg yolk
3	tablespoons ice water, plus more if needed

Combine the flour, sugar, and salt in a large mixing bowl and stir to mix.

Cut the butter into the flour mixture using a pastry blender or two knives in a crosscutting motion until the mixture resembles coarse meal. Work quickly so the butter remains cool and doesn't melt into the flour.

Combine the egg yolk and the 3 tablespoons ice water and stir to mix. Add to the flour mixture and stir with a fork just until the dough clumps together and is just moist enough to pat together. Do not mix any more than necessary. If the dough is dry and crumbly, add more ice water, 1 tablespoon at a time, just until the dough comes together; do not add so much water that the dough becomes wet or sticky.

Turn the dough onto a lightly floured work surface and, with lightly floured hands, form into a ball. Divide the dough in half and form each piece into a flat disk. Wrap each disk in plastic and refrigerate for at least 1 hour, or for up to 3 days, before proceeding with the recipe.

SARA'S SWAPS Give these pies an extra kick of spice by stirring 2 tablespoons chopped crystallized ginger into the sweet potato filling along with the other spices. You can also make these hand pies with different fillings, like baked pumpkin, butternut squash, apples, or peaches.

jen's chocolate-peanut butter pie

This pie is a peanut butter cup aficionado's dream. It was the creation of my friend Jen, who was one of the bakers at Foster's, and it has since become a Market staple—one of our most popular pies. With layers of crispy chocolate crust, smooth dark chocolate ganache, creamy peanut butter filling, and cool whipped cream, it is a true indulgence. MAKES ONE 9-INCH PIE / SERVES 8 TO 10

CRUST

1   prebaked 9-inch Black Bottom Cookie Crust, with ¼ cup ground peanuts (page 335)

CHOCOLATE GANACHE LAYER

1   cup semisweet chocolate chips (or 6 ounces bittersweet chocolate, chopped)
¾   cup heavy cream

PEANUT BUTTER LAYER

6   ounces cream cheese, softened
¾   cup creamy peanut butter, softened
¾   cup sweetened condensed milk
1   teaspoon pure vanilla extract
2   cups heavy cream

TOPPING

1   teaspoon pure vanilla extract
2   cups whipped cream, reserved from the peanut butter layer
¼   cup toasted peanuts
2   tablespoons ganache, reserved from the ganache layer
½   cup peanuts, toasted

CHOCOLATE GANACHE LAYER | Place the chocolate chips in a large bowl. Place the cream in a small saucepan and bring to a boil. Pour the hot cream over the chocolate, stirring until the chocolate melts and the mixture is fully combined and smooth. Set aside 2 tablespoons of the ganache for the topping. Let the remaining ganache cool slightly, then pour the ganache into the bottom of the cookie crust and refrigerate for about 30 minutes, until firm.

PEANUT BUTTER LAYER | Cream the cream cheese and peanut butter in a large bowl with an electric mixer or wooden spoon until soft and creamy. Add the condensed milk and beat until thoroughly blended. Add the vanilla and stir to mix.

In a separate bowl with an electric mixer, whip the cream to soft peaks. Set aside half of the whipped cream for the topping and gently fold the remaining half into the peanut butter mixture. When the ganache is completely firm, spoon the mixture on top of the chilled ganache, spread evenly, and refrigerate for about 1 hour, until firm. You can refrigerate the pie overnight or up to several days at this point.

(continued)

TOPPING | Fold the vanilla into the reserved 2 cups whipped cream. Using a spatula or pastry bag, evenly spread or pipe the cream over the pie and sprinkle with the peanuts.

Gently reheat the reserved ganache in the microwave for about 10 seconds, until soft enough to pour. Cool slightly and drizzle the ganache over the pie, sprinkle with peanuts, and chill until ready to serve.

molasses-bourbon pecan pie

I substitute molasses for the usual corn syrup in this version of classic pecan pie. The filling is every bit as sticky as you'd expect, and the molasses and bourbon add a deep, almost smoky flavor. Serve with vanilla ice cream or a drizzle of eggnog.

MAKES ONE 9-INCH PIE / SERVES 8 TO 10

1	cup molasses
1	cup sugar
4	large eggs, beaten
3	tablespoons bourbon
2	tablespoons unsalted butter, melted
1	tablespoon pure vanilla extract
	Pinch of kosher salt
2	cups pecan halves
1	unbaked 9-inch Everyday Piecrust (recipe follows)

Preheat the oven to 350°F.

Combine the molasses, sugar, eggs, bourbon, butter, vanilla, and salt in a large bowl and stir to mix. Place the pecans in the bottom of the pie shell and spread evenly. Pour the molasses mixture over the pecans.

Place the pie on a rimmed baking sheet and bake for 50 minutes to 1 hour, until firm around the edges and slightly loose in the center.

Remove from the oven and let cool for several hours before slicing.

everyday piecrust

Piecrust isn't nearly so difficult as some people make it out to be. Just be sure to have all the ingredients as cold as possible and handle the dough minimally, and you'll have flaky, buttery crust in no time. The egg in this all-purpose crust makes it especially easy to work with, and the added shortening makes it extra flaky.   MAKES TWO 9-INCH PIE- OR TART CRUSTS

3	cups all-purpose flour
2	tablespoons sugar
1	teaspoon kosher salt
8	tablespoons (1 stick) cold unsalted butter, cut into small pieces
1/4	cup vegetable shortening
3	tablespoons ice water, plus more if needed
1	egg, lightly beaten
2	teaspoons white distilled vinegar

(continued)

Combine the flour, sugar, and salt in a bowl and stir to mix.

Cut the butter and shortening into the flour mixture using a pastry blender or two knives in a crosscutting motion until the mixture resembles coarse meal. Work quickly so the butter remains cool and doesn't melt into the flour.

Combine the 3 tablespoons ice water with the egg and vinegar in a separate bowl and stir to mix. Add the egg mixture to the flour mixture and stir with a fork just until the dough clumps together and is moist enough to pat together. Do not mix any more than necessary. If the dough is dry and crumbly, add more ice water, 1 tablespoon at a time, just until the dough comes together; do not add so much water that the dough becomes wet or sticky.

Turn the dough onto a lightly floured work surface and, with lightly floured hands, form into a ball. Divide the dough in half and form each piece into a flat disk. Wrap each disk in plastic and refrigerate for at least 1 hour, or for up to 3 days.

Check the pie recipe for special rolling instructions. To prepare a basic pie shell, remove the dough from the refrigerator and let sit for about 10 minutes. Place on a lightly floured work surface. Dust a rolling pin with flour and roll the dough between ⅛ and ¼ inch thick. Fold the dough in half or gently roll it onto the rolling pin and lift it over the pie pan. Press the dough lightly into the bottom and up the sides of the pan. Trim the excess dough, leaving about 1½ inches of dough draped over the pan. Roll the extra dough under itself to form a rim around the edge of the pan. Crimp the rim of dough with your fingers or press with the tines of a fork. Prick the bottom of the crust two or three times with a fork to create small holes.

Cover the crust with plastic and refrigerate for at least 1 hour, or up to 3 days, before proceeding with a recipe or partially or fully prebaking the crust (see Know-how, page 345).

JAM TARTS Start with the trimmings or one full recipe of **Cornmeal Crust (page 331), Sweet Tart Crust (page 344),** or **Everyday Piecrust (page 341).** Dust a rolling pin with flour and roll the dough between ⅛ and ¼ inch thick. Press the dough into 2-inch tart shells and refrigerate for about 30 minutes.

Fill each shell with about **1 teaspoon of your favorite jam** and arrange on a baking sheet. Place in the refrigerator to chill completely, about 1 hour.

When ready to bake, preheat the oven to 375°F.

Bake for 25 to 30 minutes, rotating the baking sheets halfway through, until the jam is bubbling and the crust is golden brown. Remove from the oven and let cool slightly before serving warm or completely cooled.

rhubarb cornmeal tart

Southern summers are too hot for rhubarb to grow, so we Southerners must make the most of our short-lived springtime harvest. This buttery, crunchy tart is one of my favorite ways to do just that. MAKES ONE 9- OR 10-INCH TART / SERVES 8 TO 10

1	pound rhubarb, cut into 1/2-inch chunks
1 1/2	cups sugar
	Juice of 1 lemon
8	tablespoons (1 stick) unsalted butter, softened
1	large egg
3/4	cup finely ground almonds
1/3	cup yellow cornmeal
3	tablespoons milk
	Pinch of sea salt
1	partially baked 9- or 10-inch Sweet Tart Crust (recipe follows)

Preheat the oven to 350°F. Have all the ingredients at room temperature before you begin.

Place the rhubarb, 3/4 cup of the sugar, and the lemon juice in a saucepan over medium heat and bring to a boil, stirring occasionally, until the sugar dissolves. Reduce the heat to a simmer and cook for about 3 minutes, until the rhubarb begins to soften. Drain the rhubarb.

Cream the butter and the remaining 3/4 cup sugar in a large bowl with an electric mixer until light and fluffy, about 3 minutes (see Know-how, page 315). Add the egg, beating well and scraping down the sides of the bowl as needed. Stir in the almonds and cornmeal and add the milk, 1 tablespoon at a time, to form a thick batter. Add the salt and stir to mix.

Add half the rhubarb to the tart shell and gently spread the batter evenly over the fruit. Top with the remaining rhubarb and bake for 10 minutes.

Reduce the temperature to 325°F and bake for another 25 to 30 minutes, until golden brown and puffy.

Remove from the oven and let cool in the pan for about 10 minutes. Remove the sides of the tart pan by carefully lifting the tart from the center of the pan base; the ring should slide right off. Serve warm or at room temperature.

sweet tart crust

This lightly sweetened, eggy dough makes a deliciously buttery, shortbreadlike crust. It's made in the food processor, so it's important to go light on the pulsing and feel the dough with your fingers to make sure it isn't getting overmixed. MAKES TWO 9- OR 10-INCH CRUSTS

2	cups all-purpose flour
3/4	cup confectioners' sugar, sifted

½	cup cornmeal
½	teaspoon kosher salt
14	tablespoons (1¾ sticks) cold unsalted butter, cut into small pieces
2	large egg yolks
3	tablespoons ice water, plus more if needed
1	teaspoon pure vanilla extract

Place the flour, confectioners' sugar, cornmeal, and salt in a food processor and pulse to mix. Add the butter and pulse just until the mixture resembles coarse meal; do not overmix.

Add the egg yolks, the 3 tablespoons ice water, and vanilla and pulse two or three times, just until the dough comes together. If the dough is dry and crumbly, add more ice water, 1 tablespoon at a time, just until the dough comes together; do not add so much water that the dough becomes wet or sticky. Turn the dough onto a lightly floured work surface and, with lightly floured hands, form into a flat, round disk. Wrap in plastic and refrigerate for at least 1 hour, or up to 3 days, or until the dough is firm enough to roll.

Check the tart recipe for special rolling instructions. To prepare a basic tart shell, remove the dough from the refrigerator and let sit for about 10 minutes. Place on a lightly floured work surface. Dust a rolling pin with flour and roll the dough between ⅛ and ¼ inch thick. Fold the dough in half or gently roll it onto the rolling pin and lift it over the tart pan. Press the dough lightly into the bottom and up the sides of the pan and trim the excess dough. Prick the bottom of the crust two or three times with a fork to create small holes.

Cover the crust with plastic and refrigerate for at least 1 hour, or up to 3 days, before proceeding with a tart recipe or partially or fully prebaking the crust (see Know-how, below).

Know-how: preparing a pie shell

Each of the pie and tart recipes in this chapter specifies whether to use an unbaked, partially baked, or prebaked shell.

If the recipe calls for an unbaked piecrust, simply proceed with the recipe after you have fitted the dough into the pie pan and chilled the shell.

To prepare a partially baked crust: Preheat the oven to 425°F. Prepare the unbaked shell as directed in the recipe. Line the bottom of the shell with parchment paper or aluminum foil and fill with ceramic pie weights, dried beans, or dried coffee beans; this keeps the shell from shrinking as it bakes. Bake for 10 to 15 minutes, until the dough is no longer translucent but not yet golden-brown. Remove from the oven and let cool.

To prepare a prebaked crust: Prepare a partially baked pie shell, as above, but do not remove from the oven. Remove the parchment paper and pie weights and continue baking for 6 to 8 minutes more, until the crust is golden brown and flaky. Remove from the oven and let cool.

bittersweet chocolate tarts
with pecan crusts

The intense dark chocolate flavor in these little tarts is proof that the best things come in small packages. For truly sensational flavor, use high-quality dark chocolate, such as Valrhona or Scharffen Berger, rather than garden-variety baking chocolate.

MAKES EIGHT 4-INCH TARTS OR ONE 9- OR 10-INCH TART

CRUST

Pecan Crust (recipe follows)

FILLING

3/4	**cup sugar**
1/3	**cup unsweetened cocoa**
1	**teaspoon kosher salt**
2	**cups milk**
3	**tablespoons cornstarch, sifted**
4	**large eggs**
2	**ounces bittersweet chocolate, chopped**
2	**tablespoons unsalted butter**
2	**teaspoons pure vanilla extract**

TOPPING

4	**large egg whites, reserved from the filling**
1/4	**teaspoon cream of tartar**
	Pinch of kosher salt
1/4	**cup sugar**

CRUST | Preheat the oven to 425°F.

Remove the dough from the refrigerator and let sit for about 10 minutes. Place the dough on a lightly floured surface and roll 1/8 to 1/4 inch thick.

Cut the dough to fit the tart pan(s) and press and mold the dough to create shells. Refrigerate for about 30 minutes. Remove from the refrigerator, weight with pie weights, and prebake the shell(s) (see Know-How, page 345). Remove from the oven and set aside to cool.

Reduce the temperature to 350°F.

FILLING | Combine the sugar, cocoa, and salt in a heavy-bottomed saucepan and stir to mix. Combine 1 cup of the milk with the cornstarch. Stir until the cornstarch is dissolved and the mixture is smooth and add to the saucepan. Place the saucepan over medium heat and cook and stir just until the sugar dissolves, about 1 minute. Remove from the heat.

Separate the eggs, reserving the whites, and whisk the yolks in a bowl with the remaining 1 cup milk. Stir a small amount of the cocoa-milk mixture into the yolk mixture to temper the eggs.

(continued)

Slowly whisk the yolk mixture back into the cocoa-milk mixture and cook over medium-low heat, stirring constantly, until the mixture thickens and bubbles around the edges, about 3 minutes. Remove from the heat and add the chocolate, butter, and vanilla, stirring until the chocolate and butter melt.

Divide the filling evenly between the tart shell(s). Place on a rimmed baking sheet and set aside.

TOPPING | Place the reserved egg whites, cream of tartar, and salt in a glass or metal bowl and beat with an electric mixture on medium speed until light and frothy. Increase the speed to high and beat to soft peaks. Slowly add the sugar, beating constantly, until the whites are shiny and hold stiff peaks, about 3 minutes. Do not beat the whites past this point or they will separate and become grainy.

Divide the meringue between the tarts, spreading with a spatula or piping with a pastry bag, and covering the custard completely to prevent the meringues from shrinking when baked. Form peaks by repeatedly drawing a knife or spatula across the meringue and then in an upward motion, or by piping with a pastry bag and ending with an upward motion.

Bake for 8 to 10 minutes for a large tart or 5 to 7 minutes for small tarts, until the tips of the meringues are golden brown. Remove from the oven and let cool 10 minutes. Remove the sides of the tart pans by carefully lifting the tart from the center of the pan base; the ring should slide right off. Serve.

pecan crust

Toasted pecans give this crust a little bit of crunch and a lot of superrich, buttery flavor.

MAKES TWO 9- OR 10-INCH CRUSTS OR EIGHT 4-INCH CRUSTS

$2\frac{1}{4}$	cups all purpose flour
$\frac{1}{2}$	cup confectioners' sugar, sifted
1	teaspoon kosher salt
14	tablespoons ($1\frac{3}{4}$ sticks) cold unsalted butter, cut into small pieces
$\frac{1}{2}$	cup ground pecans
2	large egg yolks
3	tablespoons ice water, plus more if needed
1	teaspoon pure vanilla extract

Combine the flour, confectioners' sugar, and salt in a medium bowl and stir to mix. Cut the butter into the flour mixture using a pastry blender or two knives in a crosscutting motion until the mixture resembles coarse meal. Work quickly so the butter remains cool and doesn't melt into the flour. Stir in the pecans.

Combine the egg yolks, the 3 tablespoons ice water, and the vanilla and stir to mix. Add the egg mixture to the flour mixture and stir with a fork just until the dough begins to clump together and is moist enough to pat together. Do not mix any more than necessary. If the dough is dry and crumbly, add more ice water, 1 tablespoon at a time, just until the dough comes together; do not add so much water that the dough becomes wet or sticky.

Turn the dough onto a lightly floured work surface and, with lightly floured hands, shape the dough into 2 balls. Form the dough into 2 flat disks, wrap in plastic, and refrigerate for at least 1 hour, or for up to 3 days.

Check the tart recipe for special rolling instructions. To prepare a basic tart shell, remove the dough from the refrigerator and let sit for about 10 minutes. Place on a lightly floured work surface. Dust a rolling pin with flour and roll the dough between $\frac{1}{8}$ and $\frac{1}{4}$ inch thick. Fold the dough in half or gently roll it onto the rolling pin and lift it over the tart pan. Press the dough lightly into the bottom and up the sides of the pan. Trim the excess dough, leaving about 1 inch of dough draped over the pan. Roll the extra dough under itself to form a rim around the edge of the pan. Crimp the rim of dough with your fingers or press with the tines of a fork. Prick the bottom of the crust two or three times with a fork to create small holes.

Cover the crust with plastic and refrigerate for at least 1 hour, or up to 3 days, before proceeding with a recipe or partially or fully prebaking the crust (see Know-how, page 345).

SEA SALT CARAMEL TARTS   Follow the recipe for Bittersweet Chocolate Tarts with Pecan Crusts (page 347), but with the following changes: Spread store-bought **dulce de leche** in the prebaked tart shells in place of (or in addition to) the chocolate filling. Just before baking, sprinkle a **pinch of your best sea salt** on top of the meringues and continue with the original recipe for baking the meringues.

Know-how: working with meringue

If you know a few basic rules, working with meringue is a breeze.
- Eggs separate most readily when they are still cold, but for best results you should wait until the whites come to room temperature before beating them.
- Always use a glass or metal bowl for whipping the eggs; plastic bowls tend to be greasier, and this residual grease can weigh the whites down and prevent them from whipping to stiff peaks.
- When whipping egg whites, start on medium speed and beat until light and frothy; then increase the speed to high and beat until soft peaks form before slowly adding the sugar and continuing to beat until stiff peaks form, about 3 minutes.
- You can test the relative stiffness of the peaks by quickly dipping the beaters or a spatula into the whites. Soft peaks will curl over and begin to collapse when the beaters are lifted; stiff peaks are glossier and will stick straight up.
- Do not beat meringue past the stiff-peaks stage or it will separate and become grainy.
- Cream of tartar is often added because its high acid content helps stabilize meringue; the same effect can be achieved by adding a teaspoon or so of equally acidic lemon juice.
- Wait to add sugar and any other flavoring agents until after you've beaten the egg

whites to soft peaks; adding the sugar too soon will prevent expansion. Add the sugar slowly and beat constantly until the sugar is completely dissolved.

•   When topping a pie with meringue, mound the meringue in the center of the pie and use a spatula or the back of a spoon to spread it to the edges and make peaks. You can also use a pastry bag and tip to pipe the meringue and form peaks. Be sure the meringue touches the edges of the crust all the way around to prevent shrinking.

•   If topping a baked pie with meringue, place the meringue on the filling while it is still warm. The heat from the pie will begin to cook the bottom of the meringue and prevent a layer of weeping liquid from forming between the filling and meringue.

•   Always bake meringue in a preheated 350°F oven; temperatures below 325°F are too cool, and temperatures above 350°F are too hot. Meringue topping on a 9-inch pie typically takes 8 to 10 minutes in a preheated 350°F oven; smaller tarts will take less time, 5 to 7 minutes.

apple sour cream pie

Classic apple pie gets a serious upgrade in the form of this creamy, tangy, streusel-topped number. With swirls of sour cream, it tastes like the "à la mode" has been baked right in.   MAKES ONE 9-INCH PIE / SERVES 8 TO 10

CRUST

1   unbaked 9-inch Everyday Piecrust (page 341)

FILLING

5   cups peeled, thinly sliced tart apples, such as Granny Smiths, Jonagolds, or Pink Ladies

1   cup sour cream

½   cup granulated sugar

2   large eggs

2   tablespoons all-purpose flour

Zest and juice of 1 lemon

¼   teaspoon kosher salt

TOPPING

1   cup chopped walnuts or pecans

½   cup all-purpose flour

½   cup granulated sugar

½   cup unpacked light brown sugar

½   cup rolled oats

½   teaspoon ground cinnamon

½   teaspoon kosher salt

6   tablespoons (¾ stick) unsalted butter, cut into small pieces

FILLING | Preheat the oven to 350°F.

Place the apples in a large bowl. In a separate bowl, add the sour cream, granulated sugar, eggs, flour, lemon zest and juice, and salt and stir to thoroughly combine. Pour the sour cream mixture over the apples and toss gently to mix. Spoon the apple mixture into the pie shell and place on a rimmed baking sheet.

TOPPING | Combine the nuts, flour, granulated sugar, brown sugar, oats, cinnamon, and salt and mix. Add the butter and mix with your fingertips until the butter is incorporated and the mixture has a crumblike consistency. Sprinkle the topping over the apples and press gently to adhere.

Bake for about 1 hour, until the filling is bubbling around the edges and the apples are tender when pierced with a knife. If the top starts browning too quickly, cover with foil until the apples are tender. Remove from the oven and let cool for at least 1 hour before slicing and serving.

say's easy peach cobbler

This is my mom's recipe for what she calls a "dump cobbler," where all you do is mix the batter, dump the fruit on top, and pop it in the oven. It's soft and moist—almost like a pudding—with big peach flavor. Try different summer fruits, like cherries, blueberries, blackberries, or plums, in place of the peaches. Serve with Farm-Stand Peach Ice Cream (page 363) or lightly sweetened whipped cream. SERVES 6 TO 8

FILLING

2	tablespoons unsalted butter
6	ripe peaches (about 1½ pounds)
½	cup sugar
	Juice of ½ lemon

BATTER

1	cup all-purpose flour
½	cup sugar, plus more for sprinkling on top
1	teaspoon baking powder
¼	teaspoon kosher salt
¼	teaspoon ground cinnamon
¼	teaspoon freshly grated nutmeg
1	cup milk
1	large egg
2	tablespoons unsalted butter, cut into small pieces

Preheat the oven to 375°F.

FILLING | Melt the butter, pour it into a 2-quart soufflé or deep casserole dish, and brush over the bottom and sides of the dish to coat evenly.

Peel and slice the peaches. Toss with the sugar and lemon juice and let sit for 10 to 15 minutes, until the peaches start to release their juices and the sugar is no longer grainy.

BATTER | Combine the flour, ½ cup of the sugar, the baking powder, salt, cinnamon, and nutmeg in a large bowl and stir to mix. Whisk the milk and egg in a separate bowl. Stir the milk mixture into the flour mixture until just combined.

Pour the batter into the prepared dish and dump the peaches in the center of the batter; do not stir. Sprinkle with additional sugar, dot with the butter, and bake for 40 to 45 minutes, until the batter has risen over the peaches and is golden brown. Remove from the oven and serve warm.

blackberry cobbler with
drop cream biscuits

As homemade desserts go, cobblers are about as easy as they come; even better, they are endearingly homey and invariably good. The fluffy cream biscuits floating over this blackberry cobbler couldn't be simpler—just mix and drop. Serve warm with sweetened whipped cream or vanilla ice cream. SERVES 6 TO 8

FILLING

2½ pints (5 cups) fresh blackberries
½ cup sugar, or to taste (depending on the sweetness of the berries)
2 tablespoons unsalted butter, melted
    Zest and juice of 1 lemon
2 tablespoons cornstarch, sifted

DROP CREAM BISCUITS

2½ cups self-rising flour (see Know-how, page 53)
2 tablespoons sugar, plus more for sprinkling on top
    Pinch of freshly grated nutmeg
    Pinch of kosher salt
2 cups heavy cream
2 tablespoons unsalted butter, melted

FILLING | Preheat the oven to 375°F. Lightly grease a 2-quart baking dish or a 9- or 10-inch ovenproof skillet.

Combine the blackberries, sugar, butter, lemon zest and juice, and cornstarch in a bowl and stir to mix. Spoon the berry mixture into the prepared baking dish or skillet and spread evenly.

BISCUITS | In a separate bowl, combine the flour, sugar, nutmeg, and salt and stir to mix. Create a well in the center of the flour mixture, pour in the cream, and mix to form a soft dough.

Top the blackberry mixture with heaping spoonfuls of the dough, covering the fruit almost completely. Brush the tops of the biscuits with the butter, sprinkle with additional sugar, and bake for 40 to 45 minutes, until the biscuits are golden brown and the fruit is bubbling around the edges. Remove from the oven and let cool slightly before serving.

banana pudding

Banana pudding is such a Southern classic that I knew I had to include a recipe for it. At the same time, I wanted to give it a bit of a modern twist, and that's how I came up with Banana Pudding Sliders. You have to learn the rules before you can break them, so here's my favorite recipe for classic banana pudding—spiked with rum, layered with bananas and vanilla wafers, and crowned with meringue—followed by those sliders I dreamed up.

SERVES 6 TO 8

2$\frac{1}{4}$	**cups milk**
1	**vanilla bean, split lengthwise, seeds scraped and reserved**
4	**large eggs, separated**
$\frac{3}{4}$	**cup sugar**
$\frac{1}{4}$	**cup cornstarch, sifted**
$\frac{1}{2}$	**teaspoon kosher salt**
3	**tablespoons unsalted butter**
2	**tablespoons dark rum**
8	**ounces vanilla wafers (about two-thirds of a 12-ounce box)**
3	**ripe bananas, sliced into $\frac{1}{4}$-inch rounds**
$\frac{1}{2}$	**teaspoon cream of tartar**

Lightly grease a 2-quart baking dish.

Combine 2 cups of the milk with the vanilla bean and reserved seeds in a heavy-bottomed saucepan, place over medium heat, and bring to a low boil. Remove from the heat and discard the vanilla bean.

Whisk together the egg yolks and ½ cup of the sugar in a large bowl. Combine the remaining ¼ cup milk with the cornstarch and ¼ teaspoon of the salt in a small separate bowl and stir to dissolve the cornstarch. Stir the cornstarch mixture into the egg mixture.

Stir a small amount of the heated milk into the yolk mixture to temper the eggs. Whisk the yolk mixture back into the saucepan with the milk mixture, place over medium-low heat, and cook, stirring constantly, for about 5 to 7 minutes, until the mixture thickens. Remove from the heat, transfer to a bowl, and add the butter and rum, stirring until the butter melts.

Preheat the oven to 350°F.

Cover the bottom of the prepared dish with one-third of the wafers. Arrange half the banana slices in a layer over the wafers and cover with half the pudding. Place another third of the wafers on top of the pudding, followed by the remaining bananas and the remaining pudding. Arrange the remaining wafers in a ring around the edges of the dish, inserting them halfway into the pudding.

Place the egg whites, cream of tartar, and remaining ¼ teaspoon salt in a glass or metal bowl and beat with an electric mixer on medium speed until light and frothy. Increase the speed to high and beat to soft peaks. Slowly add the remaining ¼ cup sugar, beating constantly, until the whites are shiny and hold stiff peaks, about 3 minutes. Do not beat the whites past this point or they will separate and become grainy.

Spread or pipe the meringue on top of the pudding with a spatula or pastry bag and tip, making sure to cover the pudding completely to prevent the meringue from shrinking when baked. Form peaks by repeatedly drawing a knife or spatula across the meringue and then in an upward motion, or by piping with a pastry bag and ending with an upward motion.

Bake for 8 to 10 minutes, until the tips of the meringue are golden brown. Remove from the oven and let cool for 10 minutes before serving.

BANANA PUDDING SLIDERS   Makes about 2 dozen sliders

Place **24 vanilla wafers** on a rimmed baking sheet. Place about **1 teaspoon of the pudding** on top of each wafer. Top each with a **slice of banana** and another vanilla wafer to make a sandwich. Add a **swirl of the meringue** on top of the sandwich. Bake for about 5 minutes, until the tips of the meringue are golden brown. Remove from the oven, let cool, and serve.

SARA'S SWAPS   One of the bakers at Foster's Market used to make this banana pudding with broken cookie bits rather than the usual vanilla wafers. It had never occurred to me to do it that way, but it was delicious. Give it a try with pieces of Sweet and Salty Pecan Shortbread (page 364) or Molasses Ginger Crinkles (page 365) and see for yourself.

carolina rice pudding brûlée

Humble rice pudding gets a serious makeover with the addition of flavorful, fat-grained Carolina Gold rice and a glassy, sugared brûlée crust.

MAKES SIX 6-OUNCE SERVINGS

3	**cups milk**
3/4	**cup Carolina Gold or other long-grain white rice**
1	**vanilla bean, split lengthwise, seeds scraped and reserved**
1	**teaspoon kosher salt**
1	**cup heavy cream**
1/2	**cup granulated sugar**
4	**large egg yolks**
2	**tablespoons unsalted butter**
1/2	**teaspoon freshly grated nutmeg**
	Pinch of ground cloves
6	**tablespoons natural cane sugar or granulated sugar**

Preheat the oven to 350°F. Lightly grease six 6-ounce ramekins and place on a rimmed baking sheet.

In a heavy-bottomed saucepan, bring the milk to a low simmer over medium heat with the rice, vanilla bean and reserved seeds, and salt. Raise the heat to medium and cook, uncovered, stirring occasionally, until the rice is tender and the mixture is thick and creamy, 20 to 25 minutes.

Remove from the heat and discard the vanilla bean. Add the heavy cream and granulated sugar and stir until the sugar dissolves. Cool slightly, then stir in the egg yolks, butter, nutmeg, and cloves until the butter melts.

Divide the pudding evenly between the prepared ramekins and bake for about 20 minutes, until slightly puffed but still soft in the center. Remove from the oven.

Preheat the broiler or prepare a small kitchen torch. Sprinkle each pudding evenly with about 1 tablespoon of the natural cane sugar.

If using a broiler, place under the broiler in the upper third of the oven until the sugar caramelizes, rotating the baking sheet to evenly brown, 1 to 2 minutes. If using a kitchen torch, torch each pudding individually to caramelize the sugar, being careful to keep the torch at the distance recommended by the manufacturer. Serve warm.

buttermilk panna cotta with balsamic strawberries

This simple panna cotta is all about the tangy flavor of creamy buttermilk topped with a sweet-tart spoonful or two of bright red balsamic-glazed strawberries.

MAKES SIX 4-OUNCE SERVINGS

2	cups well-shaken buttermilk
1½	teaspoons unflavored gelatin
1	cup heavy cream
⅓	cup sugar
1	vanilla bean, split lengthwise, seeds scraped and reserved
	Pinch of kosher salt
	Balsamic Strawberries (recipe follows)

Place the buttermilk in a bowl and sprinkle the gelatin evenly on top without stirring. Let stand for 10 minutes, undisturbed.

Place the cream in a small, heavy-bottomed saucepan and add the sugar, vanilla bean and reserved seeds, and salt. Place over medium heat and bring to a boil for about 1 minute, stirring to dissolve the sugar. Remove from the heat, discard the vanilla bean, and pour the cream mixture into the buttermilk mixture, stirring to dissolve the gelatin.

Pour the panna cotta into six 4-ounce ramekins. Cover with plastic and refrigerate for at least 4 hours or overnight, until the panna cotta sets.

When ready to serve, dip the bottom of each ramekin in hot water (taking care not to reach the rims) for about 5 seconds to loosen the panna cotta. Run a knife around the inside edge and invert each panna cotta onto a serving plate. Spoon the Balsamic Strawberries and their syrup over the panna cotta and serve.

balsamic strawberries

MAKES ABOUT 2 CUPS

2	pints (4 cups) ripe strawberries, hulled and sliced
2	tablespoons sugar
1	tablespoon aged balsamic vinegar

Place the strawberries in a bowl and sprinkle the sugar and vinegar on top, tossing to mix. Let stand for about 10 minutes, until the berries start to release their juices and the sugar is no longer grainy. Serve immediately or refrigerate in an airtight container until ready to serve.

aunt june's boiled custard

My Aunt June used to make this boiled vanilla custard almost constantly from Thanksgiving to Christmas so as to keep a steady supply on hand. Ever the ready hostess, June kept the custard stored not in the refrigerator, as you might expect, but in a Tupperware container in the trunk of her car. This ensured that she was never without party supplies, whether she was entertaining at home or calling on friends. We were always glad to see Aunt June coming at that time of year, not least because we knew her famous custard was sure to follow. **SERVES 8 TO 10**

6	**cups milk**
2	**cups heavy cream**
1	**vanilla bean, split lengthwise, seeds scraped and reserved**
1½	**cups sugar**
1	**teaspoon kosher salt**
6	**large egg yolks**

Heat the milk, cream, and vanilla bean and reserved seeds in a large, heavy-bottomed saucepan over medium heat just until scalded (just before the boiling point). Remove from the heat, add the sugar and salt, and whisk until the sugar dissolves. Discard the vanilla bean.

Place the egg yolks in a medium bowl and whisk to mix. Slowly whisk about 2 cups of the milk mixture into the eggs to temper the eggs. Whisk the egg mixture back into the pan with the remaining milk mixture.

Place over very low heat and cook, whisking constantly, for 5 to 7 minutes longer, until the mixture thickens. Remove from the heat and cool to room temperature. Cover and refrigerate until ready to serve, or for up to 3 days. Serve chilled.

SARA'S SWAPS Let this easy recipe do double duty around the holidays and use it to make eggnog in addition to custard. When the custard comes off the heat, stir in bourbon to taste and let cool. Meanwhile, place 6 large egg whites in a glass or metal bowl and beat to soft peaks with an electric mixer. Add 1 cup heavy cream whipped to soft peaks and lightly sweetened. Gently fold the egg whites into the custard and serve chilled, topped with freshly grated nutmeg and more lightly sweetened whipped cream.

cornmeal thumbprint cookies

The unexpected crunch of cornmeal gives this version of classic thumb-print cookies a distinctly Southern accent. When making these jam-filled cookies, try using several different jams and preserves, such as blackberry, raspberry, and Brandied Figs (page 301). MAKES ABOUT 2½ DOZEN 2- TO 2½-INCH COOKIES

½	cup blanched, unsalted almonds
½	cup confectioners' sugar, sifted
1¼	cups all-purpose flour
½	cup yellow cornmeal
	Zest of 1 lemon
½	teaspoon kosher salt
¼	teaspoon freshly grated nutmeg
8	tablespoons (1 stick) cold unsalted butter, cut into small pieces
1	large egg
1	teaspoon pure vanilla extract
⅔	cup peach or your favorite fruit preserves

Combine the almonds and confectioners' sugar in a food processor and pulse until the almonds are finely ground, about 1 minute.

Add the flour, cornmeal, lemon zest, salt, and nutmeg and pulse several times to mix. Add the butter and pulse until the mixture resembles coarse meal.

Stir the egg and vanilla in a small bowl and add to the almond-butter mixture. Pulse just until the dough begins to stick together.

Transfer the dough to a lightly floured work surface and knead several times to form a flat disk. Wrap tightly in parchment paper or plastic and refrigerate for about 1 hour, until slightly firm.

When ready to bake, preheat the oven to 375°F.

Pinch off small pieces of the dough and roll into 1-inch balls. Place the balls on ungreased baking sheets, spaced about 2 inches apart. Using your thumb, press the center of each cookie to form an indentation.

Spoon a heaping ½ teaspoon of preserves in the indentation of each cookie. Bake for about 15 minutes, until golden brown around the edges.

Remove from the oven and let cool on the baking sheets for about 5 minutes. Serve warm or transfer to a baking rack to cool completely. Store in an airtight container until ready to serve, or for up to 4 days.

farm-stand peach ice cream

Throughout the South, but especially along rural strips of highway, you'll find a plethora of roadside farm stands advertising their homegrown wares with colorful, hand-painted wooden signs. I love these quirky little catchall stands, where you're almost as likely to encounter folk art or a mini petting zoo as you are watermelons and eggs. If you're lucky, you can also find some of the best peach ice cream you'll ever eat—creamy, cold, and ultrafresh. I like to think my version, which makes the most of sweet, sun-ripened fruit, is just as tasty. MAKES ABOUT 2 QUARTS / SERVES 6 TO 8

3   **cups half-and-half**
1   **cup heavy cream**
1   **vanilla bean, split lengthwise,
    seeds scraped and reserved**
6   **large egg yolks**
1   **cup sugar**
6   **tablespoons ($^3/_4$ stick) unsalted butter**
6   **ripe peaches (about 1$^1/_2$ pounds),
    peeled and sliced**
    Pinch of kosher salt

Heat the half-and-half, cream, and vanilla bean and reserved seeds in a large, heavy-bottomed saucepan over medium heat just until scalded (just before the boiling point). Remove from the heat and discard the vanilla bean.

Place the egg yolks and ½ cup of the sugar in a large bowl and beat with an electric mixer until light and fluffy, about 3 minutes. Slowly whisk about 2 cups of the half-and-half mixture into the yolks to temper the eggs. Whisk the yolk mixture back into the pan with the half-and-half mixture and cook over very low heat, whisking constantly, for 5 to 7 minutes, until thick. The custard should coat the back of a spoon and hold a line drawn with your finger.

Whisk in the butter until melted, then remove from the heat and let cool. Transfer the custard to an airtight plastic container and refrigerate for at least 4 hours or overnight.

Place the peaches in a large bowl and toss with the remaining ½ cup sugar and the salt. Let sit for at least 30 minutes, until the fruit releases its juices and the sugar is no longer grainy. Cover and refrigerate for about 1 hour.

Pulse the peaches in a blender or food processor five or six times, until smooth but still slightly chunky. Pour the custard into an ice cream maker and churn according to the manufacturer's instructions. Add the peaches for the last 5 minutes of churning. Scoop and serve.

sweet and salty pecan shortbread

These understated little cookies are made with three kinds of sweeteners—natural cane sugar, flavorful maple syrup, and coarse, raw demerara sugar—a feat that gives them their subtly complex flavor and crunchy texture. Crisp and buttery, they make the perfect teatime snack or ice cream accompaniment. MAKES ABOUT 2½ DOZEN 2-INCH COOKIES

1/2	pound (2 sticks) unsalted butter, softened
1/2	cup natural cane sugar
2	teaspoons sea salt
1/2	cup maple syrup
2	teaspoons pure vanilla extract
2 1/2	cups all-purpose flour
1 1/2	cups chopped pecans
1/3	cup demerara or turbinado sugar, plus more for sprinkling on top

Cream the butter, natural cane sugar, and 1 teaspoon of the salt in the bowl of a mixer fitted with the paddle attachment or in a large bowl with a wooden spoon and beat until light and fluffy (see Know-how, page 315). Mix in the maple syrup and vanilla until evenly incorporated. Slowly add the flour on medium speed or with a wooden spoon, stopping to scrape down the sides of the bowl several times, just until all the flour is incorporated; do not overmix. Add the pecans and stir to mix.

Turn the dough onto a piece of wax paper or plastic and roll into a 2-inch round log about 12 inches long. Combine the demerara sugar and remaining 1 teaspoon salt and stir to mix. Sprinkle the log evenly with the demerara sugar mixture and roll the log back and forth to adhere. Wrap and refrigerate for several hours or overnight, until firm.

When ready to bake, preheat the oven to 350°F. Lightly grease two baking sheets or line with parchment paper.

Cut the dough into ¼-inch-thick slices and arrange on the baking sheets, spaced about 1 inch apart. Sprinkle the tops of the cookies with demerara sugar and bake for 15 to 18 minutes, shifting racks and rotating the baking sheets halfway through, until lightly golden around the edges.

Remove from the oven and let cool on the baking sheets for 5 minutes. Serve warm or transfer to a baking rack to cool completely. Store in an airtight container until ready to serve, or for up to 4 days.

molasses ginger crinkles

Puffed and crackled exteriors make these chewy, intensely spiced cookies as pretty as they are delicious. I got the idea to add coffee to the dough because of how beautifully the flavors of ginger and molasses come together with bitter, smoky coffee. Serve with iced coffee to double the effect.   MAKES ABOUT 2 DOZEN 2-INCH COOKIES

12	tablespoons (1½ sticks) unsalted butter, softened
1	cup granulated sugar
½	cup unpacked light brown sugar
1	large egg
½	cup molasses
1	teaspoon coffee extract or pure vanilla extract
2½	cups all-purpose flour
1	tablespoon ground ginger
1	tablespoon grated fresh ginger
1½	teaspoons baking soda
1	teaspoon ground cinnamon
¾	teaspoon ground cloves
½	teaspoon kosher salt
1	tablespoon finely chopped crystallized ginger

Cream the butter, ½ cup of the granulated sugar, and the brown sugar in the bowl of a mixer fitted with the paddle attachment or in a large bowl with a wooden spoon and beat until light and fluffy (see Know-how, page 315). Slowly add the egg, molasses, and coffee extract, beating well to combine.

Combine the flour, ground ginger, fresh ginger, baking soda, cinnamon, cloves, and salt in a separate bowl and stir to mix.

Add the flour mixture to the butter mixture and beat just until combined. Cover the dough with plastic and refrigerate for at least 1 hour or overnight, until firm.

When ready to bake, preheat the oven to 375°F.

Combine the remaining ½ cup granulated sugar and the crystallized ginger in a small shallow bowl and stir to mix. Pinch off small pieces of the dough and roll them into 1-inch balls. Roll each ball in the sugar-ginger mixture to coat evenly and arrange on ungreased baking sheets, spaced about 2 inches apart.

Bake for 12 to 15 minutes, until the edges are set and the center is still soft. Remove from the oven and let cool on the baking sheets for about 5 minutes. Serve warm or transfer to a baking rack to cool completely. Store in an airtight container until ready to serve, or for up to 3 days.

red velvet cupcakes

Southerners love a good red velvet cake the way they love good, juicy gossip. That's because there's inherent drama in a towering white cake that, beneath swaths of innocent cream cheese frosting, possesses a shockingly crimson interior. Of course, they also love red velvet cake for its twangy buttermilk and cocoa–infused flavor and exceptionally smooth, supple crumb. MAKES ABOUT 1½ DOZEN CUPCAKES

CUPCAKES

1½	**cups granulated sugar**
12	**tablespoons (1½ sticks) unsalted butter, softened**
3	**large eggs**
1	**teaspoon pure vanilla extract**
2½	**cups all-purpose flour**
3	**tablespoons unsweetened cocoa**
1	**teaspoon baking soda**
1	**teaspoon baking powder**
½	**teaspoon kosher salt**
1¼	**cups well-shaken buttermilk**
1	**teaspoon distilled white vinegar**
1	**tablespoon red food coloring (optional)**

FROSTING

8	**tablespoons (1 stick) unsalted butter, softened**
8	**ounces cream cheese, softened**
2½	**cups confectioners' sugar, sifted**
1	**teaspoon pure vanilla extract**

CUPCAKES | Preheat the oven to 350°F. Line one 12-cup muffin tin and half of a second 12-cup tin with paper liners and lightly spray the tops of the tins with nonstick spray. Have all the ingredients at room temperature before you begin.

Cream the granulated sugar and butter in a large bowl with an electric mixer until light and fluffy, about 3 minutes (see Know-how, page 315). Add the eggs one at a time, beating well and scraping down the sides of the bowl after each addition. Beat in the vanilla.

Combine the flour, cocoa, baking soda, baking powder, and salt in a separate bowl and stir to mix. Add the flour mixture to the butter mixture in thirds, alternating with the buttermilk and beginning and ending with the flour mixture, stopping to scrape down the bowl several times and stirring just until all is incorporated. Do not overmix. Stir in the vinegar and food coloring, if using, until thoroughly blended.

Scoop the batter into the prepared muffin tins using a ¼-cup measure or ice cream scoop to fill each cup about three-quarters full. Bake for 20 to 25 minutes, until springy to the touch and a wooden skewer inserted in the center comes out clean. Remove from the oven and let cool completely before frosting.

FROSTING | Cream the butter and cream cheese in a large bowl with an electric mixer until light and fluffy. Slowly add the confectioners' sugar 1 cup at a time and cream until smooth. Add the vanilla and mix until blended.

Using a spatula or pastry bag and tip, spread or pipe the frosting on the cupcakes and serve.

---

chew on this: **about red velvet cake**

Although the origins of red velvet cake are up for debate, the cake has been around since long before the popularization of commercially produced food coloring, in the 1950s and 1960s. In fact, the cake's red tint was most likely initially the result of a chemical reaction sparked by mixing acidic buttermilk and vinegar with natural cocoa powder. (The acid also had the effect of softening the cake's crumb.) Over the years, the color was intensified with beets and, finally, the red food coloring that is most often used today.

SARA'S SWAPS Damon Lee Fowler, my friend and expert on all things Southern, makes a brown velvet cake in which he simply omits the food coloring. Because I don't typically keep food coloring in my pantry, I often follow his lead with this recipe, and both versions are equally tasty. But the bright color is a true crowd-pleaser, especially among kids.

Know-how: *piping frosting on the fly*

You don't need a pastry bag and tip handy to pipe frosting. Just snip the bottom corner off a plastic sandwich bag and use a spatula to fill the bag with frosting. Use the bag as you would a pastry bag, pushing the frosting out through the hole in the corner to create swirls or rosettes.

must-haves

You probably already own much of what you need to cook and eat like a Southerner. Most of the recipes in this book can be tackled without much more than a trusty knife and some serviceable pots and pans, but here are a few essentials that most Southerners like to keep handy—and some, like good cast-iron cookware, that they simply wouldn't dream of doing without.

BISCUIT CUTTERS AND ROLLING PIN   You can use drinking glasses to cut biscuits in a pinch, but biscuit cutters help ensure a light, airy, and uniform finished product. This is because biscuit cutters, like cookie cutters, have open tops, which allow air to escape as biscuits are punched out, thus preventing the dough from compressing. A good wooden rolling pin lasts forever—meaning it is sometimes treated as a family heirloom in its own right.

BUNDT OR TUBE PANS   Southerners have a special affinity for molded foods, from pound cakes and tomato aspic to cranberry sauce and shimmering, gelatin-spiked salads. A little collection of small and large Bundt pans, tube pans (I prefer the really deep ones, like the ones my grandmother used for angel food cakes), and salad molds enables you to make all sorts of "fancy" molded dishes.

CAKE STAND AND COVERED CAKE PLATE   Southerners take their cakes very seriously, meaning that presentation is every bit as important as flavor and texture. Decorative cake stands make cakes of all descriptions look their very best. A covered cake plate—the Tupperware version from the seventies seems to be among the most popular—is also important for transporting cakes to parties and other events. I still use the same one I bought at a yard sale over twenty years ago.

CANNING EQUIPMENT   A good home-canning set can be bought at your local hardware store or online for less than fifty dollars, and it's all you need to get started putting up your own garden preserves and pickles.

CAST-IRON SKILLETS, SEVERAL OF VARYING SIZES   If you go out of your way to get only one thing from this list, this is it. A well-seasoned cast-iron skillet is the indispensable heart of the Southern cook's arsenal. Because heavy cast iron conducts and maintains heat easily and evenly, these workhorses of the Southern kitchen fry, braise, and, best of all, sear with unequaled flair and perfect reliability. What's more, frequently used cast-iron skillets only improve with age as repeated applications of fire and grease season the surface to a smooth, nonstick gleam. Accordingly, Southerners treat well-seasoned cast-iron skillets as heirlooms, second in importance only to family silver or a beloved grandmother's fine jewelry. I use one or another of my cast-iron skillets almost every day—to fry the perfect egg, sear sea scallops, bake cornbread, or cook greens. When buying a new cast-iron skillet, be sure to follow the manufacturer's instructions for the pan's initial seasoning. After that, maintain the skillet's finish by washing it by hand (never in the dishwasher) with little or no soap and applying a thin layer of oil to the cleaned and dried cooking surface between uses.

CHARCOAL GRILL   Before I sing the praises of charcoal grills, let's just be clear on one thing: charcoal grills produce grilled what-have-you, *not* barbecue. Barbecuing involves a pit, a slow-burning wood fire, and, most often, a pig—and it is best left to the masters. Grilling, on the other hand, is an intramural sport with a considerably lower bar of entry. (It is also a method of cooking that is characterized by quick cooking over medium to high heat, as opposed to the low-and-slow mantra of pitmasters everywhere.) I prefer charcoal to a gas grill for the smoky flavor it imparts.

COVERED CASSEROLE DISHES   Covered casserole dishes are all about socializing on the go. Whether they are plastic, ceramic, or Pyrex, they are designed to package and easily transport one's best dishes to and from social functions, from potlucks and dinner parties to neighborhood block parties and church suppers, and most Southerners amass a large collection over the years.

DEVILED EGG PLATE   A deviled egg plate is a platter with lots of evenly spaced, egg-shaped indentations for nestling deviled eggs so they don't slide around. They come in all sorts of clever designs, and some people collect them. I still have my grandmother's deviled egg plate, which has her name written on a strip of masking tape stuck to the bottom from when she took it to church suppers and family dinners. It may not seem like it today, but for Southern ladies of my mother's generation, for whom entertaining was paramount, serving dishes like this really do qualify as essential kitchen equipment.

DUTCH OVEN   Like cast-iron skillets, Dutch ovens retain even, high levels of heat, so these roomy pots with tight-fitting lids are ideal for making roasts, stews, and even fried chicken.

ELECTRIC DEEP FRYER   Having a small countertop deep fryer or one of those big electric or battery-operated fryers is not imperative, but it's good fun and helps lend a crunch to a range of fried dishes. Use the smaller one to make Squash Puppies (page 65) and Crispy Fried Vidalia Onion Rings (page 246), and the larger one to throw an outdoor fish or chicken fry or make Carl's Deep-Fried Turkey (page 149) for Thanksgiving.

GRIDDLE   A flat griddle, preferably made of cast iron, conducts heat beautifully and is ideal for making everything from juicy Pimiento Cheese Burgers (page 186) to French toast and fried eggs.

ICE CREAM MAKER   Traditional hand-cranked, wooden-bucket-style ice cream makers are more nostalgia-inducing than practical; unless you have plenty of eager helpers on hand to take turns with the cranking, an electric model is your best bet. I keep the gel-filled canister from my ice cream maker in the freezer so it's ready to go at a moment's notice.

MORTAR AND PESTLE   This pair is perfect for crushing spices and making pastes and rough mixes like pesto, shrimp paste, and nut butters.

MUDDLER   This pestlelike wooden instrument is used by bartenders to smash and bring out the flavors of fruits and herbs in cocktails. I use mine to make Mint Juleps (page 27) and also to mash fresh strawberries to spread on hot biscuits, just like Granny Foster used to do.

OYSTER KNIFE   These indestructible little knives are short and sturdy—built to do battle with craggy, tight-lipped oyster shells. Without one, you'll end up with as many broken paring knives as shucked oysters. For more information about shucking oysters, see Know-how, page 22.

PIE PANS AND PYREX DISHES   The more the merrier when it comes to pie pans and Pyrex dishes, which are ideal not only for baking pies (do you need any more reason than that?) but also for making casseroles, toasting nuts, baking sweet potatoes—you name it.

PRESSURE COOKER   This works by utilizing the built-up pressure of trapped steam to raise the boiling point of water, thus speeding up the time it takes to cook anything from vegetables to meat. Pressure cookers make cooking things like dried beans and stews a snap, and they are especially useful for canning vegetables like tomatoes that require higher-than-boiling-point temperatures to be safely preserved.

essentials

Keeping your pantry stocked with the following items will allow you to easily incorporate Southern-style cooking into your weekly repertoire. These complement basic kitchen staples, such as olive oil, butter, dried herbs and spices, rice, beans, and vinegar, which are found in most kitchens regardless of region. For help finding items that aren't carried by your local grocer, consult Sources (page 377).

dairy

BUTTERMILK   Southerners have long favored buttermilk for drinking, cooking, and especially baking. In addition to its refreshing tart flavor, buttermilk adds body and helps tenderize everything from biscuits to cakes.

flour bin

CAROLINA GOLD RICE   This old, lowcountry variety of long-grain white rice is flavorful, fat grained, and buttery. It's perfect for eating on its own or as an accompaniment to all manner of meats, vegetables, and stews. Try my Carolina Gold Rice (page 215) and see for yourself.

CORNMEAL   As with pork, molasses, and a few other foods, it would be nearly impossible to overestimate the importance of cornmeal in Southern cooking. The evidence is everywhere, from cornbread and spoon bread to the golden crust on fried green tomatoes and fried catfish.

GRITS   Thanks to a few key dishes, such as shrimp and grits, this Southern grain of ground hominy is finally coming into vogue on a national scale. Just make sure you start with good, coarse-grained, stone-ground grits—the package should not say "quick" or "instant"—and you can't go wrong.

HOMINY   Hominy, or corn that has been hulled mechanically or with a lye solution, has a wonderfully nutty, rich flavor and is typically used in soups, stews, and casseroles. You can get it in ready-to-eat canned form or dried, in which case the plump kernels should be soaked overnight and then cooked, like dried beans.

SELF-RISING FLOUR   Soft white self-rising flour, which is low in both gluten and protein and comes blended with leavening and salt for extra lift, is the secret to Southern baked goods, from airy biscuits to sky-high, tender-crumbed cakes. Most every Southerner has a preferred brand, whether it's White Lily (my favorite) or Martha White (my mom's choice). You can also make your own self-rising flour (see Know-how, page 53.)

larder

ANDOUILLE SAUSAGE   Just a little bit of this spicy, smoky pork sausage, which hails from Louisiana via France and Germany, adds unmistakably big flavor to soups, stews, gumbos, ragouts, and other Southern specialties.

BOUDIN   Boudin is the name for several kinds of French-derived sausages made by Cajun and Creole chefs. They can be made with anything from pork and rice (sort of like a dirty rice sausage) to crawfish and alligator.

COUNTRY HAM   Country ham is salt- and smoke-cured and aged over several months, until it is intensely salty and almost flaky. Southerners eat fried slivers of country ham on buttermilk biscuits or use shards of it to flavor beans or soup. It keeps up to a few months in the fridge wrapped tightly in plastic, so it's easy to keep some on hand. Many online Southern vendors will ship country ham right to your door; see Sources (page 377) for a few of my favorite sellers.

LARD   Pig fat that has been rendered for use as high-heat cooking grease or baking fat, lard is known for the flaky texture and rich flavor it produces. Because of its soft, shorteninglike texture, it is also sometimes spread on biscuits, like butter. The most sought-after lard is leaf lard, which is made from fat deposits found around the kidney and loin.

PAN DRIPPINGS   Drippings are the bits of browned meat, rendered fat, and juices left in the pan after cooking meat, such as bacon. Drippings can be deglazed and used as the foundation for savory sauces or saved and used as a flavor-packed cooking oil. Many Southerners have a dedicated Mason jar in which they pour drippings to refrigerate for later use. Adding just a little bit to the pan amps up the flavor of fried eggs, greens, sauces, and stews.

SALT PORK   This is the name for fatty cuts of meat, like streak o' lean, pork belly, and fatback, that have been salt cured. It is used to add flavor to greens, soups, and field peas.

STREAK O' LEAN   This is the Southern term for cuts of pork that are mostly fat, with just a few streaks of "lean," or meat. It is used for frying, flavoring dishes, and making lard.

TASSO HAM   Despite its name, this smoked pork is made from the shoulder rather than the hindquarters of the pig. Like andouille sausage, tasso ham is used in Cajun and other Southern cooking to add deep, spicy flavor.

THICK-CUT BACON   There's no real need to explain this one; most everyone loves bacon, whether fried with eggs, crumbled over soup or salad, or used to flavor soups, stews, and casseroles. But that's not all; for many Southerners, the fat that is rendered in cooking the bacon is every bit as valuable as the meat itself. See Pan Drippings, above.

pantry

CHOW-CHOW   A Southern pickle relish most often made with cabbage, chow-chow is traditionally used to flavor beans and rice. See Green Tomato Chow-Chow (page 300).

HERBSAINT   This herb- and spice-infused liquor tastes like anise and was originally created as an absinthe substitute, made without wormwood, when absinthe was made illegal. See Sazeracs (page 28).

HOT SAUCE   Hot sauce is a must for frequent and liberal sprinkling on beans and rice, fried eggs, hoppin' John, Bloody Marys, fried fish, and whatever else suits your fancy. Everyone has a favorite kind, from Tabasco to Louisiana and even Sriracha (or rooster sauce), a Thai hot sauce that is becoming ever more popular in the United States. My favorite is Texas Pete, which is made not in Texas but in North Carolina; it has just the right amount of heat for me.

MOLASSES AND SORGHUM SYRUP   Molasses—a thick, dark, earthy-flavored syrup—is a by-product of processing sugarcane into table sugar. It is used as a sweetener for cooking and baking, and also as a condiment. (My dad loved to drizzle molasses on his pancakes and waffles, and I like to spread it on cornbread.) Molasses varies in color and flavor depending on whether it is made from the first, second, or third pressing of the sugarcane. Sorghum is a similarly dark, smoky-sweet syrup that is often confused with molasses, but it is actually pressed from sorghum grain rather than sugarcane.

PEANUTS   Peanuts are legumes, as the "pea" in their name suggests. They grow underground, like potatoes, and can be boiled like field peas or roasted to assume their signature nutty disguise. I keep my pantry stocked with roasted peanuts, peanut butter, and peanut oil for snacking, garnishing, baking, and frying.

PECANS   Southerners can rightly be said to be obsessed with these nuts, which grow on majestic native pecan trees throughout the South. With their sweet, rich, nutty flavor, pecans are excellent in both sweet and savory preparations. I toss toasted pecans in everything from salads and rice pilafs to granola, grind them to make crispy crusts for fish or meat, or bake them into pies, cookies, and cakes.

PEPPER VINEGAR   Like hot sauce, pepper vinegar is an everyday-and-everyway condiment that Southerners douse on everything from greens to pulled pig to add vinegary flavor and lots of spicy chile heat. To make your own, see Hot Pepper Vinegar (page 309).

PICKLES, PRESERVES, AND CHUTNEYS   Pickles and preserves have a special place at the Southern table, where they appear as condiments at nearly every meal. Whether you make your own or buy them at the farmer's market or grocery store, stocking up on pickles and preserves is an easy way to spice up basic dishes and put a little bit of summer on the table year-round.

PIMIENTOS   Small and sweet, red pimiento peppers used to be an important cash crop in the South. Now, however, they are most commonly encountered in a can and are best known for their starring role in Pimiento Cheese (page 18).

root cellar

SWEET POTATOES   I'm sure my sweet potato obsession has something to do with my Southern background, because this native plant plays a prominent role in the region's agriculture and cooking. I consider sweet potatoes a pantry item, like onions and garlic, because they keep beautifully when stored in a cool, dark place and can be used as building blocks for a wide variety of dishes.

ANSON MILLS

Organic heirloom grains, including rice, hominy, grits, and wheat

Columbia, South Carolina

(803) 467-4122

ansonmills.com

BENTON'S SMOKY MOUNTAIN COUNTRY HAMS

Smoked, unsmoked, and aged country hams, prosciutto, and bacon

Madisonville, Tennessee

(423) 442-5003

bentonshams.com

BLACKBERRY FARM

Pickles, jams, preserves, cheese, cured meat, heirloom seeds

Walland, Tennessee

(800) 273-6004

blackberryfarm.com

CAFÉ DU MONDE

Chicory coffee

New Orleans, Louisiana

(800) 772-2927

shop.cafedumonde.com/coffee.html

CALLIE'S CHARLESTON BISCUITS

Great Southern biscuits, including country ham biscuits

Charleston, South Carolina

(843) 577-1198

calliesbiscuits.com

CAROLINA PLANTATION RICE

South Carolina–grown grits and rice, including Carolina Gold

Darlington, South Carolina

(877) 742-3496

carolinaplantationrice.com

CLEMSON BLUE CHEESE
Roquefort-style blue cheese
Clemson, South Carolina
campusdish.com/
en-US/CSSE/Clemson/BlueCheese/
ClemsonBlueCheese.htm

DEAN & DELUCA
Guinea hen, grits, and pickles
(800) 221-7714
deandeluca.com

FOSTER'S MARKET
Pepper jelly, pickles, grits, and cookbooks
Durham, North Carolina
(919) 489-3944
fostersmarket.com

GOURMET WILD GAME
Quail, venison, goat, pork, rabbits, and frogs
(877) 355-6328
gourmetwildgame.com

THE GRATEFUL PALATE
Bacon and more, including Bacon-of-the-Month Club
Fairfield, California
(888) 472-5283
gratefulpalate.com

HAM I AM
Whole or half hams (my favorite is the peppered ham), quail, ducks, turkeys, tamales, smoked brisket, and bacon
(800) 742-6426
hamiam.com

JACOB'S WORLD FAMOUS ANDOUILLE
Andouille sausage, boudin sausage, smoked chicken, tasso ham, filé powder, cracklings, and dried field peas
LaPlace, Louisiana
(877) 215-7589
cajunsausage.com

K&L WINE MERCHANTS
Peychaud's Bitters, small-batch bourbons (including Knob Creek, Booker's, Baker's, and Basil Hayden's)
Redwood, California
(877) 559-4637
klwines.com

THE LEE BROS. BOILED PEANUTS CATALOGUE
Southern grocery, pantry essentials, and embellishments
Charleston, South Carolina
(843) 720-8890
boiledpeanuts.com

LOCAL HARVEST
National directory of small organic farms, with online store featuring meats (including pork belly), produce, honey, and more
Santa Cruz, California
(831) 515-5602
localharvest.org/store

LODGE CAST IRON
Cast-iron cookware
South Pittsburg, Tennessee
(423) 837-7181
lodgemfg.com

LOUISIANA CRAWFISH CO.
Live Louisiana crawfish, gulf shrimp, boudin sausage, andouille sausage, tasso ham
Natchitoches, Louisiana
(888) 522-7292
lacrawfish.com

MARIAH JADE SHRIMP CO.
Certified wild American shrimp, oysters, soft shell crabs, crabmeat, gumbo, and étouffée base
Chauvin, Louisiana
(800) 445-6119
mariahjadeshrimp.com

McEWEN & SONS
Organic stone-ground grits and cornmeal
Wilsonville, Alabama
(205) 669-6605
mcewenandsons.com

MUDDY POND SORGHUM MILL
Pure sorghum syrup
Monterey, Tennessee
(931) 445-3589
muddypondsorghum.com

SAVANNAH BEE COMPANY
Artisanal honey, including tupelo honey
Savannah, Georgia
(912) 233-7873
(800) 955-5080
savannahbee.com

A SOUTHERN SEASON
Gourmet groceries, Southern and others
Chapel Hill, North Carolina
(919) 929-7133
southernseason.com

SWEET GRASS DAIRY
Fine handcrafted cow and goat cheeses
Thomasville, Georgia
(229) 228-6704
sweetgrassdairy.com

ACKNOWLEDGMENTS

So many people helped to make this book possible, knowingly and unknowingly, and I am truly and forever grateful to each and every one of them. Special thanks (in no particular order) to:

The customers and staff of Foster's Market, who inspire me every day and make it all possible—and more than that, make it a joy. My business partner and nephew, Patrick Edwards, for being my right hand at the Market and a taster par excellence in the test kitchen. The farmers and purveyors, whose hard work and dedication shine through in all of their food, making what we do in the kitchen easy.

The behind-the-scenes team that worked in harmony to bring the book to life. Tema Larter, my co-author, who developed a distinctive voice throughout the pages of this book. Her knowledge and love of Southern food brought my memories and experiences to life. Peter Frank Edwards, the photographer, who captured the dishes in this book so beautifully, and whose inventive images always inspired me to look again with fresh eyes. Wendy Goldstein, for rigorously testing the recipes with precision and creativity, ensuring each one was ever more tasty and reliable, and whose styling skills helped to make them look as good as they taste in the photos. Our editor at Random House, Pamela Cannon, whose sure-footed guidance and keen observations helped make this book all it could be. Porscha Burke, for her fast responses to all my calls and emails. And others on the team at Random House, from production (Janet Wygal and Richard Elman) to design (Barbara Bachman, Anna Bauer, and Paolo Pepe) to publicity (Maria Braeckel). My agent, Janis Donnoud, and publisher, Susan Kamil, for believing in this project and making it happen.

Finally, and above all, my family and friends. This book and the recipes and memories in it are so personal, and each and every one of you was in my mind while I worked on it. Thank you for your recipes, your culinary inspiration, your love, support, guidance, and friendship; I could not do what I do without you. My husband, Peter Sellers, whose humor, enthusiasm, and support keep me grounded each and every day. Judy Edwards, my sister, who is my source and sounding board for all things Southern. My parents, whose love of great food and good times taught me the basics. My aunts Ginny, Anne, and June, for sharing not only their recipes, but also their homes. And my grandparents, but most especially my inimitable Granny Foster, whose hand in the kitchen often guided mine, and who seemed to be ever by my side in crafting this book.

Note: Page references in *italics* refer to photographs.

SARA FOSTER is the owner of Foster's Market, the acclaimed gourmet take-out store/cafés in Durham and Chapel Hill, North Carolina, and the author of several cookbooks, including *The Foster's Market Cookbook,* winner of the Best Cookbook Award from the Southeast Booksellers Association. She has appeared numerous times on Martha Stewart Living Television and NBC's *Today* show. She has also been featured in magazines such as *More, House Beautiful,* and *Southern Living,* and is featured regularly in *Bon Appétit.*

TEMA LARTER works in acquisitions at the University of North Carolina Press and as a freelance food writer. A native Southerner and avid foodie, she has previously worked as a pastry baker and a farmhand on organic vegetable farms from northern Virginia to southern Spain. She was married on one of those farms and now lives in Durham with her sweet husband, Jay.